＇ ‾ript‾

Making Waves

Also available from Continuum:

Toward a New Film Aesthetic
Bruce Isaacs

*The Strange World of David Lynch: Transcendental Irony from
Eraserhead to Mulholland Dr.*
Eric G. Wilson

A New History of Documentary Film
Jack C. Ellis and Betsy A. McLane

Directed by Steven Spielberg: Poetics of the Contemporary Hollywood Blockbuster
Warren Buckland

The Films of Tim Burton: Animating Live Action in Contemporary Hollywood
Alison McMahan

The Films of Krzysztof Kieslowski: The Liminal Image
Joseph Kickasola

The Films of Peter Weir
Jonathan Rayner

The Pleasures of Horror
Matthew Hills

Making Waves

New Cinemas of the 1960s

Geoffrey Nowell-Smith

continuum

NEW YORK • LONDON

The Continuum International Publishing Group Inc
80 Maiden Lane, New York, NY 10038

The Continuum International Publishing Group Ltd
The Tower Building, 11 York Road, London SE1 7NX

www.continuumbooks.com

Copyright © 2008 by Geoffrey Nowell-Smith

Printed in the United States of America on 50% postconsumer waste recycled paper

Library of Congress Cataloging-in-Publication Data

Nowell-Smith, Geoffrey.
  Making waves : new cinemas of the 1960s / Geoffrey Nowell-Smith.
     p. cm.
  Includes bibliographical references and index.
  ISBN–13: 978–0–8264–1819–7 (hardcover : alk. paper)
  ISBN–10: 0–8264–1819–8 (hardcover : alk. paper)
  ISBN–13: 978–0–8264–1820–3 (pbk. : alk. paper)
  ISBN–10: 0–8264–1820–1 (pbk. : alk. paper)
  1. New wave films—Italy—History and criticism. 2. New wave films—France—History and criticism. 3. New wave films—History and criticism. I. Title.

PN1993.5.I88N69 2007
791.43'611—dc22

                    2007034378

Contents

Acknowledgements

The chapter in this book on Antonioni is adapted from an article first published in *Sight and Sound* in December 1995. It is republished here with the kind permission of the editor. Stephen Crofts, Lúcia Nagib, David Nowell-Smith, Erminia Passannanti, and Sam Rohdie read and made useful comments on parts of the manuscript of the book while I was writing it. Cecily Nowell-Smith helped prepare the Index, for which I am particularly grateful. I should also like to thank the staff of the BFI Library in London and the Bibliothèque du Film (BiFi) in Paris for their kind assistance throughout. The cover still from Jean-Luc Godard's *Contempt (Le Mépris)* was provided by the Iconothèque at BiFi and is reproduced by permission of Studio Canal Image.

Geoffrey Nowell-Smith
London, May 2007

This book is dedicated to the memory of Tom Milne (1926–2005), film writer and translator without peer

A Note on Names and Film Titles

Throughout the book I have tried wherever possible to refer to films under a generally accepted English-language release title, where such exists. Many films, however, were never released commercially, or had different titles in Britain and in North America, have acquired new titles on re-release, or were given titles which for one reason or another simply didn't stick. Faced with a potentially confusing situation, I have applied a mixture of common sense and personal prejudice. Some films are uncontroversially referred by their original title: for example *L'avventura*, *Hiroshima mon amour*, *Les Carabiniers*. Others have an equally uncontroverisal release title: *Before the Revolution*, *The Discreet Charm of the Bourgeoisie*, *Antonio das Mortes*. In cases where choices have had to be made, I have used original titles for a number of films where the available English title or titles seemed to be in some way unsatisfactory. Thus François Truffaut's *Les Quatre cents coups* has two English titles. One is *The Four Hundred Blows*, which is a literal rendering of the original, but means nothing at all in English. The other is *Wild Oats*, which captures the sense of the original but never caught on. Since neither is satisfactory, I have stuck with the original. I have also stuck with the original for Jean-Luc Godard's first feature *A bout de souffle*, rather than using the translated title *Breathless*, which is the name of Jim McBride's 1983 remake. As between British and American titles, I have tended on the whole to prefer British as (again on the whole) they tend to be more accurate. Thus, for Louis Malle's *Ascenseur pour l'échafaud* I have chosen *Lift to the Scaffold* rather than *Elevator to the Gallows*: in France criminals are executed by guillotine, not hanged on gallows. But sometimes I have preferred American: thus *Loves of a Blonde* for Miloš Forman's *Lásky jedné plavovlásky*, rather than *A Blonde in Love*, and *Sandra* rather than the abstruse *Of a Thousand Delights* for Luchino Visconti's *Vaghe stelle dell'Orsa*. Not much hinges on these decisions, but since the issue can be problematic in some cases, the index of film titles at the end of the book contains original, US, and UK titles for most films referred to in the book.

Accents and diacritical marks on foreign names have been preserved unless it seemed overly pedantic to do so. I have followed everyday French usage in not putting accents on letters when they are capitalized: so *A bout de souffle* rather than *À bout de souffle*, *L'Ecran français* rather than *L'Écran français*. Accents and diacriticals are also the first casualty when a person has to change country. On leaving Poland, Roman Polański became Roman Polanski, which is how he is also spelt in the book. I have tried to get the diacriticals right on Eastern European personal names and film titles, but I cannot promise 100 per cent accuracy.

Introduction
What Were the Sixties?

The subject of this book is the new cinemas of the 1960s, mainly though not exclusively in Europe. As to what constituted a new cinema and even as to what constituted the 1960s, I have been flexible. There can always be a debate as to what constituted a new cinema, and there also can be (and indeed there always is) a debate as to what constitutes the 1960s in more than a pedantically chronological sense. Basically, in this book I have started by treating under the rubric 'new cinemas' those films and film movements which had the label attached to them, formally or informally, at the time of their emergence, any time from the late 1950s onwards. Thus, obviously, the French New Wave or Nouvelle Vague, Brazil's Cinema Novo, the Czechoslovak New Wave, Germany's Young German Cinema (*Junges deutsches Kino*), and, at the end of the period, New German Cinema (*Neues deutsches Kino*). Also identifiable new cinemas such as the breakout into feature film-making of British Free Cinema; the undoubtedly new (though not so often named as such) cinema that grew up in Italy in the void left by the demise of neo-realism; Cuban cinema in the immediate post-Revolution period which was new almost by definition; and other related novelties in Yugoslavia (with Dušan Makavejev) or Japan (with Nagisa Oshima). All these figure in the book, though not all are discussed in detail. As for the chronology, I have stretched it to make it fit my understanding of what counted as important in the general period under consideration. From a film point of view, the 1960s begin emblematically in May 1959, with the triumph at Cannes of François Truffaut's *Les Quatre cents coups* and Alain Resnais's *Hiroshima mon amour*. Arguably, a starting point could be set even earlier, possibly as far back as February 1956, with the first Free Cinema screenings at the National Film Theatre in London. The period ends, not spectacularly but with a gentle fade-out, some time in the early or mid-1970s, when the impulse behind the new cinemas runs out and when, moreover, New Hollywood emerges and the Empire Strikes Back.

1

This deliberately loose approach begs a number of questions, to which it is worth attempting to give at least approximate answers early on. The first question is, what exactly is new about these new cinemas apart from the fact that they were perceived as such by certain people at the time? Forty or more years on, ought we continue to take the judgement of these people on trust, or might we not do better to make a more substantive definition of what really was new in the cinemas of the period? Was the novelty of the new cinemas the same in France as in Brazil? Was it aesthetic or political? Did the novelty reside in the films themselves, or was it something broader, to do with changes in the surrounding culture and in the audience and the expectations it had of cinema? Might there have been other novelties, less remarked on at the time, which better deserve the title 'new cinema' than the phenomena generally recognized as such?

To start with the question of how reputations were acquired, commentators at the time did have their blind spots. The reputations of the new cinemas were made at festivals and press shows, by the opinions of critics and fellow film-makers, and consolidated at the box office by what can generically be called the 'art cinema' audience. This audience took its cue from critics and commentators but it was in its own right a shaping force in making the new cinemas what they were. It is possible with hindsight to point to serious over- and under-valuations by opinion-formers and public alike. The judgements of the time were limited by ignorance, fashion, and snobbery in various combinations and it is not too difficult for a writer arriving later on the scene to reorder the picture in all sorts of ways in the light of changing tastes. If I have refrained from doing so to any great degree, it is because the judgements of the time are themselves part of what created the time and made it what it was. 'The cinema' was (and is) much more than just the films that are made at a particular moment in time. It includes the assumptions that film-makers individually or collectively bring to their craft, the expectations they have of favourable or unfavourable reception, and the reception itself. I have tried on the whole to position myself inside this cinema rather than outside or above it, and to recreate the world of the new cinemas as it appeared to participants in that world rather than view it with conscious and critical distance.

Against 'false perfection'

This said, it is also possible to make certain assertions about the ways in which the new cinemas were new other than simply in name. For a start, almost without exception the new cinemas were a rebellion. Principally this rebellion was aesthetic and was in opposition to what I have elsewhere called the 'false perfection' of the studio film.[1] The falsely perfect studio films against which the new cinemas rebelled were made above all in Hollywood, film factory to the world. But sometimes the rebellion was against a target closer to home, as with the French Nouvelle Vague's oedipal revolt against Daddy's cinema – *le cinéma de papa* – encapsulated in the native 'quality tradition'. Meanwhile the rebellion was also political, with most of the new cinemas (the French again a partial exception) aligned on the new, non-Stalinist left. In Eastern Europe the rebellion was necessarily aesthetic and political at the same time, since to break out of the confines of official socialist realism was already a political gesture and no forward movement, aesthetic or political, was possible without it.

The rebellion was also vociferous. The new cinemas announced themselves polemically. The old cinema was not only rejected but denounced. Many of the new film-makers were critics, and some of them, such as François Truffaut in France or Lindsay Anderson in Britain, quite vehement and even violent about what they disapproved of or simply didn't like. The British (Free Cinema, February 1956) and the Germans (Oberhausen, February 1962) produced manifestos; the French were less formal but the volume and directedness of the criticism in *Cahiers du cinéma* was equally, in fact more, effective. Having denounced the opposition, the new film-makers then had to prove themselves capable of doing better, which in many cases they did.

One reason why the new cinemas rebelled against perfection was because they could not afford it. The new cinemas were on the whole poor cinemas. The size of the audience was unpredictable, varying from the modest to the minuscule, and the small budgets available for films pitched at this uncertain market often made technical perfection unattainable. But the perfection achieved with the aid of higher budgets and all-round professionalism was felt by many of the new film-makers to be a cover for an interior void. Refined dialogue, perfect match cuts, impeccably even lighting, spectacular action, these were attributes that might be worth pursuing if you had the money, but on the other hand they might not. From early on – in fact from as early as Jean-Luc Godard's first feature, *A bout de souffle*, released in March 1960– the new cinemas learnt to make a virtue of necessity. If a film was rough-and-ready in the way it was put together, then so be it. If it breathed more life as a result, so much the better. But because the new films were often imperfect, they drew attention to themselves – not only to what they were saying but to who was saying it. The relationship between film-maker and public was redefined. In place of an unspoken compact between the film industry and the audience there came into being a more personal relationship between the film-maker and the spectator. With the mass audience in decline, a greater proportion of cinemagoing became an elective activity, supported by listings magazines which were perused by prospective moviegoers in search of the 'new Antonioni', the 'new Godard', or whatever it might be. Around the new-style compact arose a new film culture, enabling a new type of cinema to thrive as never before.

At the time they first appeared the new cinemas were celebrated rather then theorized. Critics sensed their novelty without being able to define it. A few instances of profound intuition, as in Susan Sontag's brilliant essay on Godard's *Vivre sa vie*,[2] alternated with regular examples of vapid impressionism and frequent reduction of the unknown into more familiar terminology. It was only after the event, with the arrival on the scene of 'film theory' in the late 1960s and early 1970s that concepts were developed which could be used coherently to define the ways in which the new cinemas differed systematically from cinemas which preceded them (and co-existed with and even survived them). In this book I shall be sparing in my application of these after-the-event concepts to the cinemas and films under consideration, but it is worth looking briefly at some of the ways in which they provide retrospective illumination on what was happening at the time.

Principally the new conceptual frameworks operated by negation. By focusing in the first instance on the kind of cinema that the new cinemas were not, and against which they were in many cases reacting, they highlighted certain key elements of difference between the old cinemas and the new, systematizing many things which film-makers and critics were aware of in a diffuse way but not necessarily with any great degree of theoretical awareness.

The first breakthrough was to see Hollywood (and by extension other conventional cinemas) as a fundamentally inexplicit cinema, that is to say one in which the marks of enunciation are suppressed or naturalized and stories are told which appear to be telling themselves rather than being developed from a position which the audience can locate and, if necessary, challenge. By contrast, the new cinemas, or some of them, told stories in which the points of enunciation were always in some way and to some degree explicit. This might take the obvious form of direct reminders to the spectator of the way the images were being put together and of the image-maker who was responsible for putting them where they were, or that of less obvious but nevertheless unambiguous indicators that the film unrolling in the spectator's presence represented not a substitute reality but an alternative take on what reality might be. To the former category would belong, in very different ways, Jean-Luc Godard or Federico Fellini; to the second, and again in quite different ways, Michelangelo Antonioni or Ingmar Bergman.

The vocabulary employed in this approach was that of semiotics, which began to influence thinking about film in France from about 1964 onwards, though somewhat later in Britain and the USA. A similar set of conclusions about the fundamental differentness of the new cinemas from a presumed norm represented by Hollywood can be found in David Bordwell's 1985 book *Narration in the Fiction Film*, which uses a less semiotically inflected language to characterize various forms of non-classical, non-Hollywood narration present in films both from the 1960s and from earlier decades.[3] For Bordwell, what distinguishes these other forms of narration is not so much the film-maker's activity in making enunciation present to the spectator as the activity demanded of the spectator in order to decipher formal procedures which signal themselves as deviations from an enduring norm. In this respect the new cinemas are mainly remarkable for the sheer number of 'deviant' practices which were able to flourish between the time of, say, Godard's *A bout de souffle* in 1960 and Miklós Jancsó's *The Confrontation* in 1968.

A year or two earlier in 1983, the French philosopher Gilles Deleuze published the first of two volumes of reflections on the nature of cinema, subtitled 'L'image mouvement'. This and a second volume 'L'image temps', which followed in 1985, set out to ground a fundamental distinction in the cinema between films (the great majority at all times) characterized by what he called the 'movement image' and those (a minority, almost all of them relatively recent) characterized by a different form of image entirely, the 'time image'.[4] Put very crudely, in movement-image films there is movement in space as required by the necessities of the action, but time has no real presence in the film except as a vector along which action takes place. Tentatively, however, beginning in a small way with Italian neo-realism in the 1940s, and more emphatically with, for instance, Antonioni or Alain Resnais in the early 1960s, time begins to make its presence felt as something in itself, above and beyond the forward movement of the action. The new cinemas of the 1960s are not all time-image cinemas, but many of them are, and across a wide spectrum. Alongside those of film-makers already cited, one could add the names of Miloš Forman and Ivan Passer in Czechoslovakia, Glauber Rocha in Brazil, Alexander Kluge and later Wim Wenders in Germany, Andrei Tarkovsky in the Soviet Union, and others almost too numerous to mention. Here the break with normal cinema is not formal but existential or, to coin a phrase, consistential, since it is a change in the very stuff of which cinema consists.

The 1960s

The most important single consideration, however, concerns the relationship of the new cinemas to the decade in which they were born and, in some cases, died. I have called this decade the 1960s, in numerals rather than spelled out as Sixties, partly as a matter of stylistic or graphic convention, but also to pre-empt the kind of personification that tends to accompany spelled out names: the Twenties that roared, the Thirties that were always depressed, or in our case the Sixties that had to swing – which of course they did, but not everywhere.

The fact is, the 1960s of popular mythology, the 'Swinging Sixties' of sex, drugs, and rock'n'roll, did not happen all at once or to everyone at the same time. Indeed for many people in the world they did not happen at all. Life was very different for peasants in Vietnam sheltering under a hail of American bombs than it was for the hippies of Haight Ashbury or the mods cruising London's King Road on their Lambrettas and Vespas. Even in the heartlands of the west the sixties revolution spread slowly. There were real changes in attitudes to sex but they often had more to do with what became admitted into discourse than with sexual behaviour itself. The female contraceptive pill, perhaps the most emblematic of all developments in the decade, did not become available to young unmarried women before 1964 or 1965, and then only in non-Catholic countries and from a handful of enlightened doctors. As for rock'n'roll, the new music associated with the Beatles, the Rolling Stones and the Beach Boys, not to mention the ultimate 1960s folk hero Bob Dylan, did not really establish itself as a cultural force before 1963 at the earliest, soon becoming quite mainstream in English-speaking countries but remaining decidedly exotic in continental Europe and Latin America. The same could be said of recreational and 'mind-expanding' drugs, whose use became more and more prevalent as the decade went on, but again mainly in Britain and North America.

Subsuming the 1960s under the sex, drugs, and rock'n'roll mantra is even more questionable when one looks at how these themes were treated in the cinema, whether old or new. There was certainly more sex, and sex-talk, in 1960s films than in those of the 1950s, thanks to a widespread liberalization of censorship regimes, not only in the western world but in eastern Europe and in Japan. But the mainstream cinema shied away from the drugs culture, on the one hand recognizing that dope-smoking could no longer be treated according to the traditional 'problem film' agenda but remaining on the other hand wary of seeming to endorse an activity of which many people disapproved and which was in any case illegal just about everywhere. The drug culture for which the period was famous does make an appearance in a few British films of the late 1960s and early 1970s, most famously *Performance* (1970), and in Underground films and in one or two mainstream or semi-mainstream American films such as *Easy Rider* (1969). But it barely figures in European films, with a couple of exceptions such as Agnès Varda's *Lions Love* (1969), which is really an American Underground film made by a Frenchwoman, and Antonioni's *Blow Up* (1966) and *Zabriskie Point* (1970), which are respectively British and American films made by an Italian fascinated by what was going on in the exotic worlds of first London and then Los Angeles.

As for the music, the original rock'n'roll of the 1950s had been enthusiastically adopted by the cinema, not only in the USA and Britain but also in continental Europe, where Luchino Visconti (of all people) staged a spectacular dance number to the sound of Bill Haley's rendition of 'Thirteen women' in his film *White Nights* in 1957. But the new music proved harder to squeeze into a show-biz format and it took the highly original talent of Richard Lester, with the two Beatles films *A Hard Day's Night* (1964) and *Help!* (1965), before the anarchic energy of 1960s pop could be harnessed to cinematic purposes. After that other films followed, including Godard's idiosyncratic *One Plus One* with the Rolling Stones in 1968. There were also documentaries, such as D.A. Pennebaker's *Don't Look Back* (1967), tracking Bob Dylan's contested concert tour of Britain in 1966. But on the whole cinema and rock music continued throughout the 1960s to occupy separate spheres, with remarkably little overlap.

In any case, the 1960s was not just pop culture, even if that is what it is remembered for. The period also saw a resurgence of the artistic avant-gardes, which had led a rather stifled existence in the postwar period. The spirit of the avant-gardes did not always translate itself rapidly into the cinema, which is on the whole a conservative institution. There was a film avant-garde in the 1950s, but it was pretty well invisible outside New York and a few other metropolitan centres such as San Francisco, Paris, London, or Vienna. In the 1960s this burst out in a new form as the Underground, while literary, dramatic, and visual art avant-garde ideas (again originating in the 1950s) also found their way into the cinema, along with a new Marxist-influenced radical politics.

The 1960s thus saw a popularization of the French 'Nouveau Roman' of Alain Robbe-Grillet, Michel Butor, Marguerite Duras, and others, which was translated into other languages and found its way into cinema first with films by Alain Resnais using the *nouveaux romanciers* as scriptwriters and then with films by Robbe-Grillet and Duras themselves. The decade also saw a powerful influence on the theatre of the ideas and practices of Bertolt Brecht, whose famous Berliner Ensemble had visited Paris in 1954 and London in 1956, bringing with it a revolutionary new approach to dramatic performance. Brechtian influence spread slowly but became quite pervasive in the early 1960s and made the leap into the cinema through the work of Godard, Jean-Marie Straub, and Rainer Werner Fassbinder from mid-decade onwards. Brecht was a Marxist, and the influence of his theatre was inseparable from the revival of interest in Marxism associated with the New Left. The new Marxism – sometimes called 'western Marxism' – took various forms but all were united in criticizing the economism of orthodox Marxist doctrines and emphasizing the importance of ideology and culture in formulating a critique of advanced capitalist societies. As such, it provided a strong counter-current to the consumerism prevalent in the more prosperous parts of the west.

Two narratives

Making sense of the turbulent mix of things that constituted the 1960s is not easy. Basically there are two main narratives of the period, a narrative of liberation and a narrative of modernization. Of these it is the liberation narrative which had most force at the time, whereas the modernization narrative is mainly after the event and follows the recognition that much of what in the 1960s appeared to be going somewhere in fact led nowhere and the actual legacy of the period can be interpreted quite differently.

According to the modernization narrative, the 1960s are to be seen mainly as a great step forward in a process of modernization which continues uninterrupted up to the present. Sex, drugs, and rock'n'roll fit into this narrative to the extent that the period represents the beginnings of a liberalization, now almost total, in the ways sex and sexuality can be publicly represented, not to mention a liberalization of laws governing what consenting adults are allowed to consent to. Less agreeably, they can also be seen as the relatively innocent harbinger of a world in which the trade in illegal drugs (very little change there: they are still illegal) has become a massive business of enormous concern to governments across the world. Back in the realm of culture they can be argued to presage the triumph of pop over culture as a whole. In these respects an unbroken line can be seen to connect the 1960s to whatever the name or number is of the decade in which this book is being written and published.

But in other respects too a continuity can be posited, with the presumed modernity of the 1960s being seen as a starting point or staging post on the long road to the present. The 1960s can thus be seen – I think legitimately – as at the very least an important step in the long process of secularization of western society, when religion began to lose both its attraction and its coercive power. Also – and again this is fair enough – there is continuity with the present in the spread of consumerism, as larger and larger segments of the population not only had more money to spend but became more flamboyant in how they spent it. One could, furthermore, see the 1960s as a crucial early stage of the gradual process of colourization of representation, whose results we now take for granted. The world of the 1950s was one when media representations, except for Hollywood films and a small proportion of British and European ones, were black and white; TV was black and white; newspaper ads and press photographs were black and white; holiday snaps were black and white; had there been computers or security cameras with screens, those screens too would have been black and white or at any rate monochrome. Now all these things are in colour, and quasi-lifelike representations of things in the world surround us at every turn. This is a huge change in the phenomenology of everyday life which has crept up almost unnoticed and where, again, if a starting point can be located anywhere, it must surely be the 1960s. It is also no accident that the 1960s were also a period in which the world itself, or at least the western world, became more colourful, as oil and smokeless fuel gradually replaced the smokier forms of coal that shrouded cities in fog and blackened their buildings. In fashion and street life, as in representation, the 1960s were bright, just as the art and music of the period were for the most part jolly, or at any rate remembered as such.

This narrative has a lot to recommend it, but it is essentially a narrative of what has survived. It is teleological in implicitly seeing modernity (or what we now call modernity) as a goal, to which the world in the 1960s was already tending. The problem with it is that it does not recognize the extent to which some developments (such as consumerism) were fiercely resisted while others (such as colourization) were unforeseen and at the time no more than incidental to the main thrust of events. Crucially, too, it neglects the elements of discontinuity between the 1960s and the present which are every bit as important as the presumed continuities.

The most important of these discontinuities is provided by the demise of socialism both as reality and as an ideal. This is not the place to go into the reasons why the command economies and repressive political systems of the Soviet Union and its satellites had to be wiped off the historical map. What matters is that in the 1960s they still existed and exercised an ambivalent power over thinking in the period. On the positive side they represented an oppositional force that kept the domination of capitalism in check. On the negative, this 'actually existing socialism', as it was sometimes called, had very little power of attraction over the young intellectuals of the period. But the limited appeal of socialism as it existed did not lessen the power of the ideal, and the 1960s was above all an idealistic decade. For millions of people throughout the world the idea that there might be no alternative to capitalism was unthinkable. From speeded-up rhythms in the factory, to military intervention in Central America in defence of US investments, to the 'bourgeois' organization of knowledge in the universities, the evils of capitalism were seen as manifest and to be resisted by all available means. The same intolerance of the established order extended to personal life: the expression of sexuality was a right, as was the choice of preferred intoxicants, and these rights had to be asserted against the repressive forces that denied them.

The concept which in the 1960s linked together such disparate phenomena as opposition to the American war on Vietnam and the presumed right to sexual self-expression was liberation, and history was widely seen as progressing in this direction. Hence the notion of a narrative of liberation as the lodestar of the period. Brought up to believe that they lived in the Free World, young people in particular experienced their life as one of unfreedom. Taking their cue from the resistance movements in the Second World War, independence movements in oppressed and colonized countries – in Algeria, Vietnam, Mozambique or Palestine, for instance – set out their goal as national liberation and this is reflected in their names: Front de Libération Nationale, National Liberation Front, Frente de Liberação de Moçambique, Palestine Liberation Organisation. As well as national liberation there were other liberations on offer. There was liberation to be pursued in countries suffering from dictatorship (Fascist or Communist); there was liberation theology (mainly in Latin America); and there were various liberations touted around in the world of sex and gender – generic sexual liberation in the mid-1960s, followed by Women's Liberation at the end of the decade, and Gay Liberation hot on its heels.

Not all these liberations were of the same kind. Independence from foreign rule is not much of a liberation if it is immediately transmuted into homegrown dictatorship. The interesting thing, though, is the way they were collapsed into each other, as if a single goal was being pursued in all these different walks of life, although even at the time a moment's reflection sufficed to realize that this was not the case. This reflection, however, came only later, and in two forms: first, a recognition that the world was not in fact progressing inexorably towards liberation; and second, an unease with some of the results which liberation had achieved. The reflux against the liberationist narrative began even before the decade was out, with the defeat – temporary or permanent, nobody knew for sure – of some of the utopias of May 1968 and the crushing of dissent in Czechoslovakia a few months later. There are signs of it too in the puritanical reaction of parts of the women's movement to the one-sided way in which men (some men) interpreted sexual liberation to their own advantage. But for the most part the early 1970s was a time in which the liberationist aims of the 1960s continued to be pushed forward. In Spain, Franco died and his regime collapsed; in Portugal, Salazar was deposed and Angola and Mozambique became independent; the Americans were thrown out of Vietnam. But as the new decade wore on the picture became cloudy. Vietnam, although liberated, remained desperately poor; the socialist government of Chile was overthrown by a military coup; Angola and Mozambique were undermined by South African sponsored rebellions; Eastern Europe stagnated, while in the west capitalism regrouped and the gains won by workers were nullified by inflation and low productivity. The election in Britain in 1979 of a Conservative government

dedicated to monetarist economics, erosion of the welfare state, reassertion of traditional moral values (whatever those might be), and a redefi-
nition of freedom as consumer choice was not the end of everything,
because other countries, France and Germany in particular, restabilized
in a more social-democratic direction. But much of what the 1960s
had stood for, or were felt to have stood for, simply disappeared. By the
end of the 1980s, with the collapse of Communism, not only in its 'actually
existing' version but as a credible ideal, the liberationist narrative of the
1960s had currency only as myth.

Periodizing the 1960s

In spite of all that can be said against it from a present or presentist
standpoint, the liberationist narrative is still convincing as a means of
understanding the 1960s as they happened, and to the extent that this
book aims to look at the period from the inside and not to second-guess
it in the light of later history, it is the narrative I shall broadly follow here.
It remains to relate the chronology of the new cinemas to that of the
period at as a whole. This is not as difficult as one might expect – provided
one recognizes that not everywhere in the world developed in the same
way or at the same pace.

In general terms the 1960s can be seen as falling into three parts. There
is a 'pre-1960s', which in world terms can be seen as lasting from the
Hungary and Suez crises at the end of 1956, to the achievement of
Algerian independence in 1962. This is the period of the Free Cinema
movement in Britain, of the Nouvelle Vague in France, and the 'Polish
school' which flourished during a brief period of liberalization in Poland
and other parts of East Central Europe. These cinemas share a strong
impulse towards, in Truffaut's phrase, 'realism and life', in opposition to
the stale formulae of the studio films of the period (in the Polish case,
those of a 'socialist realism' which was neither realist nor socialist). The
1960s proper lasted roughly from 1963 to 1968, coinciding with the steady
escalation of the American war in Vietnam and culminating with the May
Events in Paris and the Soviet invasion of Czechoslovakia. To this period
belong the Czechoslovak New Wave, the Young German Cinema, the
first stirrings of new cinemas in Latin America, and a plethora of often
rather confusing developments in other countries. In this period realism
ceases to be an unquestioned value, but the move away from it takes
contradictory forms, from the exploration of sexual fantasy in Roman
Polanski's *Repulsion* (1965) and Luis Buñuel's *Belle de Jour* (1967), to the

ritualism of Glauber Rocha's *Black God, White Devil* (1964), to the sheer wackiness of Richard Lester, to the beginnings of a Brechtianized cinema in Godard and Straub. After 1968 there is a third phase as opposition to the Vietnam War reaches its climax, the thwarted militancy of the May Events finds outlet in terrorism, and Europe begins to rethink the founding myths of its post-1945 resurgence. Even more than the 1963–68 period, this 'post-1960s' is hard to characterize in cinema terms and I would be hesitant to make patterns where none exist. But of the traumatic character of 1968 there can be no doubt. Optimism and the belief in a better world round the corner are in diminishing supply. Films become more reflective and finally, after a long silence, the cinema follows the lead of literature in critically examining the recent past.

Why Europe?

Finally I need to say something about the last of the questions posed at the beginning of this introduction: why, if the new cinemas were a worldwide phenomenon, does this book concentrate so heavily on western Europe? There are two reasons for this, good and less good.

The less good reason is a self-limiting one. This is not a learned book. I have not read massively in the secondary literatures or chased down abstruse films that have disappeared from circulation. I am dependent on what I know or have been able easily to find out. I am reasonably confident that in matters to do with western European cinema I at least know what I am talking about. But when it come to Czech, Japanese, or even Brazilian cinema, I am at a loss. I can only follow the films (if available at all) through subtitles which are frequently unreliable, and the literature about them in a (to me) more accessible language rarely seems to address the questions that I think need answering. For that reason alone I have not given Eastern European, Latin American, or (especially) Japanese cinemas the space they undoubtedly deserve. If this is Eurocentrism, all I can plead is guilty with mitigation.

There is, however, a good reason for Eurocentrism in talking about the new cinemas of the 1960s and this is that Europe really was the centre of most of what went on during the decade. Paris, London, and Rome were the centre, and Rio de Janeiro and Tokyo were the periphery. Los Angeles was also on the periphery and even New York was not as central as New Yorkers would like to believe. As a movement, the new cinemas spread outwards, beginning in Britain, France, and Italy and gradually taking in other parts of the globe. But even as new cinemas emerged outside the original nucleus they continued to look to the centre for validation. Reputations and access to markets were gained and lost at European Festivals, especially Cannes or Venice but also Berlin, Locarno, or San Sebastian, or on first release in major European cities. North America was relatively insignificant. As producers, Canada and the USA were pioneers of the new documentary and there were moments when it looked as if American experimental films were going to break out of the world of the artistic avant-gardes into that of regular film distribution. Commercially, North American release was very valuable to new cinema film-makers and the European subsidiaries of the major US releasing companies, especially Warner Bros., played an important and underappreciated role in guaranteeing distribution for many new cinema films. But on the whole the 1960s was a period when Europe led, other countries followed, and the USA looked on.

Last of all I should point out that in talking about 'the cinema' (new or otherwise), I have confined myself mostly to the world of films which were made for commercial release. Although in dealing with documentary I cover a number of films made either for television or for release on non-commercial 16 mm circuits, I have with some reluctance excluded the Underground and the artistic avant-gardes from consideration. In so doing I have fallen into the trap laid by Godard for Michel Piccoli in *Deux fois cinquante ans de cinéma français* (1995). Godard interviews Piccoli on video about his role as head of the celebrations of the centenary of cinema in 1995. Exactly what centenary are you celebrating?, Godard asks. That of the Lumière brothers' first screening of films to a paying public, replies Piccoli. Aha, says Godard, so by cinema you mean capitalist cinema. In this book, too, cinema is capitalist cinema. But that is what the cinema is, even when it rebelled, as it did in the 1960s.

Notes

1. Geoffrey Nowell-Smith, *L'avventura* (London: British Film Institute, 1997), p. 11.

2. Susan Sontag, 'On Godard's *Vivre sa vie*', *Moviegoer* 2, summer/autumn 1964. Reprinted in *Against Interpretation* (New York: Farrar, Straus & Giroux, 1966).

3. David Bordwell, *Narration in the Fiction Film* (Madison, WI: University of Wisconsin Press, and London: Methuen, 1985).

4. Gilles Deleuze, *Cinéma 1: l'image-mouvement* (Paris: Editions de Minuit, 1983) and *Cinéma 2: l'image-temps* (Paris: Editions de Minuit, 1985); translated as *Cinema 1: The Movement-Image* (London: Athlone Press, 1986) and *Cinema 2: The Time-Image* (London: Athlone Press, 1989).

Part I

Before the Revolution

1

World Cinema in the 1950s

There were troubles ahead, but the 1950s were on the whole good years for world cinema. European cinemas (with the partial exception of Germany) had recovered from wartime devastation and were fighting back against Hollywood competition. The American cinema itself had never been better. Boosted by refugees from Nazism, many of whom preferred to remain in California rather than return to their home countries, Hollywood was flowering artistically even as its economic dominance was beginning to be challenged. The studio system had become less rigid than it had been before the War. Creatively minded producers, whether outside the studios like John Houseman or inside like Arthur Freed at MGM, worked to allow artistic talent to flourish as never before. Among directors, established masters like John Ford and Howard Hawks were still at the height of their powers. Emerging talents included John Huston, Nicholas Ray, and the prodigious Orson Welles, while among the émigrés there were not only refugees from Nazism such as Fritz Lang, Billy Wilder, Otto Preminger, and Douglas Sirk, but there was also Alfred Hitchcock who had been enticed across the Atlantic by David O. Selznick and showed no sign of wishing to leave.

The American cinema was on the whole market-led and organized around recognizable popular genres such as family dramas, comedies, crime films, westerns, and musicals. American comedies were perhaps not quite as brilliant as they had been the 1930s and early 1940s, but most of the other genres were at their peak of achievement. The classic gangster genre had given way to what was to become known as film noir, in a late flowering of masterly black and white cinematography. Across the board of dominant genres, one has only to think of *Singin' in the Rain* (Gene Kelly and Stanley Donen, 1951), *All I Desire* (Douglas Sirk, 1953), *Rebel without a Cause* (Nicholas Ray, 1955), *The Searchers* (John Ford, 1956), *Touch of Evil* (Orson Welles, 1958), or Hitchcock's *Vertigo* (1958) to realize that this was a time not only of good films but of great ones. If there was one thing wrong with the scene from the cinemagoer's point of view it was that the American audience was (or was thought to be) only interested in American product. Outside the major cities or on the 16 mm circuit there were few foreign films to be seen.

In Europe the situation was very different and in some respects opposite. The return of American films to continental Europe in 1946 was a welcome relief after wartime austerity. Since these included not only new films but films from the war years themselves – *Citizen Kane* (1941), *Casablanca* (1942), *Meet Me in St. Louis* (1944), to name but three – the late 1940s offered audiences a veritable bonanza. Faced with the Hollywood deluge, European industries at first found it hard to compete without the benefit of protectionist legislation, reluctantly conceded by the Americans. By the mid-1950s, however, the industries in France and Italy had recovered and home-produced films were as popular as American at the box office. These were for the most part the same sort of films as had been popular before the war, but there were some films that were different. The most famous of these were the products of Italian neo-realism, a movement in aesthetic rebellion against the studio confections of the 1930s and politically committed to the anti-Fascist culture that had emerged from the liberation struggle in 1943–5. Neo-realist films were only sporadically popular at the box office but they had a worldwide resonance among critics and actual or future film-makers, not just in Europe but in Latin America and even in India, where Vittorio De Sica and Cesare Zavattini's *Bicycle Thieves* was to prove a life-long influence on the young Satyajit Ray.

Whereas in the United States or Britain films had to be made for the mass market if they were to be released at all, the situation in many European countries was more flexible. Modestly budgeted films could pay their way on the basis of a limited big-city release in their home country followed, with luck, by export sales picked up when the film was shown at one of the many festivals which grew up in the postwar period. This was a chancy business for producers since the available home market could be quite small even when it was enhanced by a co-production agreement enabling a partner producer to claim home-market protection in another European country.

Attempts to maximize the market for non-mainstream production led to the development of a phenomenon generically, and rather confusingly, known as art cinema. While some of the films placed under this rubric could indeed be distinguished by their claim to be somehow more like 'art' than ordinary films were, the main distinction operating in practice lay in the way they were promoted and distributed. Films that appeared on 'art cinema' circuits were not necessarily more artistic than mainstream films. Indeed they often *were* mainstream films, at least in their country of origin, but acquired extra cachet when circulating abroad in subtitled versions. The art cinema circuits in Britain in the 1950s, for example, showed films of many different kinds. Some were genuinely artistic films of minority appeal; some were quality mainstream; some were sub-artistic tat whose only claim to distinction was that they were foreign; and some were there because they had more sex in them than mainstream films usually did. It is significant that the first, and for a long time the only, film by the great Kenji Mizoguchi to be shown commercially in Britain was *Street of Shame* (1956), which as its title suggests was a film about prostitution, then still a taboo subject in the British as well as the American cinema.

The main problem for the industry worldwide was that fewer people were going to the cinema. The trend started in Britain and the USA immediately after the war and spread to continental Europe and to Japan in the late 1950s. This was not an immediate concern in Europe before 1960 because even if attendances were beginning to fall, a higher proportion of spectators was watching home-produced films, which was good for the producers, and ticket prices were increasing, to the benefit of exhibitors. The main losers were the Americans, faced with a loss of audience numbers both at home and to a lesser degree in export markets.

But even more important than how many people were deserting the cinema was who these people were. Until the 1960s, all films in the USA were made for universal consumption, with the 'family audience' always in mind. It was this family audience that was breaking up in the postwar period. If parents with young children preferred to stay home and watch TV, and teenagers opted to go out on their own, Hollywood found itself without an audience for its core product. Various steps were taken in the 1950s to stem the decline. Films were made more spectacular, to differentiate them from what you could get from the television. Colour became almost universal (TV was still black and white); wide-screen and stereo sound were introduced in 1953, first by 20th Century–Fox and then by the other studios. Teenagers were wooed by rock'n'roll, by teen-flicks such as those starring Sandra Dee, and (mainly outside the studios) by horror films. But basically Hollywood had no answer to the problems of the changing audience.

The heart of the problem lay in the industry itself, with its cumbersome capital-intensive apparatus and above all its largely self-imposed censorship. Unlike some other countries, the American cinema did not have separate censorship or classification categories. All films had to be suitable for everybody and the criteria of suitability were very narrowly defined. Both audiences and film-makers grew increasingly restive during the 1950s. The Production Code Administration (PCA), which handled the censorship or pre-censorship of films, was besieged with demands from producers to be allowed to introduce more adult subject matter, and in 1954 and again in 1956 modifications were made to the Code, allowing 'mature' subjects such as prostitution, drug addiction, and miscegenation to be shown if 'treated within the limits of good taste'.[1] Otto Preminger, a particularly sharp thorn in the PCA's side, was able (just) to make *The Man with the Golden Arm* with its heroin-addicted hero in 1955, but even in 1958 MGM was only able to get its adaptation of the Broadway musical *Gigi* through the PCA by making the heroine marry the rakish hero rather than enter into a career as a kept woman.

The Production Code was binding on all members of the Motion Picture Association of America (MPAA) and applied not only to the films its members made but those that they distributed. But it was not easily enforced on companies who were not members of the Association. Small distributors were free to take on foreign films which contained elements that would not have passed the Code. In 1950, two basically pretty innocent scenes in *Bicycle Thieves* involving a little boy who on one occasion wanders with his father into what turns out to be a brothel and on another starts opening his fly to pee against a wall were objected to by the PCA but the distributor refused to submit and the film was shown uncut, even in mainstream cinemas. Then, the following year, objections were raised by American Catholic organizations to Roberto Rossellini's *The Miracle* in which a simple girl is made pregnant by a man she mistakes for St Joseph. The case made its way to the Supreme Court, which ruled in 1952 that films were covered by the First Amendment guaranteeing freedom of speech and the film could not be prohibited from being shown.

European countries had censorship problems too, but the issues were as likely to be political as sexual. Visconti's *Senso* (1954) was shorn of two crucial scenes deemed to be insulting to national memory and a few years later Godard's *Le Petit Soldat* (1960) was banned in France for its implication that right-wing terror groups were engaged in the struggle to prevent Algeria from gaining independence. But European censorship had always been less prudish than American, even before the imposition of the Production Code. It tended to be assumed in European films that human beings were born with sexual organs and at a certain point in their lives began to use them, not always in socially approved ways. (These were known facts in the USA as well, but the PCA did its best to disguise them.[2]) In the 1950s, both Britain and France introduced 'over-sixteen' certificates, which meant that films like Ingmar Bergman's *Summer with Monika* (1952) or Roger Vadim's *And God Created Woman* (1956) could be shown to adolescent and adult audiences, even if the nudity in them was deemed unsuitable for children.

These differential censorship practices gave a welcome boost to European cinema, both at home and to some extent in America. In America they led to a substantial trickle (but still far from a flood) of free-thinking European films entering the market and to a dent in the value of exports as European audiences turned to more 'adult' material. More liberal censorship was not the only factor behind the resurgence of the European film industries in the 1950s, but it certainly played a role. By the mid-1950s domestic production (including co-production with other European countries[3]) accounted for 40 to 50 per cent of box office revenues in both France and Italy, a significant rise since the immediate postwar years. Since the market overall was shrinking, if only slowly, this meant that Hollywood could no longer rely on exports to Europe as a stable source of income. By 1960 the European film industries found themselves in a generally good state of health, while Hollywood was entering a severe crisis.

Not that the situation in Europe was entirely rosy. German cinema had still not fully recovered from the effects of Nazism, war, and a partition that left the major studios in the Soviet Zone (later German Democratic Republic). Spain slumbered under the regime of General Franco, though it had one great (and anti-Franquist) director in the form of Juan Antonio Bardem. Eastern Europe was experiencing a post-Stalin thaw, but it was slow to take effect and had suffered a nasty setback following the repression of the Hungarian revolt in 1956. Meanwhile in

France the commercial industry, although better organized than it had been, was nostalgically tied to the values of the 1930s and unprepared for the changes taking place in cultural life. As for Japan, its problems were very much the same as those of Hollywood, with audiences deserting the tried and trusted genres and the studios uncertain of what formulas could replace them.

The need for renewal was most strongly felt in the country where it happened least, the United States. Here the 1960s turned out to be a period mostly of decline. As the great genres fell out of favour with audiences, so the films produced in them declined in both quantity and quality. Westerns and musicals were still being made, but the great directors, such as Anthony Mann and Budd Boetticher in the western, or Vincente Minnelli in the musical, were no longer making them.[4] The fate of the western is perhaps best summed up in a comparison between two films which came out in 1962. John Ford's *The Man Who Shot Liberty Valance* is a sentimental elegy both for the old west and for the genre that celebrated it. Sam Peckinpah's *Ride the High Country* (released in Britain as *Guns in the Afternoon*) is, by contrast, harsh and unsparing, a study not so much of decay as of decadence, and as such marks (perhaps perversely) the first step in a renewal of the genre that was to take place, under the unlikely stimulus of competition from the 'spaghetti' westerns of Sergio Leone, in the 1970s. For its part, family drama did not die out (how could it?) or even go into hibernation, but the issues it foregrounded had lost their urgency and, as with the western and the musical, its greatest practitioners drifted away from the genre by the mid-60s if not earlier. Sirk retired; Minnelli made a few more dramas but his career then went into abeyance; Ray was tempted by producer Samuel Bronson into making historical spectaculars in Spain, before giving up commercial filmmaking entirely in the late 1960s.

If nothing else, Hollywood was due for a generational change. Some of the leading directors who had started in the silent period went on making films into the 1960s or even 70s, but in the case of Ford and Hawks these were mostly tired copies of their earlier work. Only Hitchcock continued to surprise: with *Psycho* in 1960, *The Birds* in 1963, *Marnie* in 1964, and *Torn Curtain* in 1966, after which he too went into relative decline. When newcomers started appearing it was often on the fringes of industry, as with John Cassavetes, or as a result of some stimulus from Europe. Arthur Penn, the most original talent to emerge in Hollywood in the period, was recognized as such in Europe from the time of his first film

The Left-Handed Gun (1959) onwards, but continued to struggle in his home country. He eventually had success both at home and abroad with *Bonnie and Clyde* in 1967, but only after the project had been offered to François Truffaut, who eventually turned it down.[5] While *Bonnie and Clyde* was only possible because of the relaxation of censorship that took place steadily throughout the 1960s, its use of slow-motion and its stylization of violence almost certainly came about under the influence of Leone and the spaghetti western, as of course did the use of the same techniques by Peckinpah in *The Wild Bunch* in 1969.

Before the European cinema could start influencing Hollywood, however, it first had to renew itself, or at least shake itself up a bit. In one way this was not difficult. European cinemas operated at more different levels and had more room for experiment and innovation than did the American. But it is one thing for experimentation to take place, it is another for it to acquire critical mass – or, to use a different metaphor, for ripples to become a wave.

In the late 1950s, there were a number of signs that such a development was underway in various parts of Europe. But these signs were contradictory and pointed in a number of different directions. One sign was the emergence or re-emergence of an international audience that actually sought out artistically challenging films. Ingmar Bergman had been little known outside his native Sweden until the release of *The Seventh Seal* in 1957. That film's instant success led to a revival of other lesser known Bergman films such as *Summer with Monika* (1952) and *Summer Interlude* (1950). *Summer with Monika* was a great hit with art house audiences, due in large part to its refreshing sexual openness, but the impact of *Summer Interlude* was even greater since it inspired future film-makers as well. Both Jean-Luc Godard and Jacques Rivette waxed lyrical about it in *Cahiers du cinéma*, with Godard calling it (with some rhetorical exaggeration) 'the most beautiful of films'.[6]

The future New Wave directors, led in this case by Truffaut, were also great supporters of the French film-maker Robert Bresson, who was in many respects the polar opposite of Bergman. Whereas Bergman harked back to the 1920s avant-gardes in his fondness for picturesque artistic effects, Bresson was deliberately ascetic and austere. His films of the 1950s, such as *A Man Escapes* (1956) or *Pickpocket* (1959), avoided almost all forms of expressive or dramatic effect, using simple compositions and employing non-professional actors whose faces remained clear of any trace of simulated emotion. Bresson's films were never popular with the mass audience, or even the section of the art house audience in search of sexual titillation not available in the mainstream, but they performed adequately at the box office in France, were enthusiastically greeted by specialist film critics, and had wide circulation on the *art et essai* circuits and on 16 mm.

But the new cinemas of the 1960s did not emerge straightforwardly from an art cinema background of the kind represented by Bergman or Bresson. Indeed if the new film-makers had set out to make films for an art cinema market only, the new cinemas would never have got off the ground. Films are commercial products and the art film market, although expanding, was not large enough on its own to support more than a few films. Nor was it safe to make a film in the expectation of export sales. At least in its country of origin, a new film had to obtain some sort of release into the general commercial market.

One way into the commercial market was to make genre films, particularly in some variety of the crime genre. Crime films were consistently popular, were inexpensive to make, and offered great flexibility to film-makers. American crime films were universally popular but audiences also appreciated films about homegrown criminals, so when blacklisted American directors John Berry and Joseph Losey arrived in Europe in the early 1950s they were soon drafted in to apply their supposed expertise to the making of crime films – Berry mainly in France, Losey mainly in Britain. Losey's early British crime films are full of random melodramatic and baroque elements, but by the time of *Blind Date* (1959) and *The Criminal* (1960) these are firmly under control and form part of the style he was to bring to the 'art' films he was to make with Harold Pinter in the 1960s.

Berry's career in France was less successful, being mainly confined to low-budget Eddie Constantine vehicles, but the insatiable French appetite for crime films gave opportunities to a number of younger film-makers who would either develop the genre in new ways or use it as a springboard to other things. Among the former were Jean-Pierre Melville, who first made his mark as a crime film specialist with the finely crafted (and largely location-shot) gangster film *Bob le flambeur* in 1955, and Claude Sautet, director of the thriller *Classe tous risques* in 1960 and previously screenwriter on Georges Franju's extraordinary horror film *Eyes without a Face* (1959). Meanwhile Louis Malle came to the fore in 1957 with a thriller, *Lift to the Scaffold*, also location shot and with a stunning jazz score by Miles Davis, generally reckoned to be a harbinger of the Nouvelle Vague.

Crime films, or at any rate films with crime subjects or underworld settings, were also a significant component of film production in Italy in the middle and late 1950s, many of them spin-offs from the collapse of neo-realism as social cinema. Apart from Federico Fellini's *Il bidone* in 1955 these were generally undistinguished and the directors who debuted in the genre such as Franco Rossi and Mauro Bolognini did not fulfill their initial promise. There was one exception, Francesco Rosi, whose first two features, *La sfida* (1957) and *I magliari* (1959), were both gangster films, with a number of fairly stereotypical generic elements but at the same time a hard edge to them provided by the location settings and sharply observed social detail.

The alternative to the low-budget, low-prestige crime or other genre film, was the high-budget, high-prestige international quality production. With large sums of money at stake, this was a risky enterprise. A number of films of this type in the mid-1950s had either done not well enough (for example, Visconti's *Senso* in 1954) or even spectacularly badly (Max Ophuls's *Lola Montès* in 1955). But in 1958 the major Italian producers, encouraged by the good box-office results the previous year of Fellini's *Le notti di Cabiria* and Visconti's *White Nights*, decided to invest heavily in high-class productions bringing together 'name' directors with bankable stars such as Marcello Mastroianni, Sophia Loren, or the young Claudia Cardinale. Unexpectedly, the former neo-realists, whose careers appeared to be in the doldrums, got a new lease of life. First to benefit was Roberto Rossellini with *General Della Rovere*, produced by independent producer Moris Ergas, which went on to win the Golden Lion at Venice in 1959. De Sica, who stars in *General Della Rovere* but whose career as a director was languishing somewhat, though never as badly as Rossellini, also hit the jackpot in 1960 with a film of Alberto Moravia's novel *La ciociara*, produced by Carlo Ponti and starring Ponti's wife Sophia Loren, and released in Britain and the USA as *Two Women*. Another former neo-realist, Pietro Germi, was encouraged by producer Franco Cristaldi to turn his hand to comedy, which he did with great success with *Divorce Italian Style* in 1961. Even more successful were Fellini's *La dolce vita* and Visconti's *Rocco and his Brothers*, which were to top the Italian box office in the 1960/61 season.

But even before Italian producers had put the final touch to their strategy, the world of cinema was rocked by the triumph at the Cannes

Film Festival in May 1959 of three films which announced to the world
the existence of a distinct 'New Wave' in French film-making. These
films were *Orfeu negro*, by Marcel Camus; *Hiroshima mon amour*, by
Alain Resnais; and *Les Quatre cents coups*, by François Truffaut. These
films were very different from each other, but whether taken singly or
together they were also very different from the cinematic mainstream, in
France or anywhere else. Put together with the Italian films which appeared the following year, *La dolce vita* obviously but also, and especially,
Michelangelo Antonioni's *L'avventura*, with a side glance to John
Cassavetes's *Shadows* and (admittedly unknown in the west) Nagisa
Oshima's *Night and Fog in Japan*, and it was clear that the 1960s in the
cinema were set to be a revolutionary decade.

Notes

1. See Richard Maltby, 'Censorship and self-regulation', in Geoffrey Nowell-Smith
(ed.), *The Oxford History of World Cinema* (Oxford: Oxford University Press, 1996),
p. 247.

2. The main purpose of the code was economic. By submitting to a system of regu-
lation of content (stricter than most of them would have liked), the members of the MPAA
ensured that all the films they planned to make could be put on the market and once
released could circulate everywhere without the need for expensive re-editing to suit local
susceptibilities. (This applied not only in the USA itself, where state and city censor boards
had to be placated, but as far as possible in export markets as well.) But in order to achieve
this universality, the companies that signed up to the PCA not only bound themselves to
an often bizarre set of rules limiting what sexual activities or body-parts could be shown
(or recognized to exist) but found themselves contributing to the construction or rein-
forcement of an ideology of 'family values' in which courtship leading to marriage and
the maintenance of marriage thereafter were the only permissible sexual values. This did
not stop Hollywood films from being full of eroticized images (particularly of women)
and sexual energy, for which they were much appreciated all over the world.

3. International co-production, by which producers in two or more countries agree
to share costs and input of talent, had been informally practised in Europe since the late
1920s. It was put on a statutory basis in the early 1950s, enabling producers in each
country to claim home market protection for their film. By the end of the decade over a
quarter of Italian films had some foreign participation, usually French, while Italian
companies participated in a similar proportion of French films. Source: Aldo Bernardini
(ed.), *Il cinema sonoro, 1930–1969* (Rome: ANICA, 1992), pp. 203–18. See also Geoffrey
Nowell-Smith and Steven Ricci (eds.), *Hollywood and Europe* (London: British Film
Institute, 1998), p. 8.

4. The last of the series of Boetticher/Randolph Scott westerns, *Comanche Station*, was made in 1959; Mann's *Cimarron* dates from 1960, after which he turned his hand to the historical spectacular with *El Cid* (1961) and *The Fall of the Roman Empire* (1964). In the musical, the great combination of Arthur Freed as producer and Vincente Minnelli as director had its swan-song in 1958 with *Gigi*, after which Freed produced no more musicals and Minnelli directed only two – *Bells Are Ringing* in 1960 and then *On a Clear Day You Can See for Ever* ten years later in 1970.

5. See Antoine de Baecque and Serge Toubiana, *Truffaut: A Biography* (New York: Alfred A. Knopf, 1999), pp. 270–72. According to Baecque and Toubiana, Truffaut decided to turn down the project when Warren Beatty was proposed for the leading role. It was Beatty who then chose Penn as director.

6. See Jacques Rivette, 'L'Âme au ventre', *Cahiers du cinéma* 84, June 1958, and Jean-Luc Godard, 'Bergmanorama', *Cahiers du cinéma* 85, July 1958. English translation in Tom Milne (ed.), *Godard on Godard* (London: Secker & Warburg, 1972), pp. 75–80.

2

Criticism and Culture

The new cinemas, wherever they appeared, emerged to fill a gap. At one level, obviously, from a capitalistic point of view, this was a gap in the market. In the case of the French Nouvelle Vague at the end of the 1950s, there were changes in the demographic makeup of the audience and producers could sense an opportunity to step in with new product to meet the latent demand. But there is more to the cinema than the status of films as market commodities, even in countries where market relations are dominant. The need felt in the 1960s was not just for new product. It was also, crucially, for new thinking and new modes of experience, often in ways which went against the imperatives which ruled (or appeared to rule) the market. If there was a gap between what the cinema had been and what it aspired to be, it was ideological and cultural at least as much as it was economic. It was a gap between different concepts of art, or different concepts of the relationship between art and politics, and the impulse for change came from film-makers, or critics, or political or cinephile activists, who wanted a cinema responsive to different imperatives than those that ruled in the market-dominated mainstream.

In this perspective, the new cinemas of the 1960s can be seen as bringing to fruition a film culture that came into being mainly in France, Italy, and (to a lesser extent) Britain and the USA, in the years immediately after the Second World War. Many future film-makers were to come out of this culture, especially in France but also in Britain, Italy, and elsewhere. It was initially a culture of cine-clubs and small magazines, but it spread rapidly to occupy an important, though always slightly off-centre position in cultural life. It was not an exclusively art film culture, but it varied a lot in how it accommodated Hollywood and other popular cinemas into its value system.[1]

The film culture of the immediate postwar period had in fact a dual character. On the one hand there was a component of pure cinephilia, a love of films for their own sake, and for the touch of magic they provided in an otherwise dull existence. In this respect it was not unlike (and indeed sprang from) ordinary film-going culture, to which it added a taste for the recondite, historic, and out of the way, accompanied by a relative lack of interest in novelty.

On the other hand this new film culture was also part of the general demand for cultural renewal that accompanied the fall of Fascism in Europe. This culture was generally left-wing, in favour of realism not just in the cinema but across the artistic spectrum, and ambivalent about Hollywood which tended to be regarded as escapist. With the coming of the Cold War in the late 1940s and the McCarthyite witch-hunts in the USA, a political edge was given to an already latent anti-Americanism in left-wing film circles.

The first stirring of the new culture was in Italy, and took place even before the war ended, during the last years of Fascism. Here a small group of left-wing dissidents had infiltrated the film journal *Cinema* and prepared the ground for what was to become neo-realism. *Cinema* and its ilk did not fully anticipate neo-realism, since what they envisaged was a realistic but formally quite conventional new cinema, and the young activists were as taken aback as everyone else when what emerged immediately after the war was the rough hewn and visibly imperfect film-making typified by Rossellini's *Rome Open City* (1945) and *Paisà* (1946). When the new neo-realist films did start appearing, however, it was in the context of a culture eager to throw off the legacy of Fascism, not just its pomp and propaganda but its conformism and narrow cast of mind. The return of Hollywood films to the screen was in this respect a mixed blessing, but it led to a debate about the role and potential of cinema which permeated Italian cultural life. Debate was joined not just by film people but by leading intellectuals from other spheres, by the novelist Alberto Moravia, the poet and cultural critic Franco Fortini, and before long by the *enfant terrible* and general intellectual gadfly Pier Paolo Pasolini. This Italian film culture was predominantly left-wing and stimulated by a Communist Party which, even at the height of the Cold War, was keen to occupy the centre ground in political and cultural life rather than take up positions of splendid isolation.

In France too, the new film culture had its gestation before the end of the war, under the Occupation. There were few new films to be seen and young people began searching out forbidden fruit in the programmes of the cine-clubs or Henri Langlois' Cinémathèque. As in Italy, the new culture only really came into being on any scale after the war, when the import of American films resumed and the first neo-realist films from Italy made an appearance in cinemas and cine-clubs; and as in Italy the interest in cinema was a rebellion against the culture of the previous generation. But whereas in Italy the new film culture was almost exclusively left-wing, in France it was more divided. The career of the famous critic André Bazin is a case in point. In the immediate aftermath of war he worked alongside the Communists in an organization called 'Travail et Culture', showing neo-realist and other films to workers' group in factories and elsewhere and writing in the left-wing film magazine *L'Ecran français*. But with the onset of the Cold War, Bazin and his friends were judged too arty and too pro-American by the Communist Party hacks who had taken over the magazine, and they had to find another platform. To this end in late 1948 they conceived the idea of a high-profile cine-club called Objectif 49 and invited Jean Cocteau to be patron of both the club and of the Festival du Film Maudit, or 'Festival of the ill-fated film' that they planned to hold in the smart resort town of Biarritz the following year.[2]

Objectif 49 opened with a season of American film noir in May 1949, with the Festival du Film Maudit following in the summer. The immediate purpose of the Festival was to screen as wide as possible a range of films which, because of war or other reasons, had not been properly shown in France before. In this it succeeded triumphantly, as the programme included Bertolt Brecht and Slatan Dudow's *Kuhle Wampe*, made in 1932 and banned by the Nazis as soon as they came to power, Luchino Visconti's *Ossessione*, briefly shown in 1943 in Italy before being banned by the Fascists, Robert Bresson's *Les Dames du Bois de Boulogne*, made at the end of the Occupation, and an impressive range of other work of all types including shorts by Norman McLaren and Kenneth Anger and the unsynched rushes of a film shot in Africa by a young ethnographer called Jean Rouch. But it had a secondary purpose, which was to link the worlds of the established arts, of high society, and of left-of-centre film culture with that of the struggling cinephiles who spent their lives watching 16 mm prints of new and old films in draughty basements in Paris and other cities. In this respect it had to wait a long time for success. Film culture was to remain, if not actually marginal, nevertheless somewhat to one side of the cultural mainstream; it also remained split between left and right, as the later history of debates between the magazines *Positif* and *Cahiers du cinéma* was to show.

In Britain too a new film culture was springing up around the film societies, which increased their numbers from less than a hundred in 1945 to over 200 in 1950, many with both 35 mm and 16 mm projection facilities. In 1948 the Oxford University Film Society published the first issue of a magazine called *Sequence*, edited by two undergraduates, Lindsay Anderson and Peter Ericsson, soon to be joined by two other university friends, Gavin Lambert and Penelope Houston, with another friend, Karel Reisz, an occasional contributor. *Sequence* (which had by now moved to London) was an enthusiast's magazine, passionately cinephile like the little magazines emerging out of the cine-clubs in Paris, but also unquestioningly left of centre in politics. It ran for just over a dozen issues, finally running out of money after issue 14 in early 1952. Just before it entered its death throes, however, the director of the British Film Institute, Denis Forman, who had grand plans to give more focus to the lively but dispersed film culture he saw emerging all around him, offered Lambert and Houston a golden opportunity: forget trying to keep *Sequence* alive and instead take over and revitalize the Institute's established but stodgy magazine *Sight and Sound*. At the same time Forman persuaded the government to have a National Film Theatre created on London's South Bank, in order to give Britain a place where the full panorama of cinema could be displayed, as it was in Paris at Langlois' Cinémathèque.

In the early years there was not much to choose between the *Sequence*/*Sight and Sound* writers and their counterparts on the *Revue du cinéma*, *L'Ecran français*, or the early *Cahiers du cinéma*. If there were differences of taste they were minor and not necessarily those that one might expect. Thus Karel Reisz wrote warmly in *Sequence* about Max Ophuls' *La Ronde*, while the young Jean-Luc Godard lambasted it in the cine-club magazine *La Gazette du cinéma*.[3] The British, especially Anderson, were enthusiastic about the westerns of John Ford and MGM musicals by Stanley Donen or Vincente Minnelli. But Roger Leenhardt in *L'Ecran français* attacked Ford for being stagy and artificial by comparison with William Wyler,[4] and the French critics in general were slow to appreciate Minnelli. Both sides concurred in regarding Nicholas Ray's *They Live by Night* as the most exciting debut since *Citizen Kane*.

Everybody liked De Sica, but Eric Rohmer in the *Gazette* seemed to be out on a limb in his extravagant praise for Rossellini's *Stromboli*.[5] Slowly, however, differences began to emerge separating the French critics not just from the British but from a broader international consensus. These differences were variously political, aesthetic, or a mixture.

For a start the French cinephiles, having been drummed out from *L'Ecran français* and other left-wing outlets, felt freer to express their continued love of Hollywood films, which they compared favourably to the popular cinema of their own country. Elsewhere, however, the climate of political suspicion took its hold, and the American films that people admitted to liking became increasingly restricted to those made by real or presumed opponents of the system. The French were also less inclined to couple realism with ideals of social progress, which some of them shared but to which others were indifferent.

Key indicators of emerging difference concerned Hitchcock, deified in France by Rohmer in particular and treated with suspicion everywhere else; Ford, admired elsewhere but increasingly denigrated by the French; Howard Hawks, launched by the young Jacques Rivette in 1953 as the epitome of all that was best in American cinema, but simply not on the critical map as far as the rest of the world was concerned[6]; and Rossellini, whose early 1950s cycle of films with Ingrid Bergman was seen both in Italy and Britain as a deviation from the true path of neo-realism, whereas for Bazin, Rohmer, Truffaut, and others it was more of a fulfilment.

With the foundation by Bazin and Jacques Doniol-Valcroze of the monthly *Cahiers du cinéma* in 1951, the French cinephiles now had a regular outlet for their outpourings and an opportunity to systematize a set of ideas which were steadily differentiating themselves from those of the consensus. In summary (and in the order, roughly, in which they appeared) the key ideas were three.

Firstly, realism. Realism was of course common currency among everyone who had been bowled over by the raw immediacy of Rossellini's *Paisà* or De Sica and Zavattini's *Bicycle Thieves* in the immediate postwar period. But Bazin and Rohmer had a different notion of cinematic realism from the standard one. For Bazin cinematic realism at its best was not reproduction of reality but an encounter. Reality was all the phenomena that make up the world and the unique privilege of cinema was that its apparatus could be used to provide a transparent window on the world, enabling the film-maker to approach these phenomena with an open eye and capture them in their immanent presence to consciousness. It was this openness of the eye to the phenomenal world — and particularly a world in which phenomena were indeed cruelly exposed to the eye as in ravaged postwar Italy – that made Italian neo-realism, especially that of Rossellini, a unique cinematic achievement.

Secondly, *mise en scène*, that is to say the creation of an alternative scenic reality by the placement of people and objects within the frame, their orientation towards the camera, movement of the camera, etc., etc. Here the *Cahiers* writers held at first conflicting views. In Bazin's ideal conception, a film such as *Bicycle Thieves* abolished *mise en scène* since all the effort of staging a scene simply dissolved back into the reality presenting itself to be filmed.[7] Similarly, Bazin chafed at the idea that the film image had to be bounded by a frame and what he loved about Jean Renoir, for instance, was the way in which, in Renoir's films, there was no constricting edge to the image and reality was always free to flow in from beyond the boundary. But even Bazin recognized that these were limit-cases and that it was not just what found its way into the film but how the material was shaped and sculpted for the camera that made a film what it was. For some of the younger writers such as Jacques Rivette, however, *mise en scène* was the very essence of cinema. In the cinema, Rivette argued, what you saw was what you got. The cinema was staged action – that is to say, *mise en scène* – which did not represent an already-there reality (as Bazin would have it) or an idea of an object (the conventional view, as in countless aesthetic textbooks). The film actor was not someone interpreting a pre-conceived (scripted) notion of a 'character' but simply *was* the person to which the audience related. And the film itself was the action in space to which the actors lent their bodily qualities. Films did of course represent real things and did contain ideas but the relation between thing and idea was only possible through the medium of *mise en scène*.[8]

Mise en scène, however, did not mean artfulness of composition. With few exceptions (Cocteau was one and so, to some extent, was Hitchcock), the film-makers the *Cahiers* writers admired were those in whose work a certain naturalness prevailed and the *mise en scène* served the purpose of displaying either an as far as possible transparent reality or intelligible human action. Renoir and Rossellini came especially to represent the former, Hitchcock and Hawks the latter.

The third big idea for *Cahiers* was that of the author. Contrary to what is sometimes claimed, *Cahiers du cinéma* did not invent the idea or notion of film authorship. It was commonly accepted the world over that great directors such Griffith, Chaplin, Eisenstein, Ford, Renoir, Buñuel, Visconti, etc. were the authors of the films they had directed, and disagreement reigned only over how low down the scale the principle extended, particularly in relation to films made in industrial conditions such as those prevailing in Hollywood. In this respect the *Cahiers* writers innovated in two ways. On the one hand they greatly extended the list of directors whose films deserved to be looked at in search of a distinct authorial signature; and on the other hand they provided new reasons why this should be done.

How the full *Cahiers* 'pantheon' developed is outside the scope of this book. What is, however, relevant is the way they developed their idea of *mise en scène* to incorporate within it the notion of the director-author as controlling intelligence.

In a way the *Cahiers* notion of authorship was simply a natural outgrowth of its assertion of the primacy of *mise en scène*. But if it was true, as the *Cahiers* writers maintained, that *mise en scène* was what made a film what it was, why was it that so many directors – *metteurs en scène*, indeed, to use the French term – were not appreciated as much as the writers and producers with whom they worked? And if the production system conspired to belittle them, reducing them to the role of setting pre-selected actors to recite pre-written lines on a pre-constructed set, might it not be the case that actual films were all too often poor simulacra of ideal, Platonic films existing in the head of the *metteur en scène*, but which he was unable to realize?

A starting point for this idealized conception was provided by an idea put forward by Alexandre Astruc, a friend of Bazin's from the days when *L'Ecran français* was still a forum for new ideas. In an article for that magazine from 1948, entitled 'Birth of a new avant-garde: the *caméra-stylo*', Astruc argued that the new cinema needed to have the fluidity and individuality of expression normally associated with writing ('stylo' is French for fountain-pen).[9] How this was to achieved was not quite clear, since neither of the films Astruc cited as examples – *Citizen Kane* and André Malraux' *L'Espoir* – had quite the requisite quality, nor could Astruc achieve it himself in his own films. But the idea continued to resonate and Astruc's largely forgotten article returned to favour when the *Cahiers* writers became the leading film-makers of the Nouvelle Vague.

The idea that a film, while never a pure mental construct, nevertheless somehow needed to flow from the mind of the director like words from a writer's pen, was certainly present to François Truffaut in late 1953 when he delivered to the *Cahiers* office an article bearing the innocent-seeming title 'A certain tendency in French cinema'. This article was in fact a highly polemical assault on the whole French critical and film-making establishment, using the respected screenwriters Jean Aurenche and Pierre Bost as stalking horses. At first the magazine was unwilling to publish it but it eventually saw the light of day in January 1954, where it caused precisely the storm that Truffaut had hoped for and Bazin and Doniol-Valcroze had feared.[10] Much cited as a source for '*auteur* theory', the article contains very little theory of any kind, a lot of polemic, and two ideas that were to become central to Truffaut's later practice as a film-maker.

These ideas were, firstly, that the scriptwriter exists to serve the director and only the director can judge how a scene will play on film; and, secondly, that cynicism is an unacceptable quality in a script, since a director cannot bring to life on the screen characters who have been conceived by the scriptwriter in a mean-spirited manner. As examples of French films free of the crushing dominance of mean-spirited writing, Truffaut cited only five. These were Robert Bresson's *The Diary of a Country Priest* (1950), Renoir's *The Golden Coach* (1953), Cocteau's *Orphée* (1950), Jacques Becker's *Casque d'or* (1952), and Jacques Tati's *Monsieur Hulot's Holiday* (1953). Had he written the article a year or so later, he would probably have included Max Ophuls's *Madame de . . .* (1953) in the list, but at the time he was not yet the friend and admirer of Ophuls that he later became.

The immediate effect of 'A certain tendency' was political. It made Truffaut one important friend, the right-wing publisher of the fortnightly magazine *Arts*, Jacques Laurent, who promptly offered him a position on the paper, and many enemies, mainly on the left. In fact, if anything deserved the title 'tendency' it was now *Cahiers*, which had put itself on a collision course not only with the left-of-centre cultural establishment but with rival cinephiles associated with the neo-Surrealist magazine *Positif*.[11] What Truffaut's ideas would mean positively for the future of French film-making was something which would only emerge later.

There were in fact many components open to right-wing construal in the writing of the *Cahiers* school which had begun to be noted well before 'A certain tendency' and Truffaut's opportunistic alliance with Laurent. Bazin's phenomenological approach to cinematic realism was explicitly anti-Marxist and his criticism of montage cinema as breaking up the seamless nature of reality was developed in the context of an attack on Eisenstein and Soviet cinema more widely. His passionate defence of Rossellini as the true realist was again a polemical response to Marxist ideas – in this case the Lukacsian concept of realism espoused by the Italian critic Guido Aristarco. Bazin, however, was never right-wing in the way some of the younger *Cahiers* writers became. His criticism of what he saw as an increasingly Stalinized left was part of a battle for the centre ground, which he felt that the pro-Communist left had occupied by deception.

In his home country, Bazin continued to enjoy considerable prestige as a critic, even if his younger associates were regarded with more than a little suspicion. Outside France, however, the unique way in which Bazin, Rohmer, and their friends had interpreted neo-realism had little resonance. For the rest of the world, neo-realism was a social movement as much as an aesthetic and its prophet was not André Bazin but Cesare Zavattini.

Zavattini, popularly known as Za, was not only the scriptwriter and effective co-author of *Bicycle Thieves* and other films directed by Vittorio De Sica from 1943 onwards. He was also a tireless propagandist, carrying the neo-realist message all over Europe, including the Soviet Union, and to various parts of Latin America. Unlike Bazin, Za was not a systematic or even consistent thinker and it was not always entirely clear from time to time what the content of this message actually was; sometimes, indeed, it seemed as if neo-realism as preached by Zavattini was not so much an aesthetic doctrine and more a way of life. Wherever he went, however, (which was just about everywhere except the USA, where he was refused a visa) he inspired film-makers to think in unaccustomed terms, as much about the sorts of problem a film might address as how it might capture the reality brought before the camera.

Bazin did have a worldwide influence on the new cinemas, but it was at one remove. His ideas and personality deeply affected the young film-makers of the French New Wave or Nouvelle Vague, especially Truffaut. And these New Wave films, when they came to be seen at festivals and in specialist cinemas all over the world, had an impact greater than that of any theorist or propagandist – even Za. On the other hand Italian neo-realism, whether as interpreted by Zavattini or by Bazin, continued to have an enormous impact outside Europe even after it had fallen out of fashion in Italy itself.

It is safe to say that most writers and thinkers about the cinema in the years before 1960 had a more or less pyramidal conception of cinema. At the top were a handful of masterworks, created by great artists with an individual vision and, generally, a realistic approach to their subject matter, and at the bottom were the hundreds of films made in industrial conditions where the rules of genre prevailed over aspirations either to realism or to individual self-expression. Exceptions might exist, for example in the cases of comedy, animation, or a tiny sector called the avant-garde, which were allowed to be surrealist rather than realist, but these exceptions were few. Even the *Cahiers* school never broke entirely with the consensus. It had its own pantheon of great directors (though its membership was not the same as the standard one) and it was if anything even more extreme in its dedication to the values of individual self-expression, differing from other schools only in its greater openness to the genre film (especially westerns and crime films) and its willingness to find great authors within the ranks of genre film-makers. Some of this liking for the genre film spilled over into the film-making practice of the early Nouvelle Vague. But if one takes the very top of the pyramid to be represented by Renoir, Rossellini, Hitchcock, and Hawks, it was undoubtedly the former two who provided the most inspiration to the critics-turned-film-makers of the early Nouvelle Vague. Chabrol and to some extent Truffaut were influenced by Hitchcock and even imitated him. As for Hawks, he continued to be admired but his influence was diffuse; in so far as films such as Truffaut's *Shoot the Pianist* or Jacques Demy's *Lola* are intelligent, unfussy, and adept at mastering changes of emotional tone, this may count as a Hawksian influence, but only loosely.

East of the Iron Curtain the same values of realism and artistic self-expression prevailed, but complicated by the restrictions on both form and content imposed by the authorities. The approved doctrine of 'Socialist Realism' was realist in name only and the rebellion against it that was gathering pace in the late 1950s and early 1960s was in large part motivated by a sense that this so-called realism obscured reality more than it revealed it. The right of the artist to self-expression was defended not as an absolute but because the artist needed this right in order to approach reality directly. There were of course plenty of other reasons for rebelling against the dead hand of bureaucracy and censorship but in the first stages of the rebellion it was arguments based on extending the concept of realism that were most likely to prevail and indeed did prevail.

The new cinemas of the 1960s, then, almost all developed from a broadly realist matrix, and were generally welcomed by the critics for that reason. There were differences. The French (or at any rate the *Cahiers* school) were more cinephile than the British, and more open to genre cinema. The Eastern Europeans and to some extent the Italians all had experiences of forms of realism which for one reason or another they had to get beyond. But non- or anti-realist aesthetic doctrines had very little purchase in the late 1950s and early 1960s, and film-makers wishing to break radically with realism had very much to plough their own furrow. Among those who did were Nagisa Oshima in Japan, Alain Resnais and Chris Marker in France, and Federico Fellini in Italy. They were to be followed by Roman Polanski (but only when he left Poland), Pier Paolo Pasolini in Italy, and Alexander Kluge in Germany. By the mid-1960s a number of film-makers who had started as realists began to move away from realism for one reason or another. When they did, they found critical opinion only partially prepared.

For critical opinion to be fully prepared for the sort of things that happened to the cinema in the 1960s there had to be intellectual and cultural changes which went way beyond the world of cinema as such. These changes – notably a revival of interest in modernism and the avant-garde, the emergence of a distinct strain of western Marxism in opposition to Stalinist orthodoxy (and its Trotskyite mirror), and the arrival of structuralism and semiotics – all went in the direction of challenging traditional realist assumptions about the relationship of representations to the objects they purported to represent. They took place in the first instance in arts other than the cinema, and in thinking about arts other than the cinema, and infiltrated the cinema only slowly and often indirectly. But they also meant that, while the legacy of the 1950s weighed heavily on the new cinemas when they came into existence around 1960, by the end of the 1960s the culture of cinema had changed radically. It was more open and more attuned to artistic diversity than it had been ten years earlier. It had also pushed itself into the centre of cultural and artistic life as never before.

Notes

1. The new film culture was weakest in the USA, for obvious reasons. The 'art film' culture in the US, such as it was, tended to be conservative and anti-popular (which to a lesser extent it also was in Europe). On the other hand the resurgent avant-garde, as

represented for example by Maya Deren or Kenneth Anger, was stronger there than anywhere in Europe. Meanwhile the presence of large Italian communities in many American cities, especially New York, meant that neo-realist films could rely on a wider market than just the art film one.

2. Literally 'maudit' means accursed. The idea of 'film maudit' seems to have been coined by Cocteau on the analogy of Mallarmé's 'poète maudit' whose destiny is to be unappreciated in his lifetime. In practice, however, a 'film maudit' could be any film which had been unlucky in its distribution history.

3. Respectively in *Sequence* 14, January 1952, and *La Gazette du cinéma* 1, May 1950.

4. Roger Leenhardt, 'A bas Ford! Vive Wyler', *L'Ecran français*, 13 April 1948.

5. Maurice Schérer [Eric Rohmer], 'Roberto Rossellini: *Stromboli*', *La Gazette du cinéma* 5, November 1950. English translation in Eric Rohmer, *The Taste for Beauty* (Cambridge: Cambridge University Press, 1989), pp. 124–7.

6. Jacques Rivette, 'Génie de Howard Hawks', *Cahiers du cinéma* n. 23, May 1953, pp. 16–23. English translation (not always reliable) in Jim Hillier and Peter Wollen (eds.), *Howard Hawks: American Artist* (London: BFI, 1996).

7. André Bazin, 'Voleur de bicyclette' in *Qu'est-ce que le cinéma?*, vol 4 (Paris: Editions du Cerf, 1962), pp. 45–59, especially p. 59. Originally in *Esprit*, November 1949. English translation in *What Is Cinema?* vol. 2 (Berkeley: University of California Press, 1971), p. 60.

8. This summary of Rivette's position is based partly on an extraordinary article he wrote, at the age of 22, in the *Gazette du cinéma* (no. 4, October 1950) criticizing the aesthetic premises he saw as underlying the second Biarritz festival in 1950. Neither here nor in his later writings, however, is Rivette a particularly clear writer and I may have forced my interpretation of him somewhat.

9. 'Naissance d'une nouvelle avant-garde: la caméra stylo', *L'Écran français*, 144. English translation in Peter Graham (ed.), *The New Wave* (London: Secker and Warburg, 1968), pp. 17–23.

10. François Truffaut, 'Une certaine tendance du cinéma français', *Cahiers du cinéma* 31, January 1954.

11. What irked *Positif* in particular, however, was not *Cahiers*' hostility to the sacred cows of French cinema so much as the pious tone that sometimes emanated from its pages. See in particular the article by Gérard Gozlan, 'In praise of André Bazin', in *Positif* 47, 1962. English translation in Graham, *The New Wave*, pp. 52–70.

Part II
The New Cinemas

3

New Cinemas, New Politics

Politics in the 1960s was far too important to be left to the politicians. It was a decade of activism and mass movements, of civil-rights and anti-war demonstrations, beginning with the CND marches in Britain and culminating in the street festival of May '68 in Paris and the rallies in Prague brought to a brutal end by Soviet troops.

In such a period the cinema could not be a passive bystander. The cinema of the 1950s had been on the whole apolitical, as indeed the mainstream cinema usually is. The film industry does not like to divide its audience and the general tendency was to avoid subjects which were uselessly contentious and off-putting to too many people. Other than in Italy, with the brief flowering of neo-realism in the late 1940s, most national cinemas played safe throughout the postwar period. Anti-Fascism was confined to history (and for preference to the war film). Hollywood produced some films which in the process of exalting the American way of life identified Communism as the enemy, but this was often no more than a plot device there had to be an enemy, and Communists (like Nazis) could conveniently fit the bill, at least for domestic audiences (countries with large numbers of Communist voters were less enthusiastic).[1] There were also a number of 'issue' films, taking up accepted contentious issues such as race relations, and a few films, such as Henri-Georges Clouzot's *The Wages of Fear* (1953), which were overtly anti-imperialist or anti-American. But on the whole the cinema eschewed political themes and – even more importantly – the expression of political attitudes.

Around 1960 the situation changed radically. There was suddenly a new audience for films which were more politically assertive and expressive of a new political mood. And there were film-makers with films to satisfy this changing mood. The audience was not huge, but it did not have to be, since the films were often small-scale and independently released and could recoup their costs even if they appealed only to young, radicalized urban audiences. The film-makers did not always wait for the audiences to develop, since they themselves were often among the first people to raise the standard on behalf of the new politics.

The 1950s were on the whole placid, prosperous (though much of southern Europe remained desperately poor), and dominated by the Cold War. In the United States these were the 'Eisenhower years', famed for their complacency. Right-wing governments were in power in most of western Europe: the Conservatives in Britain, Christian Democrats in Germany and Italy, Franco in Spain. France was ruled by a variety of coalitions, but the presence in them of the social-democratic SFIO did little to alter the generally conservative tenor of official politics. Only in Sweden and the other Scandinavian countries was social democracy solidly entrenched. Communist parties were in power nowhere, except of course in Eastern Europe, where they exercised a total monopoly.

The general mood of stable complacency was rocked by two major events which took place simultaneously in the autumn of 1956, the Suez crisis and the Soviet invasion of Hungary. Both were precipitated by acts of self-assertion by small nations – in the former case the nationalization of the Suez Canal by Egypt's President Nasser, in the latter the attempt by the reformist government of Hungary to make itself neutral in the Cold War. Both led to military intervention which provoked an international crisis and major repercussions in the internal affairs of the countries directly or indirectly involved.

The invasion of the Suez Canal zone by Israeli forces, followed by British and French paratroops, seemed at first sight just another of those minor military operations with which the imperial powers kept the unruly natives in order. The British in particular both overrated and underrated Nasser. On the one hand they repeatedly compared him to Mussolini and even Hitler as a threat to international order. And on the other hand they thought it would be easy to teach him a lesson in the good old-fashioned imperial manner. But the British and French also overrated their own power to teach lessons to anyone.

The Americans refused to support the invasion, threatened economic sanctions against Britain, and forced their allies into a humiliating retreat. Domestic opinion in Britain had been divided at the time of the invasion and the idea of standing up to Nasser was on the whole warmly greeted. 'It's GREAT Britain again,' howled one of the British tabloids, the *Daily Sketch*. But the realization that Britain was not great at all, but politically and economically dependent on the United States, produced a lot of soul-searching, particularly on the left. How was it, the left asked, that the Government could be so deluded as to push the country into such a foolish enterprise, and what did it say about the British people that so many of them could happily follow political leaders with such abysmal political judgement?

Worldwide, the main effect of the Suez crisis was a reality check. It was now clear that the old imperial powers were a spent force and the only western imperialism the rest of the world had to fear was that of the United States.

At the same moment, however, another unpleasant reality forced itself on world attention. After the death of Stalin in 1953, a slow 'thaw' had begun in the Soviet Union and its satellites. On 25 February 1956, the new Soviet leader Nikita Khrushchev gave a secret speech to the 20th Congress of the Soviet Communist Party denouncing the 'errors and crimes' of the Stalin period. Although the speech was secret, word soon filtered through to other Communist parties of what seemed to be a turning point in Soviet policy. Publication of the full contents of the speech by the US State Department in June added fuel to the rapidly spreading flames.[2] Reformist and dissenting movements grew throughout the Soviet bloc, most notably in Poland and Hungary. But the optimism of the reformists was premature. When the reforming government of Imre Nagy in Hungary showed signs not only of internal liberalization but of wishing to join Yugoslavia in pursuing a neutralist foreign policy, the Soviet Union decided to use force to impose its control. On Sunday 4 November, Soviet troops entered Budapest. Hundreds of demonstrators were shot dead in the street, while the rest of the world stood idly by.

The crushing of dissent in the Soviet bloc was surprisingly easy. As a contemporary joke put it, 'The Hungarians behaved like Poles, the Poles behaved like Czechs, and the Czechs behaved like swine.' The main result of the repression was to put back the cause of liberalization in Hungary itself and in neighbouring Czechoslovakia by several years, though in Poland it was to prove unexpectedly beneficial, since the regime was increasingly aware of the strength of opposition and the need for propitiatory gestures. Meanwhile, however, the Hungarian events also created a crisis on the left in western countries. The western Communist parties split from top to bottom. There were mass resignations both of working-class militants and of intellectuals. In France, important sympathizers such as Jean-Paul Sartre publicly dissociated themselves.[3] In Italy, the damage was temporary, largely because the leadership moved tactfully to a position of less than vociferous support for the Soviet action. But overall the Communist parties emerged from the crisis deeply discredited, with large numbers of former members and sympathizers finding themselves, for the time being at least, without a home.

The vacuum on the left caused by the impact of Hungary and Suez was soon filled. Intellectuals leaving the Communist parties joined forces with independent leftists of various persuasions, an alliance which was sealed, in Britain, by the merger in 1960 of two journals, the *Universities and Left Review* (independent) and the *New Reasoner* (mainly ex-Communist) to form the *New Left Review,* whose first editor was the Jamaican-born Stuart Hall. The programme of *New Left Review,* and of the emerging new left in general, was strongly anti-imperialist, supportive of reform movements in Eastern Europe, neutralist in relation to the politics of the Cold War, and as impatient with the Labour Party as it was suspicious of the Communists. The new left in Britain also directed its attention to the peculiarly class-bound nature of British cultural life, putting forward the claims of popular culture to elite attention and enthusiastically supporting Free Cinema and the working-class realism in British cinema that emerged from it.[4]

The situation in France was complicated by the escalation of the war in Algeria. Whereas successive British governments had succeeded in disengaging themselves more or less gracefully from imperial entanglements, the French were more obdurate and also faced problems closer to home. Algeria was not a distant colony but a Mediterranean country with an Arab and Berber Muslim majority and a very substantial French minority and its political status was that of part of metropolitan France.

Opposition to the Algerian war was at first muted. Heavy government censorship kept the majority of people in the dark about what was going on. The Communist Party, although committed in principle to an anti-colonial policy, was hesitant and in any case isolated. The return to power of General de Gaulle in 1958, followed by military successes against the independence movement, seemed for a while to promise that the conflict could be contained. But de Gaulle knew that he was only borrowing time and in 1959 began to drop hints that a political solution was necessary, which would involve self-determination for Algeria if not out-right independence. The years in which the French Nouvelle Vague emerged were also those of great anxiety, with young men being sent to fight a war that was going to be lost, threatened military coups and, eventually in 1962, a peace settlement.

Meanwhile in the Americas, the United States also found itself obliged, from time to time, to use violence against its satellites, though not on the Soviet scale. At the beginning of 1959, however, it was taken by surprise when left-wing guerrillas, led by Fidel Castro, captured the Cuban capital Havana and shortly afterwards set out on a programme of mass expropriation of US-owned businesses. The Americans reacted with an abortive invasion attempt. Castro in turn responded by inviting the Soviet Union to install missiles on Cuban soil. For ten days in October 1962 it looked as if the world might be on the brink a new world war, this time nuclear, but the crisis was averted when the Soviet leader Nikita Khrushchev agreed to withdraw the missiles in exchange for unspecified concessions on the American side. This neutralized any direct military threat Cuba might pose to the United States, but it could not stop the ideological one. During the 1960s, Cuba, as a self-styled 'free territory of the Americas', was a beacon of hope for liberation movements throughout Central and South America and a source of inspiration for artists and intellectuals of many persuasions, especially in the cinema. Within months of the seizure of power, the revolutionary government founded ICAIC, the Instituto Cubano de Arte e Industria Cinematográficos, to create a new cinema and a new film culture in the country. Its first step, even before a foot of film was exposed, was to invite to Havana the Italian neo-realist Cesare Zavattini. Zavattini arrived in December 1959 and stayed for several months, lecturing, discussing with film-makers, and working on scripts for Julio García Espinosa and others. Other foreign film-makers followed, coming to celebrate the revolution, meet the Cubans, and make films of their own: Chris Marker with *Cuba si!* in 1961, Mikhail Kalatozov with *I Am Cuba* in 1962, and Agnès Varda with *Salut les Cubains* in 1963.[5]

When the new cinemas erupted on to the scene from 1959 or 1960 onwards it was against this rapidly changing political background. Not only that, but many of the new film-makers themselves were political radicals of one kind or another. Few were communists, either by formal affiliation or by conviction. (This was in contrast to the older generation, where a number of film-makers in both France and Italy had been closely linked to the communist parties even if not actually members.) Film-makers who declared their political convictions openly included Lindsay Anderson and Tony Richardson in Britain, Alain Resnais (a signatory to the Manifesto of the 121) and Chris Marker in France, Pier Paolo Pasolini and Marco Bellocchio in Italy, Dušan Makavejev in Yugoslavia, Glauber Rocha and other proponents of Cinema Novo in Brazil, and Nagisa Os-hima in Japan. Even if they hadn't declared them, the nature of these convictions would have been clear enough from the films being made, which increasingly featured characters who were marginal or dispos-sessed or in revolt against the circumstances of their existence.

Not all the new cinemas were radically leftist, or leftist from the outset. There is an obvious problem in characterizing the cinemas of East Central Europe along a left/right axis. For the most part the new cinemas in Poland, Czechoslovakia, and Yugoslavia were necessarily oppositional to the prevailing regime, but not always in ways which western leftists iden-tified with. For many on the left in the west, the enemy was American imperialism, and this made them sympathetic to the Soviet Union in a way the Eastern Europeans found naive to say the least. In general, how-ever, the non-conformist values expressed in the films of the Polish School and the Czech New Wave found an echo in the sensibilities of western film-makers and audiences. There were also strong bonds of friendship between film-makers across the Iron Curtain, with Lindsay Anderson and, inevitably, Zavattini in the forefront. As for Makavejev, his extreme championing of the sexual revolution and his coupling of Stalinism with sexual repression won him many enthusiastic admirers in the west – some of whom he lost when there was a feminist backlash against what was seen as the phallocratic ideology of his *W. R. Mysteries of the Organism* (1971).

The French New Wave, or Nouvelle Vague, was also politically equi-vocal, at least in the early stages. While Resnais and Marker, as mentioned above, were clearly identified with the left, the writers and future film-makers of *Cahiers du cinéma* were divided in their sympathies. The founders of the magazine, André Bazin and Jacques Doniol-Valcroze, were both men of the left from way back and remained so throughout. But some of the younger writers, François Truffaut in particular, became impatient with what they saw as a kind of establishment leftism and for a while in the late 1950s adopted the right-wing poses encouraged by the fortnightly magazine *Arts* which had offered them house-room. This phase did not last long. The Algerian War was beginning to radicalize young French people, especially those in danger of being called up. Jean-Luc Godard's second feature film *Le Petit Soldat* (1960) shows a quizzical sympathy with its right-wing terrorist hero, but within a couple of years he had switched his mercurial sympathies from the extreme right to the extreme left, while still remaining uncommitted, before becoming a firm opponent of the American war in Vietnam from the time of *Pierrot le fou* (1965). As for Truffaut, his conversion to left-wing causes was less visible but no less significant. Revolted by the atrocities conducted by the French in Algeria, he had his name attached to the list of the 121 intellectuals protesting the war, but since the government suppressed the press advertisement on which the signatures were to appear, this gesture went unnoticed, except by the police, who subjected Truffaut to harassment.[6] The government also censored films about Algeria, and *Le Petit Soldat* was banned for a number of years, but Jacques Rozier's *Adieu Philippine*, made in 1962 when conscripts were still being sent out to fight, and Jacques Demy's *The Umbrellas of Cherbourg*, looking back over the conflict from the comfortable retrospect of 1964, are both New Wave testimonies to the way French society had been polarized by the war, and most film-makers had come out in opposition.

More than Hungary, Suez, or Algeria, it was the American war in Vietnam which definitively radicalized the generation that came of age in the late 1950s and early 60s. The first Indo-Chinese war, against the French, had ended in stalemate, with the former colonies of Laos and Cambodia neutral and Vietnam divided into a communist-dominated North and a South nominally in the western camp. But the rebels in the South had not been defeated and low-level guerrilla operations continued to be launched after the ceasefire in 1954. The French had neither the resources nor the will to intervene, but the Americans did. Considering their global interests threatened, the Americans sent first advisers and then combat troops to back up what increasingly became a puppet regime in the South. Full-scale American involvement is generally dated from 1964, when President Lyndon B. Johnson seized on an incident reported (probably falsely) to have taken place off the North Vietnamese coast to launch retaliatory raids against the harbour and city of Haiphong. From then on there was a steady escalation of hostilities, eventually involving more than three million American ground troops, while more bombs were dropped on Vietnam by American bombers than on Germany in the Second World War.

The war in Vietnam also greatly exceeded the Algerian, or any other colonial war, in the level of protest it evoked. The protests were strongest in the United States themselves, where an entire generation was threatened with conscription – 'the draft' – to fight a war which looked increasingly unwinnable. But protest marches, sometimes violent, took place all over the world. In Britain the Labour Party had to fight off massive opposition within its own ranks to the government's apparent support for the Americans, although to his credit Prime Minister Harold Wilson resisted American demands for Britain to send ground troops. In the end only Australia and South Korea took a direct part on the American side. Other western countries dissociated themselves as much as was diplomatically possible.

In western Europe, opposition to the war was important not only in its own right but as a catalyst for a wider wave of youthful radicalism which was to reach a peak with the Paris May Events in 1968. Exasperation with American action can be traced in the various references to the war scattered through the films of Jean-Luc Godard in the mid-1960s. These begin in the background when Jean-Paul Belmondo is listening to the news in *Pierrot le fou* (1965) and become more insistent in *Made in USA* (1966) and *Masculin Féminin* (also 1966, where Jean-Pierre Léaud paints 'Peace in Vietnam' on an official American limousine), and above all in *Two or Three Things I Know about Her* (1967), with its bitterly hilarious scenes of two radio hams picking up fictitious broadcasts by Lyndon Johnson announcing, 'with a heavy heart', ever more grotesque escalations of the conflict. Godard also took part, along with Alain Resnais, William Klein, Joris Ivens, Agnès Varda, and Claude Lelouch, in the 1967 compilation film *Far from Vietnam*, which was a rallying call for opposition to the war.

In the USA itself, anti-war feeling brought white middle-class protestors into uneasy alliance with the new Black Power militancy, and in both the USA and Britain the anti-war movement interlaced with the emerging counter-culture of sex, drugs, and rock'n'roll. Mainstream cinema was slow to catch up with these developments. Hollywood steered studiously clear of anything to do with the war in Vietnam, whether the fighting on the ground or the rising tide of protest at home. But at the very end of the decade a couple of independent documentaries, Michael Wadleigh's concert movie *Woodstock* (1970) and the Maysles brothers' astonishing *Gimme Shelter* (1970) came out to give a feel for the counter-culture at the time (cosy in *Woodstock*, disturbing in *Gimme Shelter* with its footage of the Rolling Stones concert at Altamont when a fan was killed). Add to that the appearance of black militant Kathleen Cleaver in Michelangelo Antonioni's *Zabriskie Point* (1970) and that is just about all that commercially released films showed the American public of the cultural revolution taking place under their noses. The war, of course, was on television every night and eventually, when it was over, there were films about it, just as there came to be films about people smoking dope and taking their clothes off and expressing utopian thoughts. But that was in the 1970s and was just playing catch-up.

In Europe the counter-culture was weaker but regular left-wing political movements a lot stronger. Here the middle and late 1960s saw the first stirrings of political groupings which placed themselves (at least in their imagination) firmly to the left of the increasingly reformist Communist parties. The idea of revolution returned to the agenda, sometimes as a worked-out political programme but more often in the sense of a feeling that life had to change more radically than conventional political thinking was able to conceive. Before May 1968, not many film-makers associated themselves directly with Maoist, Trotskyist, or other far-left groupings, but some did. Rather surprisingly, the dogmatic Trotskyists of the Socialist Labour League (later portentously retitled Workers' Revolutionary Party) made considerable inroads in the 1960s among British actors and film and TV directors, the best known being Ken Loach and Vanessa Redgrave.

More often, however, artists were drawn to less formal politics and the expression of radical views and ideas without an obvious political armature. What constituted a political film became the subject of much debate. There were films about politics which were angry and activist, but some which were reflective and contained no obvious political lesson or message. Three out of four of Alain Resnais's early features have political, or partly political, subjects. In *Hiroshima mon amour* (1959), it is nuclear war and also the German occupation of France; in *Muriel* (1963), it is the war in Algeria; and in *La Guerre est finie* (1966), it is the Spanish Civil War. But in each film that aspect of the subject matter is approached though a filter of memory and the film is also about memory and how it works and the traces it leaves. In each case, too, the lesson is ambiguous; it could be that there are certain things that we cannot help remembering but that we would be better off if we could forget; or it could be that memory is necessary and salutary if we are not to repeat mistakes made in the past.

On the whole in the early 1960s there were still few films which could be called directly political. (One noteworthy exception, way ahead of its time, was Nagisa Oshima's *Night and Fog in Japan*, which was pulled from release by its studio, Shochiku, because it was thought to be inflammatory.) Mainly there were social films with a clear but implicit political message. Many of the films of the British New Wave are of this type, most obviously Tony Richardson's *The Loneliness of the Long Distance Runner* (1963), which affirms the anti-social (in context, anti-bourgeois) values of its working-class hero. Early films from the Brazilian Cinema Novo such as Glauber Rocha's *Barravento* (1962) or Nelson Pereira Dos Santos's *Vidas secas* (1964) belong in this category too, though here the message is more urgent. But the vogue in Britain for working-class subjects was more a throwback to the days of neo-realism than a distinct modern development, and left-leaning western European film-makers were more inclined to want to analyse the discontents of bourgeois society than to exalt a proletarian alternative. The great dissectors of bourgeois discontent in the early 1960s were the unclassifiable Luis Buñuel, Chabrol, who was not a leftist at all, and Antonioni, whose radical critique of his own class was always there to be inferred but never thrust into the audience's face.

In the middle of the decade, however, there was a change of mood, and a number of films came out in which the dissection of bourgeois life acquired a harder political edge. Marco Bellocchio's *Fists in the Pocket*, released in 1965, was a study of a dysfunctional upper-middle class family and as such could be located in a genre familiar from Hollywood melodramas of the 1950s such as Nicholas Ray's *Bigger than Life* (1956) or Douglas Sirk's *Written on the Wind* (also 1956). But in Bellocchio's film the dysfunctionality is so extreme and the anger and revulsion so pronounced that its political implications could not be ignored. It was particularly radical in the Italian context since the politics of neo-realism had always been conciliatory and humanist and a film so clearly animated by hatred was almost unthinkable. Other critiques of the bourgeois family came indirectly in Visconti's *Sandra*, released at the same time, and more assertively in Pasolini's *Theorem* in 1968. Bellocchio meanwhile turned his attention to other institutions, including the holiest of all holy cows, the Catholic Church. His next film, *China Is Near* (1967), was imaginatively even more violent than *Fists in the Pocket*, satirizing both state and Catholic education and the antics of ultra-left students as well as sober-minded conformists in the process of watching a family self-destruct. The

China of the title was the China of the Cultural Revolution, and *China Is Near*, along with Godard's *La Chinoise* (1967), marks the arrival on the scene of the youthful Maoism of 1968.

These films which set out to erode bourgeois institutions from within were revolutionary in the sense that they presented the ruling class as beyond reform, so that only a revolution could destroy its perverse grip on society as a whole. But they were in no position to prescribe realistically how such a revolution could be brought about. The mainstream left was more interested in films which promoted political change and denounced the abuse of power in ways that showed a way forward. Films of this kind were also beginning to appear, again more often in Italy than anywhere else, but also in Latin America. Francesco Rosi's first distinctive feature, *Salvatore Giuliano* (1962), had taken a major step towards a kind of political film-making that put analysis before sentiment, revolutionary or otherwise. But it was set in the recent past, rather than the actual present and the problems it addressed – banditry and corruption in postwar Sicily – could be dismissed as lacking contemporary relevance. They were Third World problems, and yet it wasn't even a Third World film. Rosi's next film, however, *Hands over the City* (1963), was unequivocally modern, since the corruption it analysed was of a kind endemic in Italy and still present forty years or more later.

Rosi called his style of film-making 'film documentato' or documented film. The structure is that of a narrative fiction and the material is reconstructed events, but always very close to events which either actually took place or could be plausibly held to have taken place. Using these events, and fitted into the narrative structure, there is then an argument, a demonstration of how such things happen. In *Salvatore Giuliano* (and later in such films as *The Mattei Affair* in 1972) the argument relates to the reconstruction, as close to documented truth as possible, of singular events; in *Hands over the City* the events are both singular and typical, in that the particular story of corruption in the construction industry in Naples on which the story is based is one that could repeat itself more or less identically again and again – and indeed has done.

A broadly similar procedure can be detected behind the making of Gillo Pontecorvo's much admired *Battle of Algiers*. Made with help from the Algerian government and released to great acclaim in late 1966, it tells the story of a crucial moment of escalation in the Algerian War based on the experience of a young recruit to the liberation forces, the FLN. In so doing it takes in the French army's recourse to torture and that FLN's decision to deploy terror against civilians. Like Rosi, Pontecorvo and his scriptwriter Franco Solinas stay very close to documented events on which they superimpose a political argument about the logic of escalation in situations of irresolvable conflict. But the film does not have the analytic detachment of *Salvatore Giuliano* or *Hands over the City* and falls back too often into the tropes of melodrama.

The Battle of Algiers was mainly a *succès de scandale*, admired for its boldness but not as widely seen as its makers had hoped. In the country where it would have had most effect, France, it was banned, and it was not until 1971 that it was commercially released in Britain. By this time two things had happened. On the one hand the escalation of the war in Vietnam had made it seem politically more relevant – though to a different war than the one it was about. But on the other hand its aesthetics – and the politics that could be deduced from them – were the subject of new controversy.

When it first appeared, *The Battle of Algiers* had a wide appeal across the political spectrum. Although firmly on the side of the FLN, it treated the French with the sort of respect accorded to honourable members of the other side in conventional war films. Meanwhile the FLN's use of civilian terror was presented as a sad consequence of a deteriorating situation beyond the control of either combatant party. By 1971, however, opinion was sharply divided. Most critics of the left and centre continued to admire it, the left finding it bold and unequivocal and the centre admiring its fairness.[7] But the world had changed since 1966. 1968 had supervened and with it a new concept of political cinema. For the post-68ers *The Battle of Algiers* was not a political film at all, just a humanist melodrama with a political subject matter.[8]

For this reaction to be possible, not only did the world have to have moved on, but there had to have been a revolution in the politics of representation. This revolution was adumbrated in the rapid changes in that took place in Godard's film-making practice in the run-up to 1968. With 1968 both cinema and political life were to take a giant leap into the unknown.

Notes

1. Samuel Fuller's *Pickup on South Street* (1953), an anti-Communist spy movie, was redubbed and released in France as a non-political story about drug-running, under the title *Le Port de la drogue.*

2. See David Caute, *Communism and the French Intellectuals* (London: André Deutsch, 1964), p. 224.

3. Ibid., p. 228. Sartre's statement of dissent was in an article in *L'Express,* 9 November 1956.

4. The first signs of a changed climate in British intellectual life had come earlier with the publication of a collection of essays edited by Tom Maschler under the title *Declaration* (London: Jonathan Cape, 1957). Although widely invoked, this book is not often read from start to finish, otherwise commentators would have noticed that at least half of the book is neither progressive nor political. Only the essays by novelist Doris Lessing, playwright John Osborne, and aspirant film-maker Lindsay Anderson look forward in any way to the new left then in gestation.

5. Varda did not actually shoot a film during her visit to Cuba. She took a lot of still pictures and it was only on her return to France that she had the idea of editing them together as a film. Other visiting film-makers included Vladimir Cech from Czechoslovakia (*For Whom Havana Dances,* 1962) and Kurt Maetzig from the GDR (*Preludio 11,* 1964). See Michael Chanan, *The Cuban Image* (London: British Film Institute, 1985), pp. 130–1.

6. The episode is described in Baecque and Toubiana, *Truffaut: A Biography* (New York: Alfred A. Knopf, 1999), pp. 162–7. The only list of the 121 that I have seen contains the name of Alain Resnais, but not Truffaut. According to Baecque and Toubiana, Doniol-Valcroze and Pierre Kast were also signatories.

7. See for example the review by Jan Dawson in *Monthly Film Bulletin,* April 1971, which praises the film for its sympathetic portrayal of the French paratroop commander modelled on the notorious Colonel Massu.

8. The most cogent expression of this new point of view is to be found in Peter Sainsbury's 'op-ed' article in *Afterimage* (London) 3, 1971, pp. 4–7.

4

Sex and Censorship

The 1960s in Britain got off with a bang. The Obscene Publications Act, passed in 1959, made it possible for 'literary merit' to be cited in defence of works prosecuted for obscenity. The first major test of the new Act came when Penguin Books decided in 1960 to bring out a complete version of D. H. Lawrence's *Lady Chatterley's Lover*, written in 1928 but only ever published in Britain or the United States in expurgated form. Prosecution followed instantly. The trial began on 21 October and after six days, during which a number of literary luminaries and a couple of Anglican clergymen spoke up for the defence, the jury decided that the book was perfectly safe reading for 'factory girls in their lunch hour'.[1] The publisher was acquitted, and the book went on general sale. Other books, such as Nabokov's *Lolita*, which bookshops tended to keep under the counter, came out into the light of day. There were further trials, and further acquittals, notably that of *Last Exit to Brooklyn* in 1964. Although the self-appointed guardians of morality continued to mount a rearguard action, that was just about it as far as literature was concerned, and by the end of the 1960s the censorship of books – or at least of books with a reasonable claim to be literature – was more or less a dead letter.

In the cinema the situation was more complicated and change came more slowly. Cinema was a public and popular art and it was widely thought that matters which might be described in a book for the private pleasure of a minority should not be directly represented visually as a publicly available display. It was only in the 1980s, with the arrival of home video, that the laws governing films in Britain were brought more into line with those covering reading matter. By that time, however, with the collapse of the Production Code Administration in the USA and the almost universal adoption of a classification system in the place of traditional censorship regimes, a consensus had begun to emerge that adults should broadly speaking be allowed to see what they liked, with separate rules for the protection of minors.

In the 1960s, however, there were still many censorship battles to be fought, and on a very different terrain. Whereas today most of the residual censorship battles are around the spectator/consumer's right to engage in certain often private and even furtive pleasures, the battles of the 1960s were more concerned with freedom of expression and the limits of public discourse. Censorship was seen as an arm of the state. It was used in France and Italy (as well as, obviously, in the Eastern bloc and in Spain and Portugal) to control social and political ideas. In Britain the theatre censorship had a strong class bias (it was operated by a curious extension of the monarchy, the office of the Lord Chamberlain) and the same values filtered though into the actions of the film censors. But above all censorship was perceived as an unnecessary barrier to honest expression, particularly, though not exclusively, in matters to do with sex.

Most of the struggles around film censorship in the 1960s were minor battles of attrition, initiated by film-makers but taking advantage of a steady shift in the public mood in favour of more openness. In many countries, particularly in Eastern Europe, the censors fought a tactical game, quietly letting through more and more items that they would previously have resisted. In Yugoslavia, Poland, and Hungary, a more permissive attitude to sex was part of a general (though still only relative) liberalization of expression. In Britain, the new Secretary of the British Board of Film Censors, John Trevelyan, gradually edged his colleagues into a more permissive attitude, bringing the X (over sixteen) category more into line with standards prevailing in continental countries such as France or Sweden. The most obvious beneficiary of this enlightened policy was the foreign art film, to which criteria of 'artistic merit', although not officially within the Board's remit (the Obscene Publications Act of 1959 did not apply to cinema), were increasingly applied, but it helped the British cinema too. In certain areas, such as the portrayal of homosexuality, the British cinema became the most progressive in Europe – though this was more due to the insistence of the film-makers than to a particularly liberal attitude on the part of the censors.

In many ways, the Lady Chatterley trial was a misleading event. Lawrence and his defenders were concerned to present sex as something special and even sacred. For film-makers in the early 1960s it was more a question of insisting that sex was ordinary and that its ordinariness as experienced in everyday life had to be reflected in film. For the most part they just wanted it recognized that young people might have sexual intercourse, which could on occasion lead to unwanted pregnancy, or that they might be sexually attracted to members of their own sex rather than the opposite one, and moreover that these were facts of life to be addressed without innuendo, gasps of horror, prurience, or moralism. These were not outlandish demands and indeed amounted to no more than the expectation that films could represent the same aspects of everyday life as were routinely represented in mainstream literature. But even these modest demands could not always be satisfied without a struggle.

The disparity of censorship regimes worked to the advantage of the industries in countries with more liberal standards, since less liberal countries often allowed in films which might not have passed the censorship at home. Very few of the early films of the French New Wave would have passed unscathed through the PCA: not *Hiroshima mon amour*, with its steamy opening sequence; not *Les Amants*, with its more-than-implied cunnilingus towards the end; not Jacques Demy's *Lola*, set in a so-called cabaret which is more like a brothel; not even *Les Quatre cents coups*, because of the scene in which the thirteen-year-old hero is asked if he has ever had sex (fortunately he says no, otherwise it might not have passed in France either). Yet they all got shown on the art-house circuit in Britain and the USA, though cuts were made in both *Les Amants* and *Shoot the Pianist* for British release, and some of the verbal innuendos in the latter were lost in translation.[2] (The novel from which *Shoot the Pianist* was adapted, David Goodis's *Down There*, has a low-life story of the kind normal in American crime novels but which would always be cleaned up in adaptation for the screen.)

Meanwhile the British censors struggled to come to terms with moderately bad language, particularly if the speaker was working-class, and with the recognition of the facts of life. Tony Richardson's film of *A Taste of Honey* was a landmark in its unaffected telling of the story of a girl who gets pregnant by a black sailor and shacks up with a gay man. On the other hand, neither the act which gets her pregnant nor the acts that got the gay man expelled from his previous lodgings are directly represented. As in classical tragedy, that sort of action is firmly off stage.

In general there is not much way of erotic spectacle in the early films of the European new waves. Nor is there much nudity or intimate love-making. Spectacle tends to be second order, so that characters may visit a strip-joint and watch someone strip off on stage, but only rarely do they strip off themselves. There is a strip-tease in Antonioni's *La notte*, but the point of it is to show a bored couple being bored with the show. In Godard's *Une femme est une femme*, Anna Karina is a night club dancer, but her performances are winsome and appealing rather than titillating. Indeed throughout the 1960s, Godard, for all the sex talk in which his characters engage, was quite reticent in what he was prepared to show. The famous scene in *Contempt* with Brigitte Bardot lying naked on a bed asking Michel Piccoli about the attractiveness of her body parts was imposed by the producers who were desperate to get their money's worth out of Bardot's expensively bought presence in the movie. And later, during the making of *British Sounds* in 1969, when feminist Sheila Rowbotham protested to him about the full-frontal, crotch-level shot of a naked woman in a supposedly political film, Godard is said to have replied, 'Don't you think I am able to make a cunt boring?'[3]

The early new waves also reacted against the tendency of the mainstream cinema to choose actors and actresses on the basis of their physical endowments. They turned their backs on what in Italy were called the 'maggiorate fisiche' and on the Hollywood standard of female beauty lampooned by Boris Vian in his novel *Et on tuera tous les afffreux*, where a woman is described as 'having been constructed with Jane Russell's breasts, Betty Grable's legs, Bacall's eyes, and the rest to match.'[4] The favoured actresses of the French New Wave – for example, Jeanne Moreau, Bernadette Laffont, Marie Dubois, Stéphane Audran – were all women who the film-makers themselves considered attractive (and often went on to have relationships with). But even where they had star quality – obviously the case with Moreau or with Françoise Dorléac – very few had regular film-star looks. Nor were they expected to undress on the screen, though it was not always clear from case to case whether this was because they didn't want to, the film-makers didn't want them to, or the censors prevented it.

An exception to the general reticence was Roger Vadim. He made his name, and Bardot's, by exploiting her radiant sexual energy in *And God Created Woman* in 1956. After making the relatively restrained *Sait-on jamais* with the established actress Françoise Arnoul in 1957, he then tried to repeat what he had done for Bardot with two other untried actresses, Annette Stroyberg (*Les Liaisons dangereuses*, 1959; *Et mourir de plaisir*, 1960) and Catherine Deneuve (*Le Vice et la Vertu*, 1962). In each case (and also with *Le Repos du guerrier* with Bardot again in 1962), a literary original was plundered to exploit its sexual content and to have Vadim's actress/protégée undress and be knocked about as much as the censorship would permit.[5]

Vadim's wanderings into the fringes of soft core won him large audiences (*Les Liaisons dangereuses* and *Le Repos du guerrier* were among the top-grossing films in France in 1960 and 1962 respectively),[6] but the film-makers who followed down the same route were on the whole neither part of the mainstream nor of the new cinemas, but hived off into a separate 'X-film' bracket which both mainstream and art-house exhibitors treated with caution. In the mid-1960s, however, a number of art-house exhibitors discovered that a large part of their audience was less interested in art films for their own sake than in the sex scenes they contained, and switched their programmes accordingly. There was nothing remarkable about this, since in the late 1950s the same cinemas had often specialized in nudist-camp frolics and had only gone 'arty' in the earlier 1960s with the New Wave boom. In Manchester in 1965, the local Cinephone art house followed Truffaut's *Soft Skin*, which did only moderately, with Bergman's *The Silence*, which ran for several weeks consecutively, but only because of the scene with Esther (Ingrid Thulin) masturbating. Thereafter it switched to sex films only. By the end of the decade a separate exhibition category had come into being in many European countries, initially mainly supplied by sex films from Sweden and Denmark, but increasingly by locally made product.

Where the new cinemas did innovate was in the discovery, or rediscovery, of sexual fantasy. The initial demand for elementary realism in the portrayal of sexual relations had been more or less satisfied by the middle of the decade. Four-letter words were still censored in British and American cinema and only began to creep in (as expletives) around 1967,[7] and the representation of sexual intercourse was elliptical in practically all films subject to censorship regimes.[8] But censorship was generally more pliant and the need to push against its limits in each and every case was not felt so strongly as it had been in the period around 1960. Generally speaking, the area of what was permitted was wide enough for most of what serious film-makers felt they needed to do. Whereas in the early 1960s most of the 'canonical' directors had been caught up in censorship difficulties on one kind of another, cases became less frequent as the decade progressed. Of course the unpredictable could happen, as when Pasolini was taken to court for alleged blasphemy in his

contribution to the compilation film *RoGoPaG* in 1963, but that had
nothing to do with the issue of the right to realistic representation of
ordinary human relations.

The shift of interest to fantasy was partly provoked by Vadim. His
search for the sexually exotic had led him first to the tremulous erotic
undercurrents of Sheridan Le Fanu's story 'Carmilla' for *Et mourir de
plaisir* and then to the Marquis de Sade – the 'divine Marquis' – for *Le
Vice et la Vertu*. But Vadim's imagination was pornographic, in the sense
of a desire to 'realize' – literally to make real – sexual events. In this respect
his approach to sexuality was less subtle than that of his contemporaries
at Hammer Films in Britain who were busy tapping into a vein of un-
conscious, or semi-conscious, fantasy where the deep ambivalence surrounding the heroine's anticipation of a fate worse than death could be
savoured in a form less realistic but psychologically more resonant.

The first person to blend realism and fantasy in a convincing way was
Roman Polanski. An exceptionally talented graduate of the Polish film
school in Łódź, he had made one feature in Poland, the psychological
thriller *Knife in the Water*, in 1962, before emigrating to Paris. There he
teamed up with the scriptwriter Gérard Brach and together they wrote
the screenplay for a film about a woman unable to cope with her sexual
fantasies. Eventually shot in London (South Kensington has never looked
the same again), *Repulsion* starred a young actress, Catherine Deneuve,
fresh from her success as the innocent teenage heroine of Jacques Demy's
The Umbrellas of Cherbourg but who the film-makers had chosen more
for the qualities displayed in her role in Vadim's *Le Vice et la Vertu*,
notably the ability to undergo humiliation without being in the least bit
humiliated. The story of *Repulsion* is told from the point of view of its
heroine who (to the extent that these diagnoses mean anything when
applied to films) is clearly a hysteric; it is only as the plot unfolds that it
becomes clear that she is severely psychotic as well. But *Repulsion* is not
a study from a psychoanalyst's casebook. Its achievement lies in its ability
to draw the spectator into a sexually charged atmosphere without revealing the extent to which this is the product of the impassive-looking
heroine's fevered imagination. Sexuality, rather than sex, is the subject of
the film.

The combination of the fantastic as a genre and the psychological
interest of sexual fantasy was to fuel a number of films from 1970 onwards, beginning with Nicolas Roeg's *Performance*. Meanwhile an even

more radical step was taken by the great Spanish director Luis Buñuel, recently returned from a long exile in Mexico. In *Viridiana* (1961) he had already created a heroine whose saintliness was inseparable from her sexual frigidity, but in *Belle de Jour* (1967) he dispensed with any attempt to psychologize. Séverine, played by Catherine Deneuve, is unable to find sexual satisfaction with her bourgeois husband. Picking up a hint from a family friend, the charming but mildly sinister Monsieur Husson, she tentatively offers her services as a prostitute in a discreet brothel in the afternoons, receiving the sobriquet 'Belle de Jour'. At first she is as timorous of her clients as of her husband and is on the verge of being dismissed, but an encounter with an uncompromisingly brutal oriental who the other girls are all afraid of suddenly opens up a new world to her and she is able to become the satisfied lover of a handsome young gangster. Meanwhile this broadly realist (if not entirely realistic) narrative is interspersed with scenes apparently set in the 18th century where Séverine is whipped by footmen and an aristocrat stands by his wife's coffin apparently masturbating. A double puzzle is posed to the audience: how much of what appears to be happening is 'real' and to what extent is Séverine herself a 'character' endowed with a psychology that explains her actions and her feelings? As Michael Wood shrewdly observes, these questions are unanswerable and yet the audience cannot help asking them.[9] But because the film seems to evade interpretation in a realistic key, it also questions the sense that one makes of sexuality. By leaving it unclear which scenes are real and which are fantasy in a narrative sense, it throws into doubt the status of sexual imaginings and their place in experience.

Few directors were as bold as Polanski or Roeg, let alone Buñuel, in exploring the uncomfortable boundaries between the real and the fantasized in sexual life. Many, however, were emboldened by the easing of censorship to move into previously taboo areas of sexual deviance and perversity. The most obvious and uncontroversial advance was the normalizing of homosexuality as a subject for film narrative. For the first time since the 1920s, homosexual relationships were allowed to take place between characters and be shown on screen in a moderately matter-of-fact way, even if not always with complete explicitness. Restrictions on explicitness had their compensations, since the less explicit a film the more it can engage the play of spectatorial fantasy in the face of uncertain events and, behind the events, uncertain desires. Some of the best films in this vein are those (Chabrol's 1968 lesbian romance *Les Biches* would be an example) in which characters are shown as hesitating in face of a newly discovered or half-discovered desire and the spectator is invited to share this hesitancy – and with it a slight oscillation of gender identity.

Homosexuality is seen as subversive in Pasolini's *Theorem* (1968), where a mysterious stranger, played by Terence Stamp, gets off with all the members of a bourgeois family – mother, father, daughter, son, and also, for good measure, the maid. It figures ambiguously in Bertolucci's *The Conformist* (1970) where the repressed homosexuality of the hero is correlated to his identification with Fascism but his wife's brief dalliance with the wife of an anti-Fascist exile is implicitly shown as a gesture of liberation. More often, however, ventures into the sexual psycho-pathology of political formations were simply reductive. Makavejev narrowly avoids this in *Switchboard Operator* (1967) by breaking the spell of realist illusion and making it clear that the connection made in the story between Stalinism and sexual repression is speculation on his part, rather than something that the audience should take as unquestioned (even if fictional) reality.

Sometimes sexual deviance was used as a new ingredient to stir into the pot of traditional melodrama. A good example of this would be the films of Visconti. In *Sandra* (1965) the plot hinges on the degree of in-cestuousness in the relationship between brother and sister: was it all in the brother's imagination, or did something happen which the sister has blotted out of her memory? In *The Damned* (1969) the central character – played by Helmut Berger, Visconti's then lover – is a repos-itory of perverse behaviours, starting with paedophilia and passing though transvestism to mother-incest. As an account of the Nazi per-sonality this is ridiculous, but it gives the film a *frisson* which a more sober rendition of events and their causes would not have had.

In 1967 a strange 'sociological' film appeared in Sweden, directed by Vilgot Sjöman and entitled *I Am Curious (Yellow)*. Constructed around a documentary film-maker's enquiry into the malaise of social democ-racy, it contained, almost incidentally, a couple of sex scenes which were unusually frank by the standards of the day. Sliding almost unnoticed into the United States, it went on to become one of the most successful foreign films at the box office there to date. In addition to trying to balance domestic opinion, the MPAA now had to take seriously the economic threat of the foreign film with its much greater sexual explicitness. For-eign films still did not account for more than a tiny percentage of US box office, but their popularity was increasing and, as with the PCA in the

1950s, they were making the MPAA look ridiculously timid. It wasn't just direct imports that were a threat. MPAA member companies themselves were investing in European films such as Visconti's *The Damned* which they would have hesitated to make in America for the American market. Gradually the MPAA began to move its standards into alignment with those in the rest of the world, though it remained in stark contrast with Sweden, where almost any sex content was allowed, but violence was still severely censored. Sex and violence together continued to provide the acid test of any censorship regime. The brutal rape scene in Sam Peckinpah's *Straw Dogs* hit more trouble with the British and Scandinavian censors than it did in the USA. Conversely John Schlesinger's *Midnight Cowboy* (1969), with its street hustler hero, was regarded in the USA and Britain as thoroughly unsuitable for impressionable adolescents but passed in some European countries as quite acceptable for teenage audiences.

The years around the 1970s, then, set down the ground rules for the situation that prevails to this day and most of what has happened since can be seen as the continuation of a process set in train by the new European cinemas in the 1960s – though not always with predictable effects. There was, however, one further watershed in the mid-1970s, which had two aspects to it, not apparently connected.

The first aspect was political. The peaceful revolution in Portugal in 1974 and the death of Franco in Spain the following year brought down the last bastions in western Europe of a kind of centralized state censorship that had existed since the days of absolute monarchy in the 17th and 18th centuries. About the same time the French and Italian governments discreetly withdrew from practising censorship of an overt or covert political nature. In all four countries, of course, regulatory systems continued to exist, as did local ordinances protecting public morals. But, noisily in Spain and Portugal and quietly in Italy and France, a matter of political principle concerning the rights of the citizen and the state in respect of the laws of the land was decided in favour of the citizen.

Secondly, however, precisely as this was happening two films came out which tested the limits of tolerance in every censorship or regulatory regime to which they were subject. These were Pasolini's *Salò*, completed just before its author's death in November 1975, and Nagisa Oshima's *Empire of the Senses*, made the following year. As well as test cases of censorship, these two films are also the swan-song of the new cinemas of the extended 1960s.

The full title of Pasolini's film is *Salò o le centoventi giornate di Sodoma* – 'Salò or the 120 days of Sodom' – combining the name of the small resort town where Mussolini set up his puppet republic in 1943 with that of one of the most notorious works of the Marquis de Sade. As the title implies, the film aims to link the anarchy of power unleashed by Fascism with the orgiastic death-dealing sexuality of Sade. Not in the main title but in secondary titles within the film is a reference to the circles of hell in which Dante's *Inferno* is arranged. *Salò* is a highly moral film, a cry of pain against the cruelty of the world and the distortion of ordinary human nature by regimes of political power. It is also a film of a terrible beauty, to borrow a phrase from W. B. Yeats. To achieve both its moral and aesthetic effect, it is totally unsparing to the spectator in its portrayal of the degradation to which human nature has been brought. Four 'libertines', as Sade calls them – in the film they also are identified as 'gerarchi' or members of the Fascist hierarchy – subject some innocent villagers to sexual abuse and humiliation, torture, and finally death in pursuit of a pleasure that eludes them at every turn since their own capacity for sexual love is impaired beyond redemption.

Needless to say, the film posed near insuperable censorship problems. It was not pornography in the normal sense, since it did not set out to produce sexual gratification. The bodies were beautiful, some of the sex acts on show were titillating, but the viewpoint offered to the spectator was so monstrous as to make simple enjoyment of the spectacle almost impossible. Throughout the world censors and regulators concurred that *Salò* was something from which the public should be protected. In Britain the film was refused a certificate for public release. A cut version was shown in a private cinema club but was seized by the police and a prosecution was threatened, which however never materialized. In the USA and Australia the film was also refused a certificate. Screenings remained rare and clandestine until the 1990s when new attempts were made to have it certificated for either cinema or video release. In 1994 a gay bookshop in Cincinnati, Ohio, was raided by police and prosecuted for possessing a video copy. In Britain it finally saw the light of day, uncut, in 2000, by which time the film was twenty-five years old and could qualify as a historic masterpiece.[10]

Empire of the Senses was also regarded as somehow having crossed one of the elusive lines that censors draw. It is a film about an obsessive love affair which ends with the woman cutting off the man's genitals rather than be deprived of them after his death from asphyxiation. But it was not the gruesome sight of her walking about with his severed cock and balls in her hand, nor the frequent shots of erections and penetration, that made the film finally unacceptable to the British censor. Rather it was a scene in which two naked children gambol in front of the heroine and she makes a grab for the little boy's penis. Again the film finally got a certificate in most countries in the 1990s, but to this day the British video optically reframes the scene with the little boy so that the offending action is not clearly seen.[11]

Both *Salò* and *Empire of the Senses* set out to test the boundaries of what was acceptable in liberal western societies. Both were by film-makers who had courted controversy before, but more for radical-political than sex-libertarian reasons. For Pasolini, the making of what turned out to be his last film was a gesture of despair. He had lost his earlier belief in the liberatory power of sex and was afraid of a recrudescent Fascism under a smiling liberal veneer. For Oshima, too, 'liberation' without revolution was a snare and a delusion. Now that our open-mindedness has reached a point where both these two great films can be freely shown, their true meaning has been lost.

Notes

1. The phrase, used in the trial, was picked up by theatre critic Kenneth Tynan, writing in the *Observer* on Sunday 9 November 1960.

2. In *Les Amants* most of what even suggests that cunnilingus is what is going on. In *Shoot the Pianist*, part of the scene where Charlie covers Clarisse's exposed breasts, 'like in the cinema'. (Truffaut had insisted on retaining the whole scene in the French version, even though it meant the film had to have an over-18 certificate. Happy days!)

3. Sheila Rowbotham, *Promise of a Dream: Remembering the Sixties* (London: Allen Lane, the Penguin Press, 2000), p. 220. The dialogue in *Contempt* was simply lifted by Godard from a similar one in *A bout de souffle*.

4. Boris Vian, *Et on tuera tous les affreux*, first published by Editions du Scorpion in 1948 under the pseudonym Vernon Sullivan. Reference is to the 1997 Pauvert edition, p. 19. The phrase 'maggiorate fisiche' (feminine plural) meaning physically overendowed is a pun on 'minorato mentale', which means mentally deficient.

5. *Les Liaisons dangereuses* was adapted from the eighteenth-century classic by Pierre Choderlos de Laclos (1982). *Le Vice et la Vertu* was from Sade's *Justine, ou les malheurs de la vertu* and therefore had to be toned down rather than up. *Et mourir de plaisir* was from Sheridan Le Fanu's story 'Carmilla' with nods in the direction of Carl Theodor Dreyer's *Vampyr*. *Le Repos du guerrier* turned a rather good contemporary novel by Christiane Rochefort into a piece of softcore schlock. Later, in 1967, Vadim adapted the recently unbanned comic strip *Barbarella* into a starring vehicle for his latest wife, Jane

Fonda. (His previous marriages had been to Bardot and Stroyberg, and he also had a child by Deneuve.)

6. Michel Marie, *The French New Wave: An Artistic School* (Oxford: Blackwell, 2003), pp. 66–67. Marie's box-office figures are drawn for an unpublished study by an American graduate student, Ignazio Scaglione.

7. According to the internet database IMDb, the first use of the word 'fuck' to slip past the censor in an English-language film came either in Michael Winner's *I'll Never Forget What's'isname* or in Joseph Strick's *Ulysses*, both of which were released in 1967.

8. Films which were not for showing in licensed cinemas could obviously be freer, because they did not have to apply for certification. But when uncertificated films were showed in a more public arena they could be subject to whatever laws the country in question had in place to control obscene display. Thus, a festival of American Underground films at the Belgian resort of Knokke-le-Zoute in 1963 descended into chaos when the organizers took fright before projecting Jack Smith's *Flaming Creatures* and it only got shown when the film-makers took over the projection booth and projected it themselves. See Jonas Mekas, *Movie Journal: The Rise of the New American Cinema 1959–1971* (New York: Macmillan 1972), pp. 111-15.

9. Michael Wood, *Belle de Jour* (BFI Film Classics, London: British Film Institute, 2000), p. 64.

10. A good account of the censorship history of *Salò* is available on the British Film Institute website – www.bfi.org.uk/features/salo.

11. According to Nigel Algar (private communication, July 2006), who was involved in the first attempt to have the film certificated in Britain in 1977, the head of the BBFC personally went to Paris, where the negative and print materials were stored after being smuggled out of Japan, to supervise reshaping the scene in the hope he could persuade his Board to pass it uncut.

5

Outside the Studio

Most of the films of the new cinemas were non- or even anti-studio in every sense of the phrase. It goes without saying that they were rarely, if ever, made by studio companies as in-house productions. Some of the big studios did (cautiously) invest in them when it seemed as if they had distribution potential and towards the end of the decade MGM took the unusual step of commissioning an 'art house' director, Michelangelo Antonioni, to make three English-language films for worldwide release by the company. But the normal pattern was for the films to be put together by small or medium-sized companies, sometimes owned by the directors concerned, with a distribution guarantee being sought to complete the financial package before the film went into production. The crucial right of 'final cut' usually stayed with the director or producer, though compromises might need to be made with distributors to meet censorship or other requirements in particular markets.[1] This was in line with general European practice, but in marked contrast to Hollywood (and to some extent British) procedures, where it was the studio, rather than the individual producer let alone the director, which laid down the basic conditions for what the film was to be like.

But the films of the new cinemas were also non- or anti-studio in the more basic, physical sense of preferring to shoot on location rather than on stage sets wherever possible. This was not an absolute rule. Sometimes a film would be shot mostly on location, with the studio being used for some interiors or for the occasional close-up cutaway. Sound was often recorded or re-recorded in the studio because location conditions had made getting a usable soundtrack difficult or even impossible. And there were one or two directors who actually chose to shoot their interiors in the studio and sometimes exteriors as well. Fellini, who had mainly shot on location in the 1950s, retreated more and more into 'inner space' from the 1960s onwards, creating his filmic world out of the imagination rather than basing himself too closely on external reality: famously, he had a massive studio set constructed to replicate Rome's Via Veneto for *La dolce vita* in 1960, instead of trying to capture life on the street in the neo-realist manner. Fassbinder, too, found working in studio interiors congenial to his theatrical mode of working with actors. In Eastern Europe, where extensive facilities could be made freely available to film-makers lucky enough to be allowed to make a film in the first place, studio shooting could also be a preferred option – depending on whether it was the studio authorities or the local police who most needed to be kept on-side.

It is sometimes assumed that the main reason for preferring to shoot on location was that it was cheaper. This, however, was by no means necessarily the case. Location shooting was cheap if you were on your home turf, used small casts and crews, shot in the street without having it cleared of traffic, and had friends who could lend you their apartments to shoot interiors in. François Truffaut's debut feature *Les Quatre cents coups* (1959) was shot in this way and came in on a budget of less than 50 million old francs (£50,000 or US$140,000 at the exchange rate of the time). Other early New Wave films such as Godard's *A bout de souffle*, Rivette's *Paris nous appartient*, Rohmer's *Le Signe du Lion*, and Chabrol's *Les Bonnes Femmes* followed the same pattern.[2] Set and shot in Paris, using actors who were not yet stars, and the lightest and most basic equipment available, they all cost very little to make. Although most of the others, even Godard, moved on to making films in different and sometimes more expensive ways, Rohmer continued to make films according to the original recipe. The great majority of his films were cheaply location-shot, in Paris or a French provincial town, with a small crew recording sound on site. Pared down budgets of this kind enabled Rohmer to go on making films for small or smallish audiences without having recourse to the French government's aid budget for film production.

But location work could also be expensive, particularly if it meant taking a large cast and crew on a long shoot away from home. Tony Richardson's *A Taste of Honey* had no stars and used (with union agreement) a relatively small crew, but it still cost £120,000 ($340,000), with much of the budget being used up on accommodating cast and crew on location in Manchester and Salford.[3] The case of Jean-Luc Godard's

Contempt (*Le Mépris*, 1963) was even more dramatic. Shot in Rome and on Capri, it did very well at the box office, but took a long time to go into profit. This was partly because of the enormous fee demanded by its lead actress, Brigitte Bardot, but it was also because Bardot, as a famous star, expected to travel with a retinue of personal attendants in train. These attendants (hairdresser, make-up artist, costumier, etc.) had to be expensively accommodated, as did other French members of the cast and crew such as Michel Piccoli or Raoul Coutard, not to mention Fritz Lang and Jack Palance.[4] The kind of savings Godard normally expected to get through his generally improvised production methods were all eaten up by these extra location costs.

Location shooting, in fact, was only an economy if practised in conjunction with other cost-saving methods. If the setting was contemporary, as it generally was, you saved not only on sets and set-dressing but also on costumes. Some directors of photography, such as Henri Decaë or Raoul Coutard, doubled up as camera operator, though this was unusual, and Sacha Vierny, director of photography on the early films of Alain Resnais, always had a full crew at his disposal, including a separate camera operator. Personal friends and other non-professional actors were cheaper than professionals, and little-known actors were cheaper than stars. Simple stories required fewer actors of any kind. Scenes with wasteful things like car crashes were generally avoided, unless it was an old car that was being sacrificed or (as in *Contempt*) the scene was faked. And so on and so forth.

Besides cheapness (where it applied), there were, however, other reasons for preferring location shooting. One such is that many of the new film-makers did not have an industry background. They had no experience of working in studios and no sense that they had the requisite skills to create a convincing fictional world in an artificial studio atmosphere. On the other hand many came from documentary and did have experience of filming what they saw in location conditions. Some, such as Lindsay Anderson and Tony Richardson, had worked both in the theatre and in documentary and saw in feature film-making an opportunity to put those two experiences together, to get outside with their actors and fit them into a real, already existing setting.

Richardson did not in fact achieve this until *A Taste of Honey*, and Anderson had cold feet when making his first feature, *This Sporting Life*, in 1963 and shot rather more in the studio than he had originally intended. But *A Taste of Honey* and (to a lesser extent) Karel Reisz's

Saturday Night and Sunday Morning both had a fresh outdoor feel to them quite unlike regular British fiction film-making of the period.

In many countries, moreover, there were simply not well enough equipped studios for it to be an advantage to film there. Conversely, in those which did, the ingrained habits of studio production, with a line-producer breathing down the director's neck and experienced technicians always ready with a safe but conservative solution for every problem, acted as an irksome constraint on innovation. To do anything new or different, it was essential for film-makers to escape these factory conditions and go elsewhere.

Underlying these contingent factors, however, was a basic contrast that had been with the cinema since the very beginning, between a cinema anchored in pre-existing reality and one which constructed a more or less lifelike world in which to base its action. To shoot on location was to encounter the world as it was; to shoot in the studio was not.

This contrast between two types of cinema runs very deep, but it takes many forms and is rarely absolute. So it is worth pointing out the particular forms it took in the 1960s and the various compromises and combinations involved at particular times.

For a start, the commitment to reality implicit in the preference for location shooting is not the same as realism. (Nor, conversely, is realism, in the conventional sense, impossible in the studio; in fact a certain type of realism is easier to achieve in the studio than outside.) Realism might or might not be a point of arrival, but observed and experienced reality had to be the point of departure. Realism may have been an aim for the early British New Wave, but it was only partly so in France, while in Italy the legacy of neo-realism was seen as something to be gone beyond.

Whether as something to follow or as something to get beyond, the example of Italian neo-realism remained paramount. It is sometimes said that the neo-realists went out into the streets because they had nowhere else to go, all the studios being bombed out, closed, or requisitioned by the Allies. But in fact location shooting had been central to the neo-realist experience, whether a studio alternative existed or not, and it was the legacy of neo-realism that acted as an inspiration to film-makers in Britain, France, and elsewhere.

One thing that neo-realism showed, however, was that location shooting could serve very different ends. For Visconti, who was a realist in the conventional sense of crafting fictions so that they looked as real as possible, shooting on location was a matter of grounding whatever he showed in something that was real and therefore looked real, but it was the look that was all important. When shooting period films on location, he dressed the set with the aid of contemporary paintings and photographs to enhance the effect of authenticity, using what he found as a starting point. On the rare occasions when he went into the studio, his aim was to meticulously produce the same effect as if he had found a suitable location to make the film in. For both Rossellini and De Sica, however, the getting out into the streets was a way of catching life as it is lived and peripheral things going on in sight of the camera or the characters are often as important as the main action itself. Antonioni, meanwhile, who was not strictly a neo-realist ('I feel the need to express reality in terms that are not completely realistic,' he told Godard in 1964),[5] location was first an foremost an atmosphere, suggesting to the director how a scene should be played and framed. Antonioni was even more fanatical about location shooting than the neo-realists proper, but his approach was that of a painter placing figures in a landscape, and supporting the picture thus created by a finely crafted use of natural sound effects.

Of these different approaches, it was that of De Sica and Rossellini which had the most effect on the new cinemas. Visconti's style was too grand to be easily copied by film-makers working on limited budgets, though Humberto Solás's *Lucía*, made in Cuba in 1969, acknowledges a clear debt to him. On the whole, however, his greatest impact was on the new Hollywood of Coppola, Cimino, and Scorsese some years later. As for Antonioni, his pictorial approach to landscape also had to wait until the 1970s, with Wenders and Tarkovsky, before acquiring much following.

As between De Sica and Rossellini, it was De Sica who basically provided the world with a model of how everyday dramatic action could be integrated into a natural setting. Not that this hadn't been done before, but no previous film which did it had the same worldwide resonance as *Bicycle Thieves*. For the French New Wave, however, Rossellini was the main inspiration. It was not just that Rossellini shot very simply on location, but he did so in a uniquely freewheeling style, not so much integrating his action into a setting as juxtaposing documentary and dramatic elements without caring too much whether the joins were visible. This is particularly apparent in the films he made with Ingrid Bergman in the early 1950s, where an element of psychodrama emerges from the way she (both as character and as actress) is forced into confrontation with her surroundings.

Although the Nouvelle Vague owed, and recognized, an enormous debt to Rossellini, they went beyond him in many respects and in so doing they found themselves breaking more radically than they had expected with the 'classical' style of film-making, whether of the French or American variety. Necessity can be the mother of invention, and much of what the Nouvelle Vague did happened as a result of ingenious adaptation to the circumstances created by their need to shoot cheaply and their desire to capture the everyday reality they saw around them.

Their first innovation was to shoot sound live on location. This was not an entirely new practice. Renoir had done it in 1934 with *Toni* and Visconti had followed suit with *La terra trema* in 1948. But most of the neo-realists, including Rossellini, had followed the general Italian practice of shooting with only a wild track and then recording dialogue and other sound in the studio. By the mid-1950s, however, the old-fashioned optical sound-recording equipment that needed a five-ton truck to carry it around had been replaced by more manageable magnetic tape, removing one major obstacle to location recording.[6] Even with the new recorders and microphones, however, film-makers were not always confident of getting a fully professional result. Chabrol boldly pioneered the use of direct sound in *Le Beau Serge* and *Les Cousins*. But the live sound in Jacques Rozier's *Adieu Philippine* proved unusable, and the whole soundtrack had to be re-recorded in the studio. Both *Les Quatre cents coups* and *A bout de souffle* used mainly postsynchronized sound from the outset. But the Nouvelle Vague film-makers soon learnt what they could and could not do, and what effect it would have. As early as his third feature, *Une femme est une femme* in 1961, Godard began to experiment with mixing live and postsynched sound in ways which broke with the conventional notion of a proper soundtrack. Within a scene street sound is switched on and off at will and from one scene to the next the sound might be location-recorded (for authenticity) or postsynched (for clarity). These experiments are taken further in *Bande à part* (1964) where the famous café sequence combines total silence (created by switching off the sound) with ambient sound collected by non-directional microphones and a song-and-dance routine recorded in playback – with some, though not all, of the bag of tricks being revealed to the audience to wonder at.[7]

Lighting on location also proved a problem, particularly for night scenes, and again it was the Nouvelle Vague which broke with convention. Prior to 1960, there were two basic ways of lighting a scene, both of which used a number of different light sources. Hollywood 'three-point' lighting used a principal key light, backlighting, and a filler to even out the illumination. The great Italian cinematographers such as Enzo Serafin and Gianni Di Venanzo aimed at a more even spread of lighting, which they considered less theatrical in its effect. Both methods, however, were cumbersome and difficult to deploy in cramped interiors or on the streets at night. Nouvelle Vague cinematographers such as Raoul Coutard and Henri Decaë therefore devised simpler systems, using fast film to reduce the amount of additional lighting needed and only two basic light sources, one for simulating directional light (such as that of a street lamp or sunlight streaming through a window) and one, diffuse and placed close to the camera, to fill in the shadowy parts of the screen.[8] Resultant scenes were not 'perfectly' lit but their visible imperfection adds immediacy to the scene, reminding the spectator that for the scene to be there, the cameraman had to be there first. One has only to compare the night scenes in a classic 'poetic realist' French film of the 1930s such as Marcel Carné's *Le Jour se lève*, shot in the studio by the great Kurt Courant in 1939, with those in Godard's *Masculin Féminin*, shot on location by Courant's son Willy Kurant in 1966, to see what an effect this innovation was to have.

Along with more portable sound and lighting equipment, the Nouvelle Vague also took advantage of lightweight 35 mm cameras such as the Eclair Caméflex, previously used mainly for newsreels. The Caméflex could be shoulder-mounted and used for travelling shots on location without the need to lay tracks. But even the most skilled and muscular operator could not walk around with a Caméflex without the camera shaking, be it ever so little. The sense that the camera was there, held by somebody in order to capture the scene being played out in front of it, became a part of Nouvelle Vague vocabulary.

So too did imperfect continuity. Conventional films, whether in Hollywood or elsewhere, prided themselves on the invisibility of their editing devices and on obtaining perfect matches from one shot in the scene to the next. This, of course, was easier in the studio, where every scene could be planned and executed in minute detail. Again it was Godard who, wittingly or not, led the march away from studio practice. With his first feature, *A bout de souffle*, in 1959, he found himself unable to edit his footage both compactly and with perfect action continuity. Faced with the choice, he opted to sacrifice continuity, and with it one of the conventions that mark traditional films as realist.

Shaky camera, flares on the lens, jump-cuts, strangely accentuated location sound. While these were in part accidental effects of difficult shooting conditions, they also arose from the Nouvelle Vague film-makers' desire to start afresh, and to make films that did not have the stale, studio look of other French films of the period. But the acceptance of visible imperfection was not universal, even among the Nouvelle Vague. It was really only Godard who carried things through to what, for him, was its logical conclusion: the systematic foregrounding of the filmic device.

Even within the Nouvelle Vague, Godard was in a minority. Not all Nouvelle Vague film-makers went in for foregrounding effects, nor did they necessarily opt for lightweight equipment if they had the opportunity to shoot more conventionally. As mentioned earlier, Resnais always shot in the traditional manner, and if he appeared to mis-match two shots it was always for narrative or anti-narrative effect rather than because footage would not match up. Rohmer, too, while shooting economically, did not like effects to show. In this he remained true to an aesthetic credo expressed as early as 1954, that films should pay less attention to framing than to landscapes and places and less attention to lighting than to light.[9] In general for the Nouvelle Vague what the location delivered was life; whatever the camerawork or editing did, it should not detract from the impression of life, even when the film drew attention to itself as an artefact.

It was not just in France that the new generation of film-makers was eager to capture the impression of life being lived. The same was true of the young British directors around Tony Richardson and Lindsay Anderson. They also wanted the effect, but were at first less successful in achieving it. Indeed it was not until he had seen some Nouvelle Vague films that Richardson really convinced himself that it was possible and worth going all out for. For his first two features, *Look Back in Anger* in 1959 and *The Entertainer* in 1960, Richardson had been forced to accept an industry cinematographer who ganged up with the producer to insist on shooting scenes in the studio that Richardson wanted to do on location. For *A Taste of Honey*, however, he found himself free to employ as cinematographer Walter Lassally, who had worked with him and Karel Reisz on *Momma Don't Allow* in 1955 and on a number of other Free Cinema documentaries. Anticipating Coutard, Lassally liked to work with very fast film stock and minimal lighting. He had also as far back as 1953 shot street scenes for a fiction film in hand-held 16 mm and on *A*

Taste of Honey devised with Richardson a technique of 'insinuating' actors into a real crowd to create a buffer between the main actors and passers-by who were unaware of being filmed.[10] By 1962, street shooting with real people rather than extras had become a regular practice, certainly in France, though a bit less regular in Britain or elsewhere.

One objection the New Wave pioneers had to face was that, as remarked above, their results were visibly not 'perfect' by industry standards. Accusations of technical incompetence were regularly thrown at Nouvelle Vague film-makers not only by industry conservatives but by critics – notably by those on *Positif*, ever eager to find sticks with which to beat the offspring of their rival, *Cahiers du cinéma*.[11] This objection had been anticipated by Anderson and his friends as early as the first Free Cinema manifesto in 1956. 'Perfection,' the authors of the manifesto declared, 'is not an aim,' meaning thereby that the high-gloss look prevalent even in documentary was an obstacle to spontaneity and therewith a sense of reality, and with the further implication that in such cases imperfection might even be a virtue. In documentary they were able to get away with imperfection since the gain in naturalness and spontaneity was there for all to see. But in fiction films a problem was posed by the prevalent convention that films should maintain a permanent illusion of constituting a self-contained substitute reality. If this illusion was to be sustained the film had to cover its tracks and not allow the audience to detect signs of the machinery that had brought the film into being as an artefact. New Wave films, however, were apt to give the game away. Flare on the lens, imperfect matches, intrusive bits of ambient sound, any of these might be enough to break the illusion of self-containment and remind the audience too obviously that what they were watching was an artefact, and someone had made it.

There were three possible responses. One was to make the film nevertheless as close to 'perfect' as possible, so that the poverty of means used in its making would not in fact obtrude and be found offensively noticeable by the likely audience. The second was to accept that some level of imperfection was inevitable but assume that the audience would regard it as a small price to pay for a film which in other respects was more real in the feeling it gave out than a better confectioned product might have been. And the third was to treat the lack of perfection as, if anything, a virtue and to regard making the means of production visible as an integral part of the aesthetics of the film.

Broadly speaking, the response offered by film-makers depended on the kind of audience for which a film was being made. Films which had to win over a mass audience tended to be the most conservative, since it was tacitly assumed, rightly or wrongly, that audiences used to the technical perfection of Hollywood product would feel shortchanged by films which broke the spell of perfect illusion which, after all, was what they had paid for. But where there was a sizable 'art cinema' audience, a different assumption prevailed: this was that the audience was looking for the work of an individual artist, so that the occasional reminder that the film wasn't just 'out there' but had visibly been put together by someone, dirty paw marks and all, helped confirm the distinctiveness of the film as artistic product. (The assumptions involved clearly allow exceptions, the most obvious being Hitchcock, whose paw marks are present in all his films, but work well enough as a rule of thumb.) It was in France and Italy, where the exhibition sector was least monopolized and a film had the best chance of surviving off a cultivated art cinema audience, that the second response was most viable.

As for the third response, it was to be developed in two ways, first in Europe by Godard, and then in Latin America by Julio García Espinosa and others. And in each case it assumed a more committed audience than either that for art cinema or that for mass-market product. For Godard it meant at first an audience dedicated to the pursuit of radical aesthetic experiment and then, around 1968, an audience committed to an even more radical politics of the image. For Espinosa it meant a politically committed audience from the outset, though not necessarily a minority one.

As already mentioned, it did not take Godard long to realize that the rolls of exposed film brought back from each day's shooting could be displayed in ways that emphasized their material character as precisely that – strips of celluloid, possibly accompanied by related pieces of magnetic tape. Increasingly he took to reminding the audience that this is what they were being offered to view and, furthermore, that what they were being offered was the combined product of a technical apparatus and a set of authorial choices on which the author was quite happy to comment in the first person Round about 1966, however, he became aware of the political implications of his procedures. The splicing together of raw reality with dramatized fiction, combined with an authorial voice drawing attention to the constructed nature of the result, challenged the audience to make sense of the word they inhabited in a new way.

Meanwhile in Latin America ideas were developing which also stressed poverty of means and imperfection of results as virtues. Ideas of 'poor cinema', 'cinema of hunger', and 'imperfect cinema' all contested traditional European and North American notions of the well made film and all argued for a cinema that rooted itself in reality but did not aim for realism.

The idea of 'imperfect cinema' first received systematic expression in an essay by the Cuban film-maker Julio García Espinosa published in 1967,[12] but the practice began earlier. For García Espinosa imperfect cinema was not principally a matter of technique and aesthetics so much as politics. What he was arguing for was a cinema whose imperfections – its rough surfaces and loose construction, whether in fiction or in documentary – reflected an honesty about its own partiality and an unwillingness to put itself forward as the bearer of achieved truth.

In putting forward imperfection as an ideal, however, García Espinosa was in part rationalizing things that were already being done, not only in Cuba but elsewhere in Latin America, and again both in fiction and in documentary. And, polemical though he was towards European models, he also recognized that he was carrying one stage further a process of reconnecting with the real that dated back to the French New Wave, to the Free Cinema manifesto, and further back still to Italian neo-realism.

Many of the developments in how films were shot and edited were the product of an openminded response to the circumstances in which film-makers found themselves. But, as the examples of Godard and Espinosa show, there were other factors at work, notably the demands of a newly radical politics of the image. If film-makers wanted to reconnect with the real, they also recognized that this real did not simply materialize by pointing the camera and microphone at it. Film-makers had to know what they were looking for and take the audience through the process of finding it and questioning what they had found. The questioning of the real was to have effects not only on narrative fiction but also and perhaps even more powerfully in documentary.

Notes

1. Ingmar Bergman, for example, personally supervised the cuts in his controversial film *The Silence* to make it acceptable both to himself and the censors in various countries. See James C. Robertson, *The Hidden Cinema: British Film Censorship in Action, 1913–1975* (London: Routledge, 1989), pp. 127–8.

2. Unusually, Chabrol's first film, *Le Beau Serge*, was shot outside Paris, in a village in the Massif Central. I have not been able to discover how much this added to the budget.

3. Tony Richardson interviewed by Penelope Houston, *Sight & Sound*, Summer 1961, p. 110. This budget was still only half that for the mainly studio-shot *Look Back in Anger* in 1959.

4. According to Michel Marie in his book on the film (*Le Mépris*, p. 18), the film's budget was 500m old francs, i.e. ten times that of *A bout de souffle*. Fifty per cent of this went on Bardot's fee. Only a successful re-release in 1981, attracting 70,000 spectators in Paris alone, and subsequent sales of TV, video, and DVD rights, made the film eventually profitable. For the information about Bardot's retinue, I am indebted to her co-star, Michel Piccoli. There is also an account of it in Colin MacCabe, *Godard: A Portrait of the Artist at 70* (London: Bloomsbury, 1973), p. 151.

5. Interview in *Cahiers du cinéma* 160, November 1964. Also in *Cahiers du cinéma in English* 1, January 1966.

6. The truly portable Nagra III tape recorder was not yet available at the start of the Nouvelle Vague. For the impact of the Nagra on documentary film-making in particular see below, pp. 83ff.

7. For Godard's experiments with sound from different sources and angles, see Jean Douchet, *Nouvelle Vague*, p. 222. The sequence in *Bande à part* (which also contains the famous one-minute silence) is not mentioned by Douchet, but I can see no way the sound can have been produced other than as described.

8. Douchet, *Nouvelle Vague*, pp. 213–16.

9. *Cahiers du cinéma* 31, January 1954, p. 39, writing under the name Maurice Schérer, apropos of the benefits of CinemaScope: 'Aussi bien, ne parlera-t-on plus de *cadrages* mais de paysages ou de sites, non d'*éclairages* mais de lumière' [Rohmer's italics].

10. Walter Lassally, *Itinerant Cameraman* (London: John Murray, 1987), p. 69. The earlier film was Gavin Lambert's *Another Sky*, shot in Morocco and never commercially released.

11. See for example Robert Benayoun, 'The king is naked' ['Le roi est nu'], originally in *Positif*, 46, 1962. English translation in Peter Graham (ed.), *The New Wave* (London: Secker & Warburg, 1968), pp. 157–81.

12. Julio García Espinosa, 'Por un cine imperfecto' *Cine cubano* 42-3-4, 1967, translated in Michael Chanan ed., *Twenty-five Years of the New Latin American Cinema* (London: British Film Institute/Channel 4, 1983).

6

Cinéma Vérité and the New Documentary

The revolution in documentary was more sudden and in many ways more radical than in any other kind of cinema. But it was not primarily a cinematic revolution. It had its roots in television and its trigger was the arrival on the scene of a technology whose application was in the first instance for television and only secondarily for the cinema.

By 1960, television was sufficiently entrenched in most developed countries to have radically altered the conditions under which documentary films were made. Nightly news programmes soon took over the function once possessed by the cinema newsreel, eventually driving the latter out of business. Meanwhile the new medium's wider need for factual programmes of all sorts meant that documentary makers were able to find shelter in broadcasting organizations, where a new generation of documentarists was trained in its turn. Although there was lamentation in Britain that documentaries were disappearing from the cinema screen, there were plenty of counter-claims that, on the contrary, the British documentary was 'alive and well and living in television'.[1]

Television in the 1950s, however, had little need for documentary as art and little appetite for documentary as anti-establishment propaganda – two qualities that had distinguished documentary film, not only in Britain, in the prewar period. Liberal non-commercial television regimes, such as those prevailing in Britain, Canada, and West Germany, gave some space in the 1950s to experiment with documentary form, but what was alive and living in television was on the whole functional journalism, often hard-hitting, but aesthetically rarely adventurous and politically always within the consensus, even if sometimes towards the edge of it.

In France the situation was different. Television arrived late and when it did it was high-minded but conformist. Meanwhile the cinema continued to offer space for documentary and experimental non-fiction. To cope with the shortage of feature films, the Vichy regime during the war had legislated to ban the programming of double bills. After the war, the ban was maintained, leaving open a slot in the regular cinema programme which was filled by short films, often directly or indirectly state-sponsored. In the mid-1950s the government moved to lift the ban, but by then the majority of exhibitors and filmgoers had become accustomed to a pattern of two-hour programmes consisting of a single feature accompanied by a short. Documentary or other short films remained part of the programme in most French cinemas until the 1970s, when feature films had regularly grown too long to be combined with a short in the standard two-hour slot.

The short films shown in French cinemas (and indeed elsewhere) were not necessarily documentaries. Short fictions could also be programmed, and could get funding from the Centre National de la Cinématographie, thus providing an outlet for apprentice work by future feature film-makers, including some of those who were to form the Nouvelle Vague. The system was not in fact all that helpful to the Nouvelle Vague, and Godard's early shorts, for example, were mostly released only after he had made his name in features.[2] But it was an outlet of a kind and there was a general recognition that the short film, fiction or non-fiction, was a legitimate part of cinema, not just something that filled up the programme while patrons took their seats and ice creams were sold.

Of French film-makers who specialized in non-fiction in the 1950s the most important, without a doubt, were Chris Marker and Alain Resnais. Rather than a documentarist in the strict sense, Marker was a film essayist, who travelled the world – China, Siberia, Cuba, Israel, Japan – to bring back footage on which he invited the audience to reflect. An archetypal Marker moment comes in *Letter from Siberia* (1958), where he shows the same sequence of shots three times, each time accompanied by a different commentary interpreting the footage in pro-Soviet, anti-Soviet, and neutral mode, and asks the audience not so much abstractly to consider the intrinsic ambiguity of the film image as to engage with the complexity of any form of coming to terms with reality. Marker's early films were of varying lengths, not always easily programmable either as a short or as a main feature. From 1960 he moved into the making of feature-length films (and after that video and digital media), but his preferred mode has remained non-fiction, with a tiny venture into fiction in the form of the sci-fi short *La Jetée* in 1962.

By contrast Resnais was deliberately impersonal and if there is a commentating voice in his films it is never put forward as his own. (In so far as there is an identifiable point of view in *Les Statues meurent aussi*, the film about the destruction of African art which he made with Marker in 1953, it is Marker's rather than Resnais's.) Resnais's short films differ from conventional documentaries in that they make no claim to be an open window on the world and indeed go out of their way to present the world as non-transparent. What they show are images rather than purported facts and it is the significance of the image and its relationship to what lies behind it that is the object of inquiry. *Toute la mémoire du monde* ('All the memory of the world', 1956) is full of shots of stacks of books, utterly opaque to the viewer and no more immediately revealing of the nature of knowledge and memory than a brain scan is of the nature of consciousness. The most famous of his shorts, *Night and Fog* (1955), with a commentary by the novelist Jean Cayrol, examines the remains of the Nazi death camps and the diminishing film record left behind, and asks embarrassing questions about the way the fading of images makes it easy for people to disavow their complicity in what took place there. Seemingly elegiac and detached, the commentary is also a challenge to the spectator and those of us who, in Cayrol's words, 'look piously at these ruins as if the concentrationary monster was dead beneath the debris, who claim to take hope in the face of this disappearing image as if the plague could go away, who like to believe that it all belongs to one time and one country only, and who would rather not look around us and hear the crying that continues without cease.'

The form of documentary film-making which burst on to the scene around 1960 was the exact opposite of Resnais's elegant and meditative style. Using 16 mm rather than the glossier 35 mm, hand holding (or shoulder mounting) the camera rather than having it fixed on a tripod or moved smoothly on a dolly, and abandoning commentary in favour of on-the-spot synched dialogue, a handful of film-makers from Canada, the USA, and France revolutionized the world of documentary. The new mode went under two different names, both originally French. In Canada the phrase used was 'cinéma direct', which soon anglicized itself as direct cinema (to the annoyance of a handful of experimental film-makers who had claimed the term to apply to films made by direct exposure of the film stock to light unfocused by a lens). The alternative term, 'cinéma vérité', was first used by Jean Rouch and Edgar Morin in the introduction to their film *Chronicle of a Summer* (1961), where they refer to it as 'une experiénce de cinéma vérité' – 'an experiment in cinema truth', or 'in relating cinema and truth'. In everyday English usage it is the term cinéma vérité (with or without its full complement of accents) which has tended to stick, but strictly speaking the terms have different meanings. A meeting of film-makers in the French city of Lyon in 1963, attended by Rouch on the one side and the American documentarist Richard Leacock on the other, attempted to formalize a distinction: 'cinéma direct' was to refer to films made where the film-makers observed a set of events, passing among the participants almost unnoticed; 'cinéma vérité' was to be reserved for films which were reflexive and in which the film-makers (as Rouch and Morin do in *Chronicle of a Summer*) interrogated the participants and indeed themselves in an attempt to determine the truthfulness or otherwise of the material brought to light by the camera. This distinction is not always easy to adhere to, since there are many films which do a mixture of both.

Whether in the form of cinéma vérité or direct cinema, the revolution was very dependent on the development of new technology – basically a 16 mm reflex camera, completely soundproofed but still light enough in weight to be comfortably shoulder mounted, and an equally lightweight sound recorder which could be synched to the camera. The ideal combination came into being around 1960 or 1961, in the form of the Eclair NPR camera, designed by the French engineer André Coutant, crystal-synched to a Nagra III-B tape recorder, designed by the Polish-born Swiss engineer Stefan Kudelski. The Eclair–Nagra combination was to become the system of choice for documentary film-makers, both in film and television, for the next twenty years, until its gradual replacement by video and, eventually, the digicam.

Before the Eclair–Nagra combination was perfected, various experiments were tried, bearing witness to the different impulses that were to lead to the revolution in the 1960s. Prior to 1958, or so it would seem, most documentary film-makers were resigned to the fact that location synch sound was impracticable if not impossible. There is a little synch dialogue in Karel Reisz and Tony Richardson's *Momma Don't Allow* (1955) but it is staged and the bulk of the film is shot silent with a soundtrack (including the music) added later. In Alain Tanner and Claude Goretta's *Nice Time* (1958), the handheld camera mingles with people in the street, but the sound, loosely associated with the images, is again an addition. In Denis Mitchell's *Morning in the Streets*, made for BBC North in Manchester in 1959, there are images and there is speech, but they are not synched and the relationship is contrapuntal rather than unifying. The effect is poetic but it is the poetry of emotion recollected in tranquillity and is avowedly distant and lacking in immediacy. These and similar films, it should also be noted, were made on 16 mm either for television or for whatever independent distribution that could be found. Films for mainstream cinema release were still mainly shot in 35 mm and street filming, even without sound, was a rarity.

The first signs of a rebellion against the constraints imposed by the impossibility of synch came from Canada. Here, film-makers associated with the National Film Board became interested in doing things which had not been done before and for which there was as yet no adequate technology. As early as 1955 the Canadians produced a lightweight (or lightish) recorder called the Sprocketape for use on location and synch location dialogue starts appearing in a number of films made as part of the TV series 'Candid Eye' from 1958 onwards. These films were more 'cinéma direct', or aspiring in that direction, than 'cinéma vérité' in the strict sense, but *The Back-breaking Leaf* (1959) not only contains a lot of location synch but speech to camera and various signs of acknowledgement of the presence of the camera and crew and the effect they had on proceedings.

The most famous NFB direct cinema film, not part of the 'Candid Eye' series, was *Lonely Boy* (1961), shot by Wolf Koenig and co-directed by Koenig and Roman Kroitor, a 27-minute study of the pop singer Paul Anka, on and off the stage, and of his relationship with his teenage fans. The film is remarkable for the balance it strikes between sympathy and social satire. The film-makers clearly struck up a good relationship with the star but seem to have found the whole phenomenon of teenage fandom perplexing and even distasteful. This question of the affective relationship between film-maker and subject was to become a major issue in subsequent debates about the supposed objectivity of direct cinema.

Not to be outdone, the French Canadians also experimented with the new method. Michel Brault worked as cameraman on an early 'Candid Eye' short, *The Days before Christmas* (1958), before returning to Quebec to join forces with Gilles Groulx and shoot *Les Raquetteurs* (the 'raquettes' in question are snowshoes) later the same year.

Meanwhile in the United States, independently of what was happening in Canada, a former combat photographer called Richard Leacock, who had worked with Robert Flaherty on *Louisiana Story* in 1948 and been frustrated by the inflexibility of method imposed by the heavy equipment, was conducting his own search for a lightweight camera and recording device. Leacock joined forces with a photojournalist from the Time–Life organization, Robert Drew, and together they urged Time–Life Broadcast to assist in the development of a lightweight synch camera. The model from which they started was a one-piece machine from the Auricon company, designed for the simultaneous recording of sound and image for TV newsgathering purposes. But it was far from ideal. Having sound and image recording together in one unit made it bulky, and it was not easily shoulder mounted. Drew and Leacock persuaded Auricon to come up with a lighter model, called the Filmagnetic, which had a viewfinder that the cameraman could look through when holding the machine on his shoulder. It was still not perfect, but in the hands of a skilled operator it worked. With it, Drew and Leacock, assisted by D. A. Pennebaker and Albert Maysles, made *Primary*, a reportage on the battle for nomination as Democratic presidential candidate between Hubert Humphrey and John F. Kennedy in 1960.

Primary was widely shown throughout the United States on the ABC network and led to Drew–Leacock Associates getting a long-term contract with Time–Life to supply more films for network broadcasting. For the film-makers this proved to be a mixed blessing. It is often claimed on behalf of direct cinema that its openmindedness towards the reality being filmed made it somehow more objective than traditional, commentary-based documentary forms. This is true to an extent, but in the world of broadcast journalism the point is very soon reached at which a programme, however the material has been gathered, becomes contentious and suspected of being biased in some direction. It is already the case in *Primary* that the charismatic Kennedy is, wittingly or not, favoured by the film-makers over the more pedestrian Humphrey. *Primary* is a very rhetorical film, even if part of its rhetoric consists in persuading the audience that it is completely spontaneous. Certainly, *Primary* made ABC feel good about having broadcast it. But within three years the network was having second thoughts. In 1963, Drew and Leacock's company, which had now been joined by D. A. Pennebaker, made a film called *The Chair*, about the last days of a condemned man facing execution. Politically, the film-makers were now on dangerous ground, since eliciting sympathy for a convicted murderer – which is what the film does, 'objectively' or not – could be seen by sections of public opinion as an assault on the administration of justice. *The Chair* scraped through. The next film, *Happy Mother's Day*, however, did not. As in *The Chair*, Leacock's evident sympathy with his subject produced a powerful result.

But the enemy of the unfortunate mother of quins who is the subject of *Happy Mother's Day* was not the justice system but the media, who were busy turning her struggle into a freak show. ABC refused to broadcast the film as edited by Leacock and his team and put out a recut version, less hostile to the press. Drew and Leacock promptly withdrew from their contract with Time–Life to supply films for the network.

Direct cinema in the United States thus soon found itself embroiled in the politics of broadcasting, with the issue further complicated by the sometimes extravagant truth claims made for the new film-making mode when the term cinéma vérité was borrowed from France to describe it. Now that the more extravagant claims are no longer made, it is possible to see American direct cinema more specifically as a form of journalism, an entry into the arena of public debate with the aid of audiovisual recorded material rather than the printed word. The close-to-camera shooting and the synch dialogue gave the new form an immediacy which neither traditional film documentary nor an author's prose could match. Whether what was shown had a particularly privileged relationship to 'truth' or to 'reality' was another question.

Shooting in 16 mm rather than 35 meant that raw stock was cheaper and more could be used. *The Chair* had a shooting ratio of 20:1. All that exposed material put a new onus onto the editing process, where selection had to be made, not as in a fiction film between different takes of the same scene, but between different scenes. Editing also produced structure and, as Steve Mamber noted in 1974, the structure in question often revolved around a crisis.[3] Although some of the film-makers, such as Albert Maysles,[4] would have liked less editorial intervention, it had to be made, and its effects could not be neutral. Structure also meant, however much the film-makers might wish to deny it, the imposition of narrativity and an accentuation of attitude. The films in which Leacock was involved generally show enormous sympathy for their subjects, those of Albert and Ed Maysles less so, while the agenda pursued by Frederick Wiseman in uncovering the workings of institutions can make his films (e.g. *Titicut Follies*, 1967; *Hospital*, 1969) occasionally ruthless.

For the most part the American direct cinema film-makers posed very few questions about the truthfulness of their films, which they were content to assert in often polemical terms. The Canadians tended to be more circumspect. For a more critical, or self-critical approach, both in theory and in practice, it is necessary to turn to the work of the French film-maker Jean Rouch.

Rouch was an ethnographer whose fieldwork in West Africa led him to experiment with gathering film footage of tribal life. His work first appeared on the metropolitan scene when a rough cut of his short film *Initiation à la danse des possédés* was screened as part of the Festival du Film Maudit in Biarritz in 1949 (see above, p. 30). Rouch believed that a visual record of collective activities, made with the consent of the participants, was precious evidence in understanding the thought patterns of tribal societies. His early films were shot silent, in 8 or 16 mm, but he soon became interested in incorporating into the film a response by the participants to the material in which they figured. He also recognized from the outset that pure tribal societies were a myth and that many of his African subjects lived double lives, most of the time in modern, westernized cities, but returning to the countryside on occasion to practise updated versions of tribal rituals, and that their experience and interpretation of this double life was something the film could be used to examine. In *Les Maîtres fous* (1954/5) he explored this double life but still without reflexivity, but in *Moi, un noir* (1958) he invited his 'subject', a West African dockworker who had adopted the name Edward G. Robinson, to produce his own commentary on footage of himself. Then, in 1959, he brought together a group of white and black teenagers in Abidjan to be filmed going about their lives and discussing race relations with each other. The resulting film was called *La Pyramide humaine*, 'The human pyramid'. Like most of Rouch's films, it took a long time to put together, but with the support of producer Pierre Braunberger, he was able to get a release for it in France in 1961.

As his projects became more complex, so did the technology needed to realize them. It was during the lengthy period of planning, shooting, and editing *La Pyramide humaine* that Rouch had three crucial encounters. The first was with cameraman Michel Brault, whom he met at a Flaherty seminar in Santa Barbara where Brault and Groulx were presenting *Les Raquetteurs*. The second was with sociologist Edgar Morin, and the third was with André Coutant. In late 1959, Rouch met Morin, and almost immediately the two set about planning a film about young people in France. It was to be produced by the prestigious Anatole Dauman and shot in synch using whatever equipment could be mustered for the purpose. Shooting had already started when Coutant's new silent-running Eclair camera was declared ready for use and Brault was hired, along with Godard's favoured cameraman Raoul Coutard, to operate it, replacing the more traditional cameramen provided by Dauman who had already shot some non-synch for the film.[5]

When the film was still in the planning stage, Morin launched onto an unprepared world the notion of 'cinéma vérité', borrowed from the Russian term 'Kino Pravda', which also means cinema truth and had been invented by the Soviet documentarist Dziga Vertov to describe some of his experiments in the 1920s to 'catch life unawares'. In a later, longer account of the making of the film, Morin explains that his and Rouch's idea was not to imitate Vertov (he cites *Nice Time* and Lionel Rogosin's *On the Bowery* as equally inspirational) but to get people to speak about themselves to the camera, in a way not possible before.[6] They would be asked a simple question, originally intended to be 'comment vis-tu?' (literally 'how do you live?') but later changed to 'are you happy?' and things would just take off from there.

This simple account is deceptive. *Chronicle of a Summer* does not just randomly ask people a dumb question. It asks it very pointedly and it brings together a group of people to whom that or a similar question has been asked. It is at this point that it becomes, in the words of the opening credit of the film the 'expérience de cinéma vérité' or 'experiment in cinema truth' which gave its name to an entire movement. As Michael Eaton points out, unlike *La Pyramide humaine*, *Chronicle of a Summer* is not a psychodrama; it does not ask the participants to act out the tensions in their relationships.[7] But the experience of being filmed does affect their lives and the film charts the way they learn to like and understand each other better – though not without the occasional bust-up on the way. There is a lot of emphasis on the African student Landry, whom Rouch had first met when making *La Pyramide humaine*. This is partly with the obvious purpose of trying to winkle out any possible racist or patronizing attitudes towards him on the part of the white participants, but it is also a learning experience for Landry himself, for example in the scene where another participant, Marceline, shows him a number tattooed on her arm and Rouch asks him if he knows what it means. It is in fact a matriculation number given to her when she was imprisoned in Auschwitz – which shocks not only Landry but some of the others, and is indeed quite a dramatic shock to the audience.

At the end of the film, Rouch and Morin, with Brault shoulder-holding the camera, walk to and fro down a corridor of the Musée de l'Homme discussing the experience they have just put the participants through and gone through themselves.

Commercially, *Chronicle of a Summer* was not a success. But its influence on documentary and indeed fiction film-makers was enormous.

Just as the world of documentary film-making was coming to terms with the direct cinema revolution, along came a film which very seriously and not at all brashly questioned the claims of direct cinema to have automatic access to reality. Direct cinema was exciting. It could be dramatic, it could be intimate. It allowed people to speak for themselves with minimal intervention (whether as help or hindrance) from mediators. But what it showed was not necessarily the truth about anything. Rouch and Morin were not necessarily telling the simple truth either, but the point they were making was, precisely, that truth is not simple.

Direct cinema was not swept away by cinéma vérité. In fact it became a preferred option for television documentary, leading to the 'fly-on-the-wall' analyses of institutions in the work of, for example, Roger Graef in the 1970s as well as to a lot of less honourable stuff. But with *Chronicle of a Summer* Rouch and Morin placed a permanent question mark over all attempts to claim truth status for representations of seen and heard phenomenal reality. At an intellectual level, this exposed a deep divide not only between the attitudes of Anglo-Saxon and continental European critics and film-makers but between two philosophical traditions. Generally in the Anglo-Saxon tradition the prevailing conception of truth is a positivistic one, which more or less equates truth with fact, or 'the facts of the case'. This commonsense attitude is not unique to the Anglo-Saxon world, but in continental Europe it is complicated by the coexistence of an alternative, post-Kantian philosophical tradition which asserts that truth is not just there to be grasped but can only be elicited by a process of critique. This alternative view finds lucid and charming expression in a scene in Godard's *Vivre sa vie* in 1962, where the philosopher Brice Parain explains to Anna Karina some of the traps that lie in the path of the unwary in their search for truth. Only two years earlier Godard had put into the mouth of the hero of *Le Petit Soldat* the notorious words 'cinema is truth, 24 times a second'. It is more than likely that it was *Chronicle of a Summer* that helped change his mind for him.

Godard remained, however, sceptical of Leacock and of the tag cinéma vérité applied to direct cinema.[8] Antonioni was also a sceptic, publicly expressing the view shared by many film-makers that truth was better served by intelligent fiction than by just recording whatever happened to be within reach of a camera or microphone.[9] Other film-makers simply kept their distance and carried on as if the new methods did not exist. Rosi, for example, remained loyal to his idea of 'film documentato' as a way of getting at truth, although what he was looking for was the truth of (or about) something that had already happened rather than truth caught on the wing, as it expressed itself in the present. But a few fiction film-makers began to explore the crossover potential of cinéma vérité with fiction by making films with a fictitious 'enquiry' structure and handheld camerawork. A good example of this practice is Vilgot Sjöman, whose films *I Am Curious (Yellow)* (1967) and its sequel *I Am Curious (Blue)* (1968) are on the one hand a pretty easily rumbled pretence of being cinéma vérité but on the other hand cannot help incorporating moments of unscripted reality into the fictional framework. In this respect the achievement of cinéma vérité was to restore to cinema some of its fundamental ambiguity as always fiction and at the same time always real, producing fictions but needing real elements in order to do so, and starting from real elements but necessarily fictionalizing as it puts them together.

Documentary proper took different directions in different parts of the world as the 1960s progressed. The pioneering American and Canadian direct cinema film-makers continued along the path they had set around 1960, making films for preference in the more flexible 16 mm format and fighting shy of the excessive reflexivity found in *Chronicle of a Summer*. Their outlets were television, if they were lucky, and the burgeoning 16 mm campus circuit which grew in importance with the radicalization of American youth caused by the escalation of the Vietnam war. To get films shown theatrically they had to be blown up to 35 mm but there were few exhibition opportunities to justify the expense. What there was a commercial market for was the rock music documentary. Pennebaker's *Don't Look Back* (about Bob Dylan's 1966 concert tour of Britain) and *Monterey Pop* (about the summer of love rock festival) were both shot on 16 but blown up to 35 for international theatrical release. Spotting the potential, the Maysles brothers actually shot *Gimme Shelter* (Altamont) on 35 and Michael Wadleigh used a mix of 16 mm and 35 mm for his massive concert movie *Woodstock*. *Woodstock* was even blown up further to 70 mm for selected cinema release, removing the film entirely from the modest world of films like *Lonely Boy* or *Don't Look Back*.

In Britain the main outlet in the 1960s was television. The documentary departments at the BBC and progressive commercial companies such as Granada welcomed the new techniques. At least they did so in theory: in practice they were often stymied by the ACTT and other trade unions which insisted on full crews for documentary film-making, thus negating most of the advantage of shooting with lightweight synch equipment. As a result, the main use of the new equipment tended to be for newsgathering, which was in a way appropriate, since that was where the search for lightweight synch had started. Meanwhile, cinema outlets for independent documentary were virtually non-existent and it was not until after 1968 that a 'political' public emerged for films structured around the first-hand testimony of working-class people gathered by direct cinema methods.

France remained the main country where full-length documentaries could still be made for theatrical exhibition, but even there they were few. In the spring of 1962, to celebrate the end of the Algerian War, Marker made the mammoth (two-and-a-half hour) documentary *Le Joli Mai*, using the new lightweight equipment to interview dozens of ordinary Parisians about their experience and in particular their response to the arrival of peace. Whereas *Chronicle of a Summer* had focused on a small handpicked group of likeminded people, and devoted a bare few minutes to inter-views with the man or woman in the street,[10] *Le Joli Mai* chooses its subjects from a wide spectrum of people, including slum-dwellers about to be rehoused in the burgeoning suburban 'projets' which later figure in Godard's *Two or Three Things I Know about Her* in 1966. As well as to Rouch and Morin, *Le Joli Mai* can be seen in part as a polemical riposte to the Nouvelle Vague, whose vision of Paris was restricted to the world of bohemian intellectuals with occasional plunges into the criminal underworld. Marker's Paris, by contrast, is more like the Rome of *Bicycle Thieves*.

Even France, however, could not support a regular flow of feature-length documentaries. Rouch's *La Punition*, made in October 1960 while *Chronicle of a Summer* was waiting to be released, got most of its audience from a showing on television by the French state broadcaster ORTF in 1962, after which he returned to his ethnographic work. Apart from the compilation *Far from Vietnam* in 1967, documentaries figure very little in French cinema until the explosion of militant film-making after May 1968. Louis Malle, however, missed out on the Paris May events because he was in India, filming what was to become *Phantom India*, a magnificent film whose pictorial qualities are best appreciated on the big screen but whose great length (nearly six hours in its complete version) makes it far more digestible as seven fifty-minute slots on TV, spread across the week.

Meanwhile, at the opposite end of the spectrum, in far-off Cuba, Santiago Alvarez was reminding the world, or that part of it prepared to pay attention, that documentaries did not have to be long, nor did they have to follow the precepts of direct cinema or cinéma vérité. Most of his films are short, they make abundant use of found footage, and they are quite startling in their effect.[11]

Notes

1. This much quoted phrase is widely attributed to Gus MacDonald at Granada Television in Manchester. I have not been able to find chapter and verse to confirm this attribution.

2. For details see the Filmography by Sally Shafto at the end of Colin MacCabe's *Godard: A Portrait of the Artist at 70* (London: Bloomsbury, 2003).

3. Stephen Mamber, *Cinéma Vérité in America* (Cambridge, MA: MIT Press, 1974), pp. 115 ff. Quoted in Brian Winston, *Claiming the Real: The Griersonian Documentary and Its Legitimations* (London: British Film Institute, 1995), p. 153.

4. Winston, *Claiming the Real*, p. 156.

5. According to Michael Eaton (*Anthropology – Reality – Cinema: The Films of Jean Rouch* [London: BFI, 1979], p. 15), the precise name of this model was the Eclair KMT Coutant-Mathot and Coutant was still modifying it as shooting progressed. The non-synch material was shot with a 10 kg Arriflex.

6. Jean Rouch and Edgar Morin, *Chronique d'un été* (Paris: Interspectacles, 1962), p. 6. English translation in Jean Rouch, *Ciné-Ethnography*, edited and translated by Steven Feld (Minneapolis: University of Minnesota Press, 2003), p. 230.

7. Eaton, *Anthropology – Reality – Cinema*, p. 15.

8. See his entry on Leacock in the Dictionary of American Film-makers in *Cahiers du cinéma* 150–1, December 1963–January 1964. English translation in Tom Milne (ed.), *Godard on Godard*, pp. 202–3 (and also Milne's notes on p. 276).

9. Michelangelo Antonioni, 'La realtà e il cinema diretto', *Cinema nuovo* 167, January–February 1964. Reprinted in his collected essays, *Fare un film è per me vivere* (Venice: Marsilio, 1994), pp. 53–5.

10. Most of the participants in *Chronicle of a Summer* were associated with the dissident left movement 'Socialisme ou Barbarie' to which Morin belonged. 'Régis' in the film is the 68-ist philosopher Régis Debray, and 'Marceline' is Marceline Loridan, collaborator (and later wife) of the documentarist Joris Ivens.

11. For more on Alvarez and other documentary film-makers in Latin America, see Chapter 14.

7

Technological Innovations: Colour, Wide Screen, the Zoom Lens

The new cinemas began the decade in black and white and ended it in colour. At neither end was this entirely a matter of choice. At the beginning the main issue was cost. Colour stock was more expensive. It was also slower, which was both inconvenient and brought other costs in its train, such as the need for stronger lights. At the end, colour had simply become a fact of life. Price differentials had dropped and meanwhile television in most countries was either already in colour or in the process of converting. And the one thing that television companies knew they did not want was too many black and white movies on their nice new coloured screens. After 1970, or indeed earlier, if a feature film was made in black and white, this could only be a matter of conscious aesthetic choice and audiences would interpret it as such.

On a wider scale, the move to colour on the part of the new cinemas was part of a general process of the colourization of representation to which reference has already been made in the introduction to this book. Hollywood had more or less completed the conversion to colour by the late 1950s, beginning with spectaculars, costume pictures, musicals, and westerns and gradually extending into regular comedy and drama.[1] Most western European cinemas followed suit, but with some delay and again starting with costume pictures and moving into regular drama later. In Eastern Europe the shift was slower Locally produced colour processes tended towards the murky and a shortage of hard currency meant that film studios could rarely afford to indulge in the more attractive Technicolor or Eastmancolor.

Colour is of course more realistic in the sense of producing a closer approximation to the look of the external world. But the reason it was introduced had nothing to do with realism in the artistic sense. In the first instance colour was adopted because it was brighter and prettier. But since the first films to use it tended to be studio spectaculars, it was in an obscure way felt to be inappropriate as a vehicle for realism. Realism was associated with reportage and documentary and the unpretty side of life. Films with aspirations to tell the truth about real life should not, it was felt, look like musical comedies or stories about Marie Antoinette. Black-and-white cinematography also had a long history of compositional values, which colour only confused. Arguments of this type weighed heavily with some film-makers, particularly those with either a strong commitment to traditional realism, such as Reisz and Anderson, or an acute feeling for composition, like Bergman or Antonioni. They were less pressing for the *Cahiers* school of Nouvelle Vague film-makers, whose commitment to realism was of a different kind and who were actively opposed to composition as a value. If the Nouvelle Vague film-makers were slow to convert to colour, it was more often for economic reasons than aesthetic.

The inspirational film for the *Cahiers* school was Vadim's *And God Created Woman*, which proved to them, if proof was needed, that films could be made in colour and widescreen and still look natural. But on the tiny budgets available to Chabrol, Truffaut, Godard, and their friends, following Vadim's example was easier said than done. Almost all the early films of the Nouvelle Vague were in black and white and the exceptions – Chabrol's *A double tour* in 1959 and Godard's *Une femme est une femme* in 1961 – are also unusual in Nouvelle Vague terms in that they were shot in the studio where more powerful lights could be used. *Une femme est une femme* was also, as the credits are at pains to point out, a 'comédie musicale' and therefore in a genre traditionally suited to colour, whereas Godard's next film, *Vivre sa vie*, was in a quasi-reportage mode and therefore generically suited to black and white. After *A double tour* Chabrol also reverted to black and white for *Les Bonnes Femmes*, for which Henri Decaë provided spectacular natural-light night-time pho-tography in the by now distinctive Nouvelle Vague mode.

In general with the Nouvelle Vague, the higher the overall budget the more likely the film would be in colour, though other factors played their part, notably genre. Thus Resnais went into colour for *Muriel* in 1963, but back to black and white for the more overtly political *La Guerre est finie* in 1966. Demy moved decisively into colour for the musical *The Umbrellas of Cherbourg* in 1964. The little scene in colour with the tarot cards at the beginning of Agnès Varda's *Cléo de 5 à 7* acts as a hint that the film is not to be read in an entirely realist key. Godard continued to alternate, using black and white for reportages such as *Une femme mariée* (1964) and *Masculin Féminin* (1966) and also for the pyrotechnics of *Alphaville* in 1965, but colour for the bigger-budget dramatic films *Contempt* (1963) and *Pierrot le fou* (1965). Of film-makers who had the choice, Truffaut was the slowest to convert. His first four features were all in black and white and it was only with *Fahrenheit 451* in 1966 that he took the plunge definitively into colour.[2] By this time, however, colour was all but universal, for all films with commercial pretensions.

In other west European countries the pattern was similar. The British New Wave, as one might expect, was solidly black and white and re-mained so as late as John Schlesinger's *Darling* in 1965. The first Beatles film, Richard Lester's *A Hard Day's Night* (1964) was also black and white, though its successor *Help!* the following year was colour. As in France, genre and subject matter played a role. Tony Richardson went into colour with the costume picture *Tom Jones* in 1963 and Schlesinger followed suit with his first costume picture *Far from the Madding Crowd* in 1967. In Italy, Antonioni converted to colour, definitively, with the experimental *Red Desert* in 1964, while Fellini, whose first experience of colour had been in his episode of the compilation film *Boccaccio '70* back in 1961, used it for choice in *Juliet of the Spirits* in 1965. Visconti had first used colour in 1954, for the historical spectacular *Senso*, and it was obvious that he would do so again for *The Leopard*, made for 20th Century–Fox in 1963. Intriguingly, he reverted to high-contrast black and white for *Sandra* two years later. Bergman's conversion to colour – together with that of his cinematographer Sven Nyquist, who had long held out against it – was late and cautious. There is colour in *The Passion of Anna* (1969) but it is not until *Cries and Whispers* in 1972 that Bergman and Nyquist develop the rich and nuanced palette that marks their later work together. A few major exceptions apart, 1965 or a year or so either side was the watershed in western Europe. Films like *Alphaville* or *Sandra,* or Buñuel's *Simon of the Desert,* were already noticeable as ex-ceptions, though not as blatant as, say, Wim Wenders' *Alice in the Cities* would be in 1974. In Eastern Europe and Latin America the tran-sition was also phased, but the watershed year in each case is later. The films of the Czechoslovak New Wave are almost all in black and white and when Miloš Forman ventured into colour with *The Firemen's Ball* in 1967 the film was a co-production with Italy and it can be assumed that the Italian co-producer – Carlo Ponti, no less – paid for the colour. In Hungary, Miklós Jancsó did not make any colour films before *The Confrontation* in 1969 – the year, as it happens, of Glauber Rocha's first colour film, *Antonio das Mortes.*

Even by the end of the decade colour was still much slower than black and white. But the Eastmancolor stocks introduced by Kodak in the mid-1950s were far more flexible than traditional Technicolor; they allowed for a greater range of effects and were better suited to natural light. The response of directors and cinematographers was accordingly varied. Godard tended to go for strong, even violent colours, similar to the effects he had admired in Nicholas Ray's films of the 1950s such as *Hot Blood*.[3] Even when his infatuation with Ray wore off he continued to stress primary colours, especially red and blue. Glauber Rocha in *Antonio das Mortes* follows suit. In sharp contrast, Antonioni in *Red Desert* deliberately smudges the Eastmancolor palette so that when the primary colours do appear it gives an effect of surprise. In between those two extremes there was plenty of room for experiment, whether with décors, filters, or in the lab, but when it came down to it most film-makers were fairly conservative in their choices and tended towards a generally naturalistic look. Obtrusive filter effects were generally frowned on and where colour is distinctive, as for example with Chabrol's colour films from the late 1960s, it is more as a result of a collaboration between director, designer, and cinematographer in planning the *mise en scène* than of camera or lab trickery.[4]

The introduction of colour was phased over a long period. That of wide screen, however, was quite abrupt. Until the mid-1950s, all films were in the so-called Academy ratio of approximately 4:3. Then in 1953 20th Century–Fox introduced its patented anamorphic widescreen process, CinemaScope, with a screen ratio of nearly double traditional Academy. Other studios rushed to catch up, either sublicensing CinemaScope from Fox or bringing in alternative processes of their own. As with colour, the introduction of wide screen had little to do with realism and everything to do with spectacle. At first widescreen processes were used only for the largest and most spectacular productions, almost always in colour and often with stereophonic sound as well.[5] But it soon spread to smaller productions and by 1960 most films were being shot either anamorphic, with a screen ratio of 2.35:1, or with some other widescreen process such as VistaVision, or with regular lenses but with the top and bottom masked off, to yield a 'widescreen' effect with a ratio of 1.85:1.

At the outset few directors welcomed the new processes and methods. Fritz Lang notoriously described CinemaScope as suitable only for snakes and funerals. Max Ophuls composed *Lola Montès* (1955) in such a way as to prevent the spectator's eye ever wandering towards the unwanted spaces at the corners of the screen. But support came from an unexpected quarter. Almost before they had had a chance to see any 'Scope films, the future film-makers on *Cahiers du cinéma* began rhapsodizing about the new process and the way it would open up cinematic space.[6] Watching films by directors they admired such as Douglas Sirk and Samuel Fuller they soon became further convinced that widescreen formats were suitable for small scale films in black and white as much as for large scale spectaculars.

When it came to making films, Truffaut went straight into an anamorphic format with his first three features, *Les Quatre cents coups*, *Shoot the Pianist*, and *Jules et Jim*. Jacques Demy also went anamorphic with *Lola*, shot by Raoul Coutard, and Godard followed with his third feature *Une femme est une femme*, also shot by Coutard. The wide screen gives a great feeling of spaciousness in the early Truffaut films and in *Lola*, but not so much in *Une femme est une femme* where the main interest lies in Godard's and Coutard's ability to manoeuvre the camera in a confined space. Then a couple of years later in *Contempt* Godard and Coutard reprised the same style of camera movement in interiors while also using the full width of the screen to good effect in the luminous location exteriors.

In spite of their early theoretical enthusiasm, the majority of Nouvelle Vague film-makers were more cautious. Rohmer and Rivette had both joined in the premature enthusiasm for the new format, but neither actually used it. Nor did Chabrol, who had avoided rash comment at the time and whose claustrophobic atmospheres were better suited to a narrower ratio.

In Italy wide screen tended to be a format which producers imposed on directors and which some directors adapted to better than others. Full, anamorphic wide screen rapidly became the norm for spectacular films of all sorts, including westerns, where it was deployed to great effect in Sergio Leone's *A Fistful of Dollars* (1964) and best of all in *The Good, the Bad and the Ugly* (1969), famous for its final shoot-out in the cemetery with the protagonists spread out the full width of the Techniscope screen.

Fellini enjoyed himself with Totalscope (Italy's CinemaScope clone) for *La dolce vita* in 1960, and Visconti with Technirama for *The Leopard* in 1963, but on the whole art cinema directors were happy to settle for the more modest dimensions of the 'panoramic' wide screen ratio, 1:1.85, of which Antonioni was the most brilliant exponent.

Needless to say, the British realist school avoided wide screen as much as possible. But Jack Clayton, who is sometimes counted a member of the school because of *Room at the Top*, directed one of the finest of all black and white CinemaScope films in *The Innocents* in 1961. John Schlesinger's *Far from the Madding Crowd* was also shot (by Nicolas Roeg) in 70 mm Panavision. Meanwhile Roeg himself seems not to have used anamorphic processes on his own films.

The superwide screen, however, had a relatively short life as a format for small-scale films. The *Cahiers* critics' hope that it would introduce a new form of spatial realism suited to all sorts of film-making proved to be soon disappointed. Films that were twice as wide as high were not easy to accommodate on television when the time came for them to enjoy their second life on the small screen, and in general the industry retreated to less extreme formats for all but spectacular films. Before this retreat the 1960s were remarkable for the sheer variety of possible screen shapes and sizes, a fact which is simply not known to many modern viewers who have only ever seen films cropped to television ratios

One further technological feature is worthy of brief mention, and that is the zoom or variable focal lens. Now a staple of television and of home video, the first truly viable zoom lens for professional film-making was introduced by the Angénieux company in 1963, just too late for the early new waves. Its arrival posed a problem for film-makers: could it be used discreetly and almost invisibly, as an occasional convenience where a dolly or tracking shot was hard to achieve, or should it be adopted whole-heartedly, as part of a new cinematic language? Some cinematographers and camera operators such as Nyquist (with Bergman) and Philippe Brun (with Resnais) invested in a varifocal lens to give them a wider choice of focal lengths and only afterwards took to experimenting with actually zooming within the shot. In the Bergman/Nyquist case these zooms tend to be pretty well invisible to the inexpert eye; with Resnais and Brun there are some visible zoom-ins in *La Guerre est finie* but more often the effect is discreet.[7] A few directors had a phase of uncritical enthusiasm for the new technology, but then had second thoughts. Visconti zooms all over the place to little purpose in *The Damned* (1969) and *Death in Venice*

(1971), but by the time of *Ludwig* (1973) he confines its use to specific occasions. Given that a compromise between visible and invisible was not easy to achieve, most film-makers at the time chose to ignore the new technology entirely and it was not until the 1970s that its use became widespread.

Two film-makers, however, took it up with enthusiasm, though for very different purpoes. These were Roberto Rossellini in Italy and Miklós Jancsó in Hungary. Rossellini in fact jumped the gun, using an early Pancinor zoom lens in *Viva l'Italia!* in 1960 and *Vanina Vanini* in 1961, before the superior Angénieux version had come on to the market. Both in these films and in the series of telefilms which began with *The Rise to Power of Louis XIV* in 1966, Rossellini used the zoom for didactic purposes. The camera may be fixed or it may be moving through a space and then at a certain point there will be a zoom in, bringing details of a scene to the audience's attention. Whatever action the camera performs, the basic assumption is subject-centred: there is a central point from which the world can be viewed and the spectator occupies that point. With Jancsó, however, space becomes fluid, subject to expansion and contraction, and a stable point of view is hard to maintain.

In the early 1970s use of the zoom became part of the general armoury of film-makers just about everywhere, in genres as far apart as documentary and horror/exploitation. The presence of the zoom – sometimes motivated, sometimes stylish, but often simply mannered – can even be seen as a marker of the period, like flared jeans or sideburns. When the tide receded a few film-makers were left who had discovered uses for the device other than as *maniera*. Examples would be Robert Altman in the USA, Theo Angelopoulos in Greece, Andrey Tarkovsky in Russia, and Raúl Ruiz in Chile and then in French exile. Its use does not form a substantial part of the legacy of the new cinemas of the 1960s. For that one must turn to narrative.

Notes

1. John Ford's choice of black and white for the western *The Man Who Shot Liberty Valance* in 1962 was already a conscious act of nostalgia. Other retarded films include Kubrick's *Dr. Strangelove* (1963), John Frankenheimer's *The Train* (1964 but in general war films were the slowest to convert), and Mike Nichols's film of Edward Albee's *Who's Afraid of Virginia Woolf* (1966).

2. Neither Rivette nor Rohmer got to make any features in the early 1960s. When they were finally able to put productions together in 1966 – Rivette with *La Religieuse*,

Rohmer with *La Collectionneuse* – the conversion to colour was more or less complete. Rohmer did however revert to black and white with *My Night with Maud* in 1969.

3. See his review of *Hot Blood* in *Cahiers du cinéma* 68, February 1957 (English translation in Milne [ed.], *Godard on Godard*, pp. 42–5).

4. I am thinking in particular of *The Beast Must Die* (1969) and *Le Boucher* (1970), both shot by Jean Rabier and designed by Guy Littaye, where the heavily saturated colours are no doubt partly due to the lab work but the visual and dramatic effects derive from decisions to use blocks of striking colour (e.g. the boy's bright yellow raincoat in *The Beast Must Die*), taken during the planning and shooting stages.

5. CinemaScope prints were able to carry four soundtracks to produce an all-round effect in theatres equipped for stereo projection. Although supposedly realistic, this form of sound was experienced as a distraction by audiences and mono (which was much easier to record in non-studio conditions) remained the rule for most films throughout the 1960s. See John Belton, *Widescreen Cinema*, pp. 208–9.

6. In *Cahiers du cinéma* 31, January 1954.

7. For Resnais, see the interview with Brun in François Thomas, *L'Atelier d'Alain Resnais* (Paris: Flammarion, 1989), p. 192. The cinematographer on *La Guerre est finie* was Sacha Vierny, but decisions about framing were made by Brun. For Bergman see the 1994 interview with Nyqvist available at http://zakka.dk/euroscreenwriters/interviews/sven_nyqvist_on_ingmar_bergman.htm.

8

Narrative

The biggest changes brought about by the new cinemas of the 1960s were in storytelling, in the way stories were told, in what these stories consisted of, in the sort of characters who figured in them, moving on to how these characters were realized by actors, and how the actors were lit and framed to present them in their roles. In a finished film, these aspects come across as inseparable, but it can be useful to separate them out in order to get a clearer idea of the elements that are combined to make a film.

The new cinemas did not replace one form of storytelling with another, but with several. They arrived at a time when film narrative had become fixed into a very restricted range of forms and opened it up in a variety of different directions. It is therefore worth starting with the state of film narrative as it was before the new cinemas came on the scene.

Film narrative in the 1950s was basically of a kind recognizable from the 19th-century novel and theatre and indeed older and more archetypal forms. It was more or less untouched by the modernism that had swept through the world of high art in the early 20th century. Not only that, but in many cases it actually piled on extra constraints to an already restricted range of possible forms.

The four main characteristics of film narrative as it existed in 1960 (and of course in most cases continues today) were that it was linear, that it was purposive, that it was oedipal, and that it tended towards a happy or, failing that, a redemptive end.

By linear I mean that the plot, however convoluted it might appear, always resolved itself into a single story which could represented as a straight line. In the 1940s and 1950s there were many films narrated in a complicated way, especially by flashback. Think, for example, of Orson Welles's *Citizen Kane* or Max Ophuls's *Letter from an Unknown Woman*. But the stories in these cases are like bits of string which have loops in them. However tangled they appear, a simple tug and they shape up as a single straight line. The enigma at the beginning – why were Kane's dying words 'Rosebud'? or who was the unknown author of the letter Stefan receives? – is resolved and the flashbacks shape up as a linear narrative after all.

Secondly, film narrative was purposeful. The action proceeded towards the accomplishment of a goal. Boy gets girl. Crime is solved. Traveller reaches journey's end. This was not merely a feature of the plot. It was also the case that, for the goal to be achieved, there had to be at least one character who had his mind set on achieving it. This was particularly the case in Hollywood films and is ideological as well as formal, in that the go-getter is an approved figure within a certain American ideology. Some go-getters in Hollywood films get their comeuppance, but that is the exception.

Thirdly, film narrative was strongly oedipal. By oedipal I mean that love stories (which the majority of films are, in whole or in part) regularly subordinated the vagaries of sexual desire to an overarching theme of growing up, acquiring experience (sexual or otherwise), and passing from the stage of being the child to that of being an adult and a prospective if not actual parent. This is a very widespread and at some level almost universal feature of narrative from any culture and in any medium, so it is not surprising to find it quite prevalent in the movies. At the same time there are numerous films which attempt to bypass it. In the films of Howard Hawks, for example, the hero and heroine enter the scene as experienced but childless adults and remain in that state at the end, though even in Hawks marriage is acknowledged as a narrative goal.

Fourthly, the happy end. Again this is a common feature of narratives of all sorts, though it is far from universal, even in fairy tales. But it was institutionalized in the cinema to an extraordinary degree. This was partly a matter of playing safe with the mass audience, which was thought to prefer uplifting endings, if not always inanely happy ones. In the USA the happy or uplifting end was not only popular (more so than in Europe), but was made practically mandatory by the Production Code, which required virtue to be rewarded and vice punished. Stories in which the hero and heroine are united at the end while the villain is defeated and even punished – already the stuff of popular melodrama – thus received an additional boost, though they could be mixed with equally melodramatic tales in which the repentant sinner is redeemed by a noble death. (In fairness to Hollywood it should be said that both film-makers and audiences increasingly found the mandatory virtuous ending a step too far and it was a reason, along with institutional prudery, for the Code's demise in the 1960s.)

These attributes of film narrative in the 1950s are all fairly typical of fiction as generally understood. They are also, in this respect, the sort of thing which tends to distinguish stories as they are told from life as it is lived. Stories in this sense have an enduring appeal because they give order to a life which is not ordered, which is entropic, made up of bits and pieces, and offers few endings of any kind, let alone happy ones. The whole thrust of the modern novel and short story, however, from the late 19th century onwards, has been to reject the convention of this form of ordered fiction and to tell stories which, while still crafted as stories, are respectful of the randomness of real life, stories which do not necessarily have clearly demarcated endings, or even beginnings, but just enter into a phase of someone's life when nothing in particular is happening and leave it at a later point when something has happened which is not an achievement, or a consummation, or a tragedy, or even a step in the re-cementing of a social order. How rare this form of storytelling was in the cinema was recognized by Jacques Rivette in 1955 when he wrote:

> For there are films which begin and end, which have a beginning and an ending, which carry a story through from its initial premise until everything has been brought back into order, and there have been deaths, a marriage or a revelation; there is Hawks, Hitchcock, Murnau, Ray, Griffith. And there are the films quite unlike this, which recede into time like rivers to the sea; and which offer us only the most banal of closing images: rivers flowing, crowds, armies, shadows passing, curtains falling in perpetuity, a girl dancing to the end of time; there is Renoir and Rossellini.[1]

In making this distinction Rivette knew, but did not need to say, that on the side of Hawks, Hitchcock, Murnau, Ray, and Griffith there were hundreds of lesser film-makers, whereas it would be hard to think of more than a handful of names to put alongside those of Renoir and Rossellini. Ten years later, however, there were many film-makers who could be mentioned on that side of the divide, among them Rivette himself.

Opening out narrative to encompass flux was only one of the respects in which the 1960s cinemas innovated, but it was a very important one. Sometimes the intention was simply to capture a 'slice of life' which, by its nature, might be extracted from the cake at any point, not necessarily a significant one. In practice, of course, most slice-of-life films did begin and end at significant points, with meetings, separations, births, marriages, deaths. But the end point tended to be precisely that, the point at which the story was brought to an end, rather than the goal, the *telos*, to whose accomplishment the film as a whole was directed.

Part of the reason why narratives ceased to tend towards a goal was that characters ceased to be goal-driven. Or, if they were shown as having a goal in mind, that goal might be trivial or disruptive. The hero of Miloš Forman's *Loves of a Blonde* (1965), for example, has a goal in mind all right, which is to get the heroine into bed with him, preferably for a one-night stand. By midway through the film he has succeeded in getting her into bed and the rest of the film is devoted to the consequences of the fact that he cannot now get rid of her.

Other films, those of Antonioni for instance, are more seriously devoted to questioning the value of purposiveness. Antonioni's characters wander through life with no clear purpose in mind. Notoriously, his heroes are often quite passive, like Giovanni in *La notte*. But even when they are not passive at all, but active and even hyper-active, like Piero in *The Eclipse* or Thomas in *Blow Up*, they are unclear about the purpose of what are doing. Characters like that are not suited to having a purposeful narrative constructed around them.

Antonioni is extreme but not unique. The new cinemas everywhere are peopled with characters who either do not know what they are supposed to be doing or are impotent to achieve their goal. There is a long tradition in literature of heroines who, because of their social position, can only be lucid observers of situations over which they can have no control. Interestingly, in the 1960s cinema, the hero as well often finds himself in this position. The character of the loser acquires a new prominence, whether in the form of the man who doesn't get the girl or in that of the intellectual who loses out in the political power game. Marcello Mastroianni and Gérard Blain specialized in the loser role and even Jean-Paul Belmondo was forced into it, losing out to the cocky Jean-Claude Brialy in *Une femme est une femme* just as Blain does to Brialy in *Les Cousins*. Even when Belmondo gets to play the romantic lead, the heroism of the character is undercut. In *A bout de souffle* Michel plays at being Humphrey Bogart, but he knows, and the audience knows, that this is just a pose and even a Bogart character, let alone a pure clean-living character as played by Alan Ladd or Gary Cooper, is a movie fantasy and not for real life. 'Unlucky the country that has need of heroes,' says Brecht's Galileo, and in the disabused but far from pessimistic world of 1960s new cinemas the traditional hero has no place. Battles may be lost or won, but films do not have to be crafted as if heroes simply went out into the world to fight them and bring back victory.

Undercutting the role of the traditional hero should not be mistaken for cynicism. Characters may not know which way they are headed, or how to get there, but this does not mean that they have given up on the prospect of a better world. The search motif, so important to narrative, does not disappear. It is just that characters do not always arrive at the end of their journey. Or the search may be an interior one, where the goal is self-knowledge rather than action on the world. And characters who do have knowledge, but find themselves living in a world over which they have no power, do not for that reason despair or cause the audience to disengage from their struggle. The intellectual heroes of Rocha's *Terra em transe* (1967) or *Antonio das Mortes* (1969) may seem destined to lose the struggle but the audience is with them in defeat and the film's clear message is that this is not the end. Think, too, of the immense relief in Eastern Europe when it was no longer necessary to make films in which the 'need of heroes' translated itself into the construction of Men of Iron or Men of Marble in accordance with Stalinist folklore.

Just as the loss of the traditional hero does not mean cynicism, so the ditching of the mandatory happy end did not imply pessimism. Arguably the opposite is the case, and the prevalence of the happy end in fiction is a compensation for the conviction that happy ends do not seem to occur often enough in real life. The unhappy, non-redemptive end was always allowable in European cinema and in certain circumstances was *de rigueur*. In the early days of cinema, melodramas would often be furnished with an 'American' (happy) and a 'Russian' (unhappy) ending, named after the supposed preferences of audiences in those countries for cheerful or sad conclusions to narratives. European film-makers carried on with the tradition of preferring unhappy ends for melodramatic stories and there are cases in the 1940s and 1950s of films being made with a happy or uplifting ending for American release and a less happy ending for some or all of Europe.[2] Alongside national preferences there were distinctions of cultural status, with audiences who prided themselves on their distinction more inclined to accept (or admire) unhappy ends than popular audiences were.

Even so, the paucity of happy ends in the films of the new cinemas is remarkable. Among films of the Nouvelle Vague, Demy's *Lola* has a happy ending with the reunion of Lola and Michel, and so does Varda's *Cléo de 5 à 7*, with Cléo's discovery that her tumour is not malignant. Godard's *Une femme est une femme* has a more or less happy ending, with the teasing suggestion that Emile may be prepared to oblige Angela by doing his bit to make her pregnant after all. But most of Godard's early films end with the death of either the hero or the heroine and for the next happy end (and then an ironic one) one must wait until *Alphaville* in 1965. Truffaut's *Les Quatre cents coups* ends with Antoine escaping from the reform school but certain to be recaptured, while his next three films end with deaths – Catherine and Jim in *Jules et Jim*, Lena in *Shoot the Pianist*, Pierre in *Soft Skin*. There are fewer deaths in Resnais, though both Bernard in *Muriel* and Diego in *La Guerre est finie* may be about to die. It goes without saying that Chabrol's films rarely end happily, although in some the murderer may be brought to justice.

But you do not need a cruel and unfair death for an ending not to qualify as a happy one. One of the most poignant of all endings is that of *The Umbrellas of Cherbourg*, where Geneviève (Catherine Deneuve), now comfortably and no doubt happily married to a rich man, encounters her former sweetheart (and father of her child) at a service station and in the movement of her head as she turns away is all the pathos of lost love and youth. And in fact many of the unhappy or ambiguous endings of new cinema films have to do with disillusionment and the end of love. Such endings, it should be said, are not necessarily unhappy, but they are not 'happy ends' either. When, at the end of Antonioni's *The Eclipse*, darkness falls and neither Piero nor Vittoria has shown up at their rendezvous, it is not the end of the world or even for the two lovers, who seem to have taken the eminently sensible decision that they were not suited to each other and would be better off somewhere else. But it qualifies as an unhappy end within the convention that lovers must be united and this should be for life, or at least for the foreseeable future.

What Antonioni is challenging, here and elsewhere, is not just the convention of the happy end but that of love as a stage on the road to maturity. If films can break into the processes of life at any point and leave them at any other point, they can also break free of the teleology of maturity and reproduction which governs so much traditional narrative.

The tradition of the *Bildungsroman*, in which life and events contribute to a learning process for the hero or heroine, is not abandoned. Characters learn, they are wiser at the end of the film than they were at the beginning, but their learning is not subordinated to a broader process of social reproduction. The great theme of the 19th-century novel was sexual object choice: how to choose the right person to love, and how to live with the consequences of choosing the wrong person or having the wrong person thrust upon one. The cinema inherited this theme but tended to shy away from its complexities, preferring to make right choices predominate over wrong ones, and even to turn wrong ones into seemingly right ones (as in David Lean's version of *Great Expectations* where Pip, instead of being liberated from his misplaced passion for Estella as in Dickens's preferred ending for the novel, is allowed to go away with her and be happy ever after). The cinema of the 1960s restores some of the complexity, but it reshuffles the pack to make the cards fall more randomly. Realistically, it recognizes that in ordinary life bad choices can outnumber good ones and inconsequential choices outnumber consequential ones, while choices not intended to have consequences can be very consequential indeed. Hence the use of the one-night stand as narrative trope. In *The Umbrellas of Cherbourg* the result of Geneviève's night with Guy is pregnancy, technically 'unwanted' but at some level surely desired; in *A Taste of Honey* it is again pregnancy, definitely unwanted and even disavowed by Jo to the extent that the innocent Geoff has to take on responsibility for its progress; in *Loves of a Blonde* there is no such drastic consequence and all that happens is that Andula forms the mistaken impression than Milda is in love with her; and in *Red Desert* there is no consequence at all, or rather the consequence is that Giuliana reaches an awareness of the total irrelevance and inconsequentiality of her fling with Corrado and if she ends the film wiser than when it started, the source of her new-found wisdom lies somewhere else entirely.

The convention of linearity was less often broken. However inconsequential or arbitrary the events they recount, the narratives of the new cinemas are on the whole linear in the sense defined at the outset of this chapter. They maintain the convention of having a single story which resolves at the end, leaving the audience in no doubt as to the outcome or to the belief that the events recounted are equally real (or unreal) within the fiction. There were, however, a number of film-makers who transgressed this broad convention in various ways, among them Resnais, Alain Robbe-Grillet, Buñuel, Godard, Pasolini, and Fellini.[3]

The narrative line in Resnais's films is usually complex, interweaving at least two levels of narrated time. In *Hiroshima mon amour* there is the present where the hero and heroine are in Japan together and a past in the town of Nevers in France during the German occupation, but except at the moment when the heroine's first memory bursts onto the screen they are usually held apart. In *Muriel* the narrative, unusually for Resnais, follows a straight line, albeit a rather jerky one, but the past keeps breaking through in the form of Bernard's traumatic and unrepresentable memories.[4]

In *La Guerre est finie* fragments of the present, recent, and further past are juxtaposed as the hero, Diego, is forced to try to make sense of his personal and political lives and the relationship between them. The story as it unfolds is confusing, but by the end it does make sense, both to the audience and to Diego. Although harder to piece together than, say, *Citizen Kane*, it is capable of resolving, just, into a linear narrative.

Last Year at Marienbad, however, does not resolve. The temporal structure is, by Resnais's standards, relatively simple. There is a present time in which a man is trying to persuade a woman about something that might have happened between them a year earlier, and there are images that can be presumed to be of this previous time in which the events may or may not have occurred. This is a story which in principle could resolve. Either the man who insists that something took place or the woman who denies the fact (or maybe just refuses to acknowledge it) could be right and shown to be right in the denouement of the film. But the film ends without giving the audience the benefit of a decision. And not just that, but the status of many shots in the film – are they past or present, are they real or part of a fantasy? – makes reconstruction of the film into a coherent narrative impossible.

The scriptwriter of *Last Year at Marienbad* was the novelist Alain Robbe-Grillet. When he turned to direction he adopted a similar structure for his own films. Both *L'Immortelle* (1962) and *The Man Who Lies* (1967) have narratives which may or may not be as they appear. In the case of *The Man Who Lies* the issue is simply whether the narrator character is to be believed or not. In the Cocteauesque fantasy of *L'Immortelle* there is more of a sense that the world the characters inhabit is a magical one – which, if it were allowed to be the case, would not make it a worse film but would undermine its claim to be a radically deconstructive form of narrative.

Buñuel is more challenging. *Belle de Jour* (1967) consists on the one hand of a more or less credible story about a woman who takes a job in a brothel in the afternoons in the hope of finding whatever it is she cannot get from her marriage and on the other hand of fragments of scenes which look like a filmic realization of some 18th-century pornography. The 18th-century scenes clearly take place in a parallel universe to that of the present-day story but they might be part of the heroine's sexual fantasy, and so might some of the scenes in the modern-day part of the narrative. Buñuel makes no attempt to label any of the scenes as more or less real than any of the others, presenting the spectator with a permanent conundrum: what aspect of the story does this scene or shot fit into? does it fit into any story at all?

In *The Discreet Charm of the Bourgeoisie* (1972) Buñuel goes further. There is a flimsy basic plot, which concerns a couple trying but failing to organize a dinner party for a group of friends. Meanwhile characters tell stories, and have or recount their dreams; there are dreams within dreams and what the audience takes to be a return to reality is often another dream. Except in one dream sequence which is told in a deliberately spooky mode, almost all of the events in the film are presented as equally real and equally normal even though many of them are either trivially or alarmingly absurd. If there is a serious purpose behind this it can perhaps be found in the title. There is indeed a certain discreet charm to the bourgeoisie, which lies in its ability to survive on top of the abyss by simply not noticing that it is there.

In *The Phantom of Liberty* (1974) and *That Obscure Object of Desire* (1977), Buñuel was to go further still. In the former, the notion of character is undermined by having the same person played (seemingly at random) by different actresses. In the latter, the events recounted form barely connected storylines, all of them to varying degrees improbable, forcing – or rather inviting – the audience to question the status of the fiction they are watching.

The stories in these films by Resnais, Robbe-Grillet, and Buñuel, whether resolving or non-resolving, share the status of being avowedly fictional throughout. If the fabric of narrative coherence is disturbed, it is by the introduction of other fictions than the one the audience thought it was engaged with. There is, however, another way in which narrative coherence can be disturbed, and that is by the intrusion of elements from outside the fictional diegesis entirely, either in the form of a non-fictional documentary real or in that of an author-narrator appearing as *deus ex machina* in his own fiction.

Both Godard and Pasolini initiate the practice of authorial intrusion discreetly and almost unnoticed, by lending their own voices to an off screen narration, but increasingly make themselves visible as a commenting presence within their own creation. In Pasolini's *La ricotta* (1963) Orson Welles, playing a camp version of himself, sits in a director's chair on a film set spouting lines of poetry which are actually by Pasolini and spoken (because Welles is being dubbed into Italian) by Pasolini himself. Then in *Hawks and Sparrows* Pasolini undermines the coherence and linearity of the main narrative by on the one hand inserting documentary footage of the funeral of the Communist leader Palmiro Togliatti and on the other hand by having his actors, Totò and Ninetto, perform in a secondary story as two medieval monks. Later, in his 1970 film version of the *Decameron*, Pasolini casts himself in the role of the painter Giotto creating a massive fresco which metaphorically represents the film the audience is watching.

Godard's assault on the self-contained fiction becomes more and more radical as the decade progresses. In *Two or Three Things I Know about Her* (1966) he mixes a story about a character ('her' – Juliette, played by Marina Vlady) with a documentary about Paris ('her' – the Paris region) commented on by himself as author. And in *Wind from the East* (1969) he undermines the idea of fiction as such by constantly interrupting, rearranging, and even erasing the narrative. Godard's ostensible target is in the first instance the lure of fiction as ideology but the film is also an assault on the hapless spectator, who is cruelly deprived of the pleasure of a flowing, resolving narrative.[5]

No such political purpose underlies Fellini's deconstruction of narrative coherence in *8½* (1963). Guido, a film director, is experiencing a crisis of creativity, which he solves by summoning up images from a mixture of memory and fantasy. The film concludes when the fantasized and remembered images invade the film set where Guido is supposed to be taking part in a ceremony inaugurating the first day of shooting of his new film. Or maybe this is not what happens, since it is never entirely clear whether the film has entered the objectively unreal world of the miraculous or whether what is happening is simply Guido yet again escaping into the subjective reality of his fantasy. Either way, the coherence of a fictional world is called into question, and in a manner which, unlike *Wind from the East*, is purely pleasurable.

Later on (for example in *Roma*, 1972), Fellini was to cast himself as storyteller/master of ceremonies, conjuring fiction out of the air while at the same time situating it in documented reality. But *8½* remains his greatest achievement, and a reminder that complex and non-linear narrative has a place in popular cinema (*8½* did well at the box office, though not as well as *La dolce vita*) as well as in refined or high-minded experiment.

Notes

1. Jacques Rivette, 'Lettre sur Rossellini', *Cahiers du cinéma* 46, April 1955. English translation (by Tom Milne) in Hillier, *Cahiers du Cinéma* I, pp. 192–204. (Quotation from Hillier, p. 194, translation slightly modified.)

2. Two examples. Ophuls's *The Exile* (1947) ends with Charles Stuart setting sail back to England to reclaim his throne, leaving the loyal and loving Katie grieving at the quayside and slowly merging back into the crowd. The studio judged this ending too downbeat and recut it to make the film end on a close-up, changing the message from (to put it crudely) 'Charles has used Katie and now moves on to higher things' to (equally crudely) 'Katie has been deserted but keeps in her heart the memory of having been loved by a king'. American audiences saw the studio version, but Ophuls's original ending was preserved in the version circulating in Europe. And in 1955, Rossellini shot his film *Angst* (also known as *Fear* or *La paura*) in two versions, one in German and one in English. To suit a presumed Germanic taste for tragedy, the German version ends with the heroine committing suicide. The English version (also used in Italy) ends with an implausible rescue.

3. Other film-makers could be added to this list, notably Polanski and Bergman. Polanski's *Repulsion* places the spectator in an uncertain world where the status of events is undecided until the very end. Throughout the film, the spectator is given access to Carol's imaginings, without them being initially labelled as such. The narrative, however, does resolve at the end, when Carol's madness is revealed, and the film more properly belongs in the genre of the non-supernatural horror film, or possibly the fantastic. And Bergman's masterpiece *Persona* has an apparently resolving story (in the end Alma simply goes away, leaving Elisabeth to sort out her problems on her own), but what has happened between the characters remains obscure and the conclusion of the narrative makes this even more disturbing.

4. The full title of the film is *Muriel ou le temps d'un retour* – 'Muriel or the time of a return' – the 'return' being both the return of a character (Bernard back from Algeria, Alphonse coming back into Hélène's life) and the 'return of the repressed' in Bernard's inner life.

5. See Peter Wollen, 'Countercinema: *Vent d'est*', *Afterimage* (London) 4, autumn 1972. Reprinted in Peter Wollen, *Readings and Writings: Semiotic Counter-Strategies* (London: Verso, 1982), pp. 79–91.

9

New Cinemas, National Cinemas

As readers can't have failed to notice, the new cinemas of the 1960s tend (in this book as elsewhere more generally) to be referred to with a national or other geographical tag attached to them. Thus there is the Czechoslovak New Wave and the Young (and the New) German Cinema, while the Nouvelle Vague is always implicitly or explicitly French, Cinema Novo is always Brazilian, and so on. This placing of cinemas in geographic locations respects certain basic facts about how the cinema operates. Cinemas are not footloose. Films tend to be set and shot in particular countries, which are also usually the countries where the film-making personnel come from and where the money was raised with which to make the film. They tend, too, to find their audiences in the first instance, and sometimes exclusively, in this their country of origin. They also tend, on this geographic basis, to construct a semantic universe which makes their place of origin a central point of reference for both home and export audiences. Thus, for example, French films reflect back to their audiences a notion of bourgeois or popular life, in Paris or the provinces, in which one of the things signified is France and some sort of Frenchness infusing the proceedings.

This basic and on the whole uncontroversial rootedness of cinemas in their particular place of origin has led to the films from these places being regularly grouped under the more restrictive heading of 'national cinemas'. As a result of this twist of nomenclature, precedence is given, wittingly or not, to underlying politico-economic and juridical factors (to do with borders, currencies, tariff barriers, citizenship, etc.) at the expense of signified elements such as language, religious/cultural tradition, or physical geography, any of which can be as defining a feature of a film, from the audience's point of view, as nationality in the technical sense.

The term 'national cinemas' is in fact highly questionable, particularly when applied to the kinds of cinema dealt with in this book, whose relationship to the nation within whose borders they originate is often complex and contested. 'National cinemas' is fair enough as a term of convenience to assist the stacking of shelves in video- or bookstores, where non-Hollywood films are regularly grouped rather like travel books: that is to say, by country if, like France or Italy, it is regarded as significant enough to merit a heading on its own, but by region if the country in question (Bolivia, say, or Senegal) is deemed to be more suitably subsumed under a broader heading – as the case may be, 'Latin America, or 'Africa (sub-Saharan)'. It is also a viable term in a technical sense, in that national cinemas have a juridical status conferred on them by the fact that national governments all over the world have legislated first to define and then to protect the products of their own film industries in opposition to those of other nations.

But in between the precise demands of national legislations (which refer to film industries rather than cinemas) and the convenience of shelf-stackers at Borders or Blockbuster, lies a vast area of conceptual confusion. This confusion is even institutionalized to the point where a reputable publishing house has brought out an entire series of books on so-called national cinemas – 'British national cinema', 'French national cinema', etc. – in which the vexatious question of what is meant by the term 'national cinema' is addressed at best sketchily and in some cases not at all.[1] It is therefore useful at this point to open up what must be a sizeable parenthesis on what national cinemas are in the first place, and what relationship the new cinemas of the 1960s bore to existing national cinema (in the sense, and to the extent, that such entities can be deemed to exist from case to case).

First of all it needs to be observed that the new cinemas, if only for reasons of comparative scale, related in many cases quite differently to the rest of the cinema in the country where they came into being. At one end, for instance, there was Cuba, where there was practically no indigenous cinema before the Revolution and the new cinema initiated by ICAIC was effectively coterminous with Cuban cinema as a whole from 1960 onwards. At the other end, meanwhile, there is the case of West Germany, where a solid if undistinguished film industry existed before, during and after the flowering of the Young German Cinema in the mid-1960s, but where the new cinema, during its brief period in the limelight, had a worldwide resonance out of proportion to its economic weight, which was insubstantial.

Secondly, as this example implies, it is important to define the respect in which the cinemas in question were or were not national. Were they, at one extreme, national only in the sense in which a car industry can be said to be national, that is to say through being based somewhere within a national territory and contributing to the national economy by providing employment and having a positive impact on the balance of payments? Or were they national in the sense of being a significant, even if passive, component of national life in the country concerned, so that audiences experienced them as in some part way part of their identity? Or, finally, did they work actively to shape the concept that audiences at home and abroad had of that country as a nation? It is not impossible for a cinema to perform this role, and the new cinemas occasionally did precisely that. But it is unusual, which makes it all the more important to be precise in one's use of terms.

To stay briefly with the case of West Germany. Here in the late 1950s and early 1960s the cinema industry undoubtedly satisfied the minimum criterion of nationality by producing films which were popular enough with audiences to enable German producers to put money back into the economy which would otherwise have been spent in the form of precious dollars to import even more movies from America than was already the case. As part of its offering, this cinema industry also provided German-speaking audiences (though few people elsewhere in the world, since the films were rarely exported) with an image of Germany as a 'home' (*Heimat*) in which they could feel comfortable. Home as portrayed in the *Heimatfilm* was a place which had never been riven with convulsions, and where everyone, even if they lived in the cities, had roots in the countryside. So although the modern city might be home to threatening delinquent youth (as in Georg Tressler's *Die Halbstarken* from 1956, one of the few German films of the period to acquire a well-deserved international reputation), West Germany could still be signified to itself in the cinema as a place at peace with itself and the world. This idyll was at variance not only with reality but with what was happening in German literature, where writers like Heinrich Böll and Günter Grass were beginning by the end of the 1950s to peel off the complacent mask put on by the official media.

In this respect, the West German cinema can count as a national cinema also in the sense of replicating a sense of national identity, intended or not. But as to the further stage, when the cinema can act, as Böll and Grass did in literature, as the conscience of a nation, the mainstream German cinema never got there, though the economically more marginal Young and New German Cinemas did, particularly the latter. Indeed for most people outside Germany, the Young and New German Cinemas (again particularly the latter) simply *are* the German cinema and what makes them emblematically the German cinema is precisely their reputation for bringing the submerged German question painfully to the surface in the 1960s and 1970s after it had been so successfully hidden for twenty years or more. But in order to bring it to the surface in the way they did they had to adopt forms which took them out of the commercial mainstream. The famous 'coming to terms with the past' (*Vergangenheitsbewältigung*) for which the German cinema became renowned through the work of Rainer Werner Fassbinder, Hans Jürgen Syberberg, and others, was largely confined to the world of art cinema until Edgar Reitz, a veteran of the Young German Cinema, produced his mammoth (and massively popular) series for television, *Heimat*, in the early 1980s.[2]

The German case was extreme. There was no country in which questions of the national past and present posed themselves more urgently than in Germany, and the industrial situation, separating old from new cinemas, was far from typical. (Not that there is any typical industrial situation, since in that respect, as in many others, every country was different.) But it was extreme only in the level of self-consciousness with which the Young and New German Cinemas pushed national questions into the foreground. Other new cinemas also redefined the relationship of cinema to nation, though less radically and with less sense of purpose, and sometimes only as a by-product of purposes which had no 'national' aspirations at all.

If there is a feature common to all the new cinemas of the 1960s, it is that they set out to rectify something false or misleading in the way life in their country was portrayed and in so doing came up with an alternative image which they hoped was more accurate or more relevant to modern life as they understood it. But the life in question didn't in the first instance have to be national life and the questions at issue did not necessarily pose themselves in national terms.

The British and French new waves provide contrasting responses to this dilemma. In Britain, the Free Cinema movement, led by Lindsay Anderson, attacked the British cinema of the 1950s for being stagy, southern, and middle-class.[3] Their remedy was to bring to the screen images of another Britain, featuring life in northern working-class settings presented in as lifelike a manner as possible. There can be arguments as to how genuinely lifelike the portrayal actually was, but there is no doubt that they did succeed, temporarily at least, in drawing attention to another Britain (strictly speaking, another England) which contradicted the accumulated stereotypes by which Britain and Britishness were defined in the cinema.[4] Outside of its country of origin, the 'new English cinema', as it tended to be called, was widely hailed as promoting, alongside a new realism, a new vision of England/Britain – which, of course, its realism served to authenticate as more genuine than the old one. This new authentic vision, however, did not stay long in the collective imaginary. Within a couple of years, the British cinema swung south, to 'swinging' London, and of the Free Cinema film-makers only Anderson continued to make Britain and Britishness an issue in his films.

With the Nouvelle Vague, France and Frenchness were at first not an issue at all. The *Cahiers* group of film-makers, particularly Truffaut, vociferously attacked the native tradition of 'la qualité française', but their quarrel was not so much with what was represented in French cinema as how it went about the business of representing anything in cinematic form. They saw the French cinema as one dictated by production values and the shibboleths of philistine scriptwriters. The clichés thrown up by these writers might on occasion be French clichés, as in stories about bourgeois husbands, docile wives, and ambitious mistresses, but that was not the problem. The problem was that a combination of stereotyped ideas and petrified studio conditions produced films which never rose above the level of cliché, French or otherwise. To remedy this, the Nouvelle Vague film-makers demanded first of all control over the production, so that they only filmed what their instinct told them was filmable. Secondly, they made films about people who were like themselves, or like the people they knew or had grown up among. This basically meant films about young or youngish people drawn from the broad spectrum of the French middle class (bourgeois or petty-bourgeois, as the case might be) which was representative of either their past roots or their present bohemian rootlessness. And, thirdly, they shot on location, showing their favoured characters in the physical environment they normally inhabited – cramped apartments, nondescript Parisian or provincial streets, cafés with pin tables, and the like.

There was nothing programmatically French about either the characters or the locations, and the scripts could have been stolen and relocated in London or New York. But they weren't scripts, they were films, and therefore produced images of what the camera saw; and what the camera saw was Paris, or a French provincial town or the French countryside, with all the national connotations that naturally adhered to the images. In his book on the Nouvelle Vague, Jean Douchet even suggests that in so far as Frenchness was an issue at all, the Paris of the Nouvelle Vague distinguished itself by being as unlike conventional images of 'Frenchness' as possible and the pervasive jukeboxes and pin tables were there to undercut national stereotypes and play up the Americanization of the world the film-makers inhabited – just they played up the role of American cinema in their cultural life. As editor of *Cahiers du cinéma* in the period, Douchet was a close friend of most of the Nouvelle Vague film-makers and he may well be right. But whatever the film-makers' intentions, the result is an imagery which has persisted to this day.[5] It is possible even today to 'read' Parisian townscape through the filter of Nouvelle Vague representations of it – except, of course, that what those films represented as modernity now looks traditional and even old-fashioned.

On the whole other new cinemas were more positive than the Nouvelle Vague in their attitude to national representation. But national representation was still often a by-product of a wish to represent something else. Throughout the socialist bloc, including Cuba, the official demand was to represent socialism and socialist ideals. Film-makers in Eastern Europe who had doubts about the reality status of this so-called socialism responded by showing ordinary people in ordinary situations, sometimes identified with local tradition, sometimes departing from it. In the case of the Czechoslovak New Wave this had a clear national component, since an explicit part of the film-makers' intention was to show Czech (and Slovak) people as Czechs (or Slovaks) first and as citizens of a socialist republic second. This in itself posed no great problem to the authorities, who were happy to encourage the belief that socialism was rooted in national soil. But problems did arise if either side was seen to force the issue and if characters were put on the screen who were thought to traduce the image of the country, and of socialism, that the authorities thought was appropriate. Are ordinary Czech women really like the two wacky girls,

Marie I and Marie II, in Věra Chytilová's 1966 comedy, *Daisies*? A sensible answer would have to be: probably not, but does it matter? But in terms of how the issue was framed, what was at stake was little short of national honour.

Elsewhere in Eastern Europe, the national question was more acute. Poland and Hungary in particular had long traditions of self-affirmed national difference, and this is reflected in their cinemas. The 'Polish school' (so-called) of the late 1950s and early 1960s was Polish not only in making films which were unlike those of neighbouring countries but in focusing on both the distant and the recent past of Poland and the Polish nation. And in Hungary the films of Miklós Jancsó in the 1960s return almost obsessively to moments in the country's history such as the aftermath of wars and attempted revolutions which could be seen as definitional of national identity.

In the case of Latin America, the national issue was part and parcel of something wider altogether. Increasingly in the 1960s Latin American intellectuals saw themselves, however strong their ties to Europe and European culture, as belonging to something that was coming to be called the Third World. The term Third World was coined in the 1950s to refer to countries which wished to affirm their neutrality in relation to the Cold War and its two massive economico-political blocs – a capitalist US-led west and a socialist bloc dominated by the Soviet Union. But what fundamentally characterized this third world was poverty and underdevelopment, by which was meant not an innocent belatedness to develop but a forced underdevelopment due to the ravages of colonialism and, in the case of much of Latin America, to an unholy alliance between local elites and the economic imperialism of the United States. The politics of the new cinemas of Latin America was continental as well as national. This is very apparent in the films made in Brazil by Glauber Rocha before he was driven into exile. They are on the one hand intensely Brazilian and, for example, explore in some depth Brazil's African legacy (a feature not shared by, say, Argentina or Mexico). But on the other hand they are infused with a no less intense Third-Worldism – for which they were to be cruelly satirized by Godard in *Wind from the East* in 1969.

The 1960s was, however, also a period of increasing internationalization in world cinema, to which both economic and political pressures contributed. In this respect it resembled the period in the late 1920s and early 1930s when there was a lot of movement of personnel from struggling industries to prosperous ones, followed by a wave of forced migration precipitated by the Nazi takeover in Germany in 1933. The forced migration in the 1960s was never on that scale, but several Eastern European film-makers chose the path of westward emigration, particularly after 1968, and military dictatorships in Latin America forced the Argentine Fernando Birri and the Brazilian Glauber Rocha into exile in Europe. Meanwhile much voluntary travel was short term and film-makers would go abroad to make one or two films and then return home to resume their regular career at home.

When film-makers did choose to move, whether voluntarily or under pressure, they rarely settled comfortably in an adopted homeland. Of the Eastern Europeans who emigrated to the west in the 1960s, Roman Polanski and Jerzy Skolimowski had interesting careers, but not in any single place. Miloš Forman settled reasonably well in the USA, but the great merit of his first American film, *Taking Off*, in 1971 is its wide-eyed amazement at the weirdness of American family life. Both Miklós Jancsó and Dušan Makavejev had great difficulty in adjusting to exile. Makavejev needed a repressive apparatus to struggle against and California failed to provide one. Jancsó spent a few years mainly in Italy during which he failed to find a subject matter. He made one interesting film there – *Private Vices, Public Virtues* (1975) – but eventually returned to Hungary, where again he had problems in adjusting. Rocha made a couple of curious rootless films in Europe before he too returned home. Buñuel, returning to make films in Europe after many years in Mexican exile, alternated between his native Spain, Mexico City, and his adopted Paris, never really feeling at home in any. Meanwhile Orson Welles, having turned his back on Hollywood after making *Touch of Evil* in 1958, wandered around Europe and ended up spending more time in Spain probably than Buñuel did on his return – though never enough to qualify him as a Spanish film-maker.

Generally, film-makers who didn't have to travel, didn't. Fellini and Bergman were notorious for their rootedness in Italy and Sweden respectively. Film-makers who travelled for just a film or two at a time were often lured by the exotic appeal of their destinations – in Antonioni's case Swinging London for *Blow Up* in 1966 and Californian hippiedom for *Zabriskie Point* in 1969 – and returned bewildered. In spite of all the movement the 1960s remained a decade in which the vast majority of film-makers saw themselves as belonging in a native soil, even if exiled from it.

Notes

1. The publisher is Routledge. An exception to this blanket condemnation should be made for Tom O'Regan's excellent *Australian National Cinema* (1996), which does address the issue head on, and to a lesser extent for Ruth Barton's *Irish National Cinema* (2004), which picks up some of O'Regan's arguments. It is, of course, quite hard to write about anything Irish without raising the national question in some form or other. For a conceptual guide through the perils of navigating the waters of national cinemas, see Stephen Crofts, 'Concepts of National Cinema' in John Hill and Pamela Church Gibson (eds.), *The Oxford Guide to Film Studies* (Oxford: OUP, 1998), pp. 385–94.

2. *Heimat*, which is sixteen hours long in all, began shooting in 1979, but the final episode was not complete until 1984. It had a brief but high-profile cinema release but its main impact was through the TV screening, which attracted audiences of 20 million. See Thomas Elsaesser, *The New German Cinema: A History* (Basingstoke: Macmillan, 1989), p. 273.

3. See in particular, Anderson's article, 'Get out and push!', in Tom Maschler (ed.), *Declaration* (London: McGibbon and Kee, 1957), pp. 153–78.

4. These stereotypes were not confined to British films, but can be found in films set in Britain by foreign directors such as René Clément (*Knave of Hearts*, 1954) and John Ford (*Gideon's Day*, a.k.a. *Gideon of Scotland Yard*, 1958).

5. Jean Douchet, *Nouvelle Vague* (Paris: Cinémathèque Française/Hazan, 1998), pp. 122–26.

Part III

Movements

10

Britain: From Kitchen Sink to Swinging London

Britain's best known contribution to the new cinemas of the 1960s started early and was over almost before the 1960s proper had got underway. This was the movement known variously as 'Free Cinema', 'British working-class realism', 'kitchen-sink realism', and (retrospectively) as the 'British New Wave'. The movement had three main protagonists: Lindsay Anderson, Karel Reisz, and Tony Richardson. Their first films were documentaries, made in the mid-1950s. They then graduated to feature film-making: Richardson with *Look Back in Anger* (1959), *The Entertainer* (1960), *A Taste of Honey* (1961), and *The Loneliness of the Long Distance Runner* (1962);[1] Reisz with *Saturday Night and Sunday Morning* in 1960; and finally Anderson with *This Sporting Life* in 1963. Other films associated with the movement include John Schlesinger's *A Kind of Loving* (1962) and *Billy Liar* (1963), and, somewhat to one side, Jack Clayton's *Room at the Top* (1959). Anderson was always acknowledged as the leader of the group and when *This Sporting Life*, his much-trumpeted first feature, turned to be a critical disappointment and a box-office failure, the movement imploded. Anderson, Reisz, Richardson, and Schlesinger went on to make further films, but of a different type than had brought them to fame.

None of the terms used to describe the movement is really satisfactory. 'Working-class realism' is restrictive but probably the least inaccurate. 'Kitchen-sink realism', a derogatory label originally given to the painting of John Bratby and a few others in the 1950s, is not even accurate, since, apart from *Look Back in Anger* and possibly *A Taste of Honey*, the films do not have particularly domestic settings. (James Hill's 1961 adaptation of Arnold Wesker's play *The Kitchen* does have a kitchen in it, but not a domestic one.) To the extent that 'working-class realism' is accurate, however, it suggests a movement that was not only limited but self-limiting and narrows the field down to a handful of films falling far short of actually being a 'new wave' in the same sense as the Nouvelle Vague in France. As for 'Free Cinema', widely used by continental writers but less often in Britain, it is strictly speaking a misnomer but has the advantage of pointing to the role the British example played in the panorama of new cinemas across the world in the 1960s. Like 'New Wave', the phrase 'Free Cinema' had a resonance that extended far further than its original application.

The original Free Cinema was an event held on 5 February 1956 at the National Film Theatre in London. Three short or medium-length films were shown: a documentary called *Momma Don't Allow* by Reisz and Richardson, about a jazz club in north London; a documentary by Anderson about an amusement park in the seaside resort of Margate, entitled *O Dreamland*; and a short-subject fiction by Lorenza Mazzetti, *Together*, loosely based on a story by Carson McCullers. The screening was accompanied by a manifesto, signed by the four film-makers, which read as follows:

> These films were not made together; nor with the idea of showing them together. But when they came together, we felt they had an attitude in common.
>
> Implicit in this attitude is a belief in freedom, in the importance of people and in the significance of the everyday.
>
> *As film-makers we believe that:*
>
> *No film can be too personal.*
>
> *The image speaks. Sound amplifies and comments.*
> *Size is irrelevant. Perfection is not an aim.*
>
> *An attitude means a style. A style means an attitude.*

The moving spirit behind the event and effective author of the manifesto was Anderson, and it was he who thought up the term 'Free

Cinema' – or rather re-appropriated it from an article by Alan Cooke published in *Sequence* five years earlier. Cooke's article was mainly about the newly emerging American avant-garde (its centrepiece was Kenneth Anger's *Fireworks*), but Anderson had re-edited it and introduced the term 'Free Cinema' to include just about anything that displayed 'an expressive and personal use of the medium'.[2]

Altogether, there were six Free Cinema programmes at the NFT between in 1956 and 1959. Three of them showcased films from abroad, including François Truffaut's early short *Les Mistons*, Lionel Rogosin's *On the Bowery*, and Roman Polanski's student film *Two Men and a Wardrobe*. Later British films (or films by British-based film-makers, since they included work by the Swiss Alain Tanner and Claude Goretta and Hungarian refugee Robert Vas) were mostly documentary and it is for documentary that Free Cinema tends to be remembered. But few of the film-makers involved, apart from Michael Grigsby and Robert Vas, were committed documentarians. The core group of Anderson, Richardson, and Reisz made documentaries in the 1950s because that's what they had the opportunity to do, not because of an ideological commitment to the documentary ideal. They did, of course, have ideas about what they wanted to achieve with the medium, ideas which were different from and sometimes opposed to those of the documentary movement of the 1930s. They were for example much more interested in the ordinary than in the exemplary and if they looked to earlier British documentarians for inspiration it was more in the direction of the radical poetic work of Humphrey Jennings (described by Anderson as 'the only real poet the British cinema has so far produced') than to the mainstream Griersonian tradition ('preachy and sociological', to quote Anderson again).[3]

Free Cinema did not create a school. But it proved that a radical film culture existed in Britain, albeit on a small scale. It also gave its name to a diffuse international movement and as such is commemorated in the 'Festival del cinema libero', which was founded in Italy in 1960 to showcase new and independent work from all over the world. In default of a better one, the term is also sometimes used to describe the feature films made by Anderson, Richardson, Reisz, Schlesinger, and others between 1958 and 1963 or thereabouts.

What set Anderson, Richardson, Reisz, and their friends on to the path of feature film making in fact had little to do with Free Cinema as originally conceived. More important was the increasing presence on the cultural scene of novels and plays by new writers of broadly working-class

background. Without exception, the feature films made by the Free
Cinema, or ex-Free Cinema, group were adaptations from the work of
these new writers, all young, most of them male, and some of them
angry. Early in 1956, about the time of the first Free Cinema screening,
Richardson teamed up with George Devine to create the English Stage
Company, whose first major success, staged at the Royal Court Theatre
in London, was a play by a young writer called John Osborne, *Look Back
in Anger*. Directed by Devine, and premiered in May 1956, *Look Back in
Anger* was slow to take off. At first it played to half empty houses, but
the vociferous support of Kenneth Tynan, theatre critic of the Sunday
newspaper the *Observer*, helped to make it first a talking point and then
an actual success. It established the Royal Court as the most important
theatrical venue in London and Osborne's hero, Jimmy Porter, as the
archetype of the 'angry young man', disgruntled, working-class and, in
the rigid class society of 1950s Britain, too intelligent and articulate for
his own good. Other theatres clamoured to be able to produce the play,
and in 1957 Richardson took the ESC production to New York.

Look Back in Anger* was the most visible symptom of a wave of dissent
sweeping through British cultural and political life, which received added
impetus later in 1956 from the ill-judged Suez adventure. This wave
brought to the fore assertively working-class writers like David Storey
and Alan Sillitoe and young actors from working-class backgrounds
such as Albert Finney and Tom Courtenay, but the sustaining force
behind it was the generation of 1945, young people of a variety of
non-establishment backgrounds who had profited from the Labour
Government's postwar reforms, particularly in education, but found
themselves frustrated by the rock-like unshakability of the British class
system in all its manifestations.

Richardson's *Look Back in Anger* and *The Entertainer* were both from
plays by Osborne; his next film, *A Taste of Honey* was from a play by
Shelagh Delaney; and his fourth, *The Loneliness of the Long Distance
Runner*, was from a story by Alan Sillitoe. Sillitoe was also the author of
the novel from which Karel Reisz's first feature, *Saturday Night and
Sunday Morning*, was drawn, while Anderson's first feature, *This Sporting
Life*, was from a novel by David Storey, and Schlesinger's *A Kind of
Loving* from a novel by another northern writer, Stan Barstow. All these
films were set in the industrial Midlands or North of England, though the
gloom of smoke-laden cities was occasionally relieved by excursions into
the Lancashire or Yorkshire upland countryside. It goes without saying
that they were all in black and white.

In an article in *Declaration* in 1957, Anderson had railed bitterly against the restricted class and geographical background of contemporary British cinema, middle-class to the core, with working-class Cockneys providing occasional comic relief.[4] By drawing on the new working-class and regional literature, he and his friends hoped to introduce a new sense of reality into British cinema – in the choice of situation, character, dialogue, and physical location. They were helped in this ambition by the slow but nevertheless real relaxation of theatrical and film censorship and by the availability of actors such as Finney, Courtenay, and Rachel Roberts every bit as rough and hungry as the characters they were asked to portray. But they were hindered on two fronts by a conservative film industry concerned about the lack of glamour and name-recognition in the scripts and casting proposed by the new film-makers and even more anxious about the young documentarists' enthusiasm for shooting on location. It did not take Anderson, Richardson, and their friends long to discover that transferring the spirit of Free Cinema to the British feature film was not going to be easy

The first popular success in the new northern working-class realist mode had actually been Jack Clayton's adaptation of John Braine's 1957 novel *Room at the Top*, completed in 1958 and released in January 1959, and starring South African-born Laurence Harvey as the Yorkshire hero and French actress Simone Signoret in a specially rewritten role as his classy mistress. The film has stood the test of time remarkably well; it is tightly scripted and well acted, but its style is stagy and conventional and its artificiality is exacerbated by the studio sets with back-projected exteriors.[5]

It was to avoid interference from cautious producers and distributors that in 1958 Richardson joined up with a young producer called Harry Saltzman to create a company called Woodfall Films with the initial aim of making the film of *Look Back in Anger* as an independent production free of any form of studio control. Richardson wanted the film to have the original stage cast and Walter Lassally, who had worked with him on *Momma Don't Allow*, to be the cinematographer. Saltzman, however, realized that he was unlikely to get guaranteed distribution without better names in the cast and a recognized safe pair of hands behind the camera. So Richard Burton was brought in to play Jimmy Porter, alongside Mary Ure (from the original cast) and Claire Bloom, and Oswald Morris was hired to shoot the film. The result was compromise. Burton rants and raves in a confined, but not sufficiently confined, studio space, and there are occasional forays out into the street as a concession to cinematic realism.

After *The Entertainer*, shot in much the same way as *Look Back in Anger*, Richardson became increasingly frustrated. Saltzman had worked wonders to get the first Woodfall films made in the first place but Richardson, encouraged by the success of the Nouvelle Vague in France, wanted to go further down the road of free-wheeling location film-making. The two had a falling out over the production of Reisz's *Saturday Night and Sunday Morning*, and agreed to go separate ways. Richardson took over sole control of Woodfall, and Saltzman, famously, went on to join Albert 'Cubby' Broccoli as producer of the first Bond pictures. Now in total command, Richardson was able to plan *A Taste of Honey* the way be wanted to. A passionate believer in location filming, and reckoning that if Truffaut and Godard could do it, so could he, he assigned nearly a quarter of his modest budget of £120,000 to the expenses of maintaining cast and crew on location away from London, hired the versatile Lassally as cinematographer, and set out for Manchester – or, more precisely, Salford.[6]

A Taste of Honey is the most 'Free Cinema' and also the most 'new wave' (in the French sense) of the British realist films. It is the lightest in touch, the nearest to improvisation, and the best rooted in its chosen setting. It also came at things from a subtly different angle. The author of the original play, Shelagh Delaney, was young, northern, and working-class but also female, and if she had anger to express, did not rant. She set the play in her native Salford, but it was first produced in a deliberately non-naturalistic and 'inauthentic' way by Joan Littlewood at the Theatre Royal in the East End of London. Littlewood's carnavalesque directing style aimed to celebrate the pleasures of working-class life rather than denounce its restrictions. Richardson, however, was convinced that the play would not lose any of its spirit from being restored to a natural set-ting, and on the whole was proved right.

The great strength of the film (as of the play) lies in its lack of moralism and its refusal to see life as such as a problem. Problems, in the film, are what people create for other people. Jo (Rita Tushingham) gets pregnant by a black sailor, and Mum disapproves (while claiming not to). Jo is befriended by Geoff, a young gay man (Murray Melvin), who persuades her to take her condition seriously and go to ante-natal classes. Neither her pregnancy nor his gayness is seen as a problem until and unless busybodies begin to interfere. In this Jean Renoir-inspired world, the naturalistic acting of the young protagonists fits smoothly into the real-life settings. The only thing that jars is the more theatrical acting of Dora Bryan as the mother and Robert Stephens as her fancy-man, who could not be restrained from playing their roles as camp stage villains. The ending, when Mum decides to take her daughter and imminent grand-child back into the family fold and Geoff is left outside on his own, retains its pathos, but only just, and only because Dora Bryan has finally been persuaded to stop overacting.

The characters of *A Taste of Honey* are all marginal, flotsam-and-jetsam on the edge of society. Although all (except perhaps the mother's fancy-man) could be broadly described as working-class, none of them is representative, nor is there any sense of a social system or class forces at work. By contrast, Reisz's *Saturday Night and Sunday Morning* presents working-class life in 'classic' form, centred around the workplace and the community. Sillitoe and Reisz, however, have no interest in showing communities as warm and friendly or factories as hubs of soli-darity. Arthur Seaton, the hero, or anti-hero, works so he can pick up a wage-packet to blow on getting drunk. His sense of solidarity is not strong enough to prevent him getting off with his best mate's wife and his com-munity feeling finds its highest expression when he takes aim with an airgun at a nasty old gossip and hits her in the bum.

Albert Finney's prodigious performance as Arthur made him a star overnight. On a slightly smaller scale the same happened to Tom Courtenay after his role as the petty delinquent Colin Smith in Richardson's next film, *The Loneliness of the Long Distance Runner*, again taken from a Sillitoe story. Colin is a less extroverted figure than Arthur and his anger and resentment are contained, finding expression only in the final gesture, when he throws the race against the posh boys from a nearby public school. Both characters, though, have the same quality of striving, unable to find themselves in the fog of their own semi-articulacy. In Colin's case in particular, what society has done to him is merely a given; what is interesting is his desperate and failed attempt to come to terms with it and find a way out.

In choosing the two Sillitoe stories to turn into films, Reisz and Richardson did not have grandiose thoughts that they were thereby rep-resenting 'the working class' or fears that they might be so interpreted. But when a third bolshie working-class anti-hero appeared on the screen in the form of Frank Machin, protagonist of Lindsay Anderson's *This Sporting Life*, it did not look like coincidence.[7] Machin, moreover, played by Richard Harris, had none of the charm of Arthur Seaton or Colin Smith and instead was merely boorish. To add insult to injury, Anderson seemed to take pleasure in the character's humiliation. By this time both the audience and the previously sympathetic critics had had enough of representations of the working class centred on ill-mannered, hard-drinking philanderers. The film bombed, and that was the end, more or less, for 'working-class realism' and the ex-Free Cinema movement.

It was not the end of everything. Richardson reprized the boozing philanderer character in the costume picture *Tom Jones*, with Finney in the role of Fielding's picaresque hero. Finney, again, played the psychotic hero of Reisz's next film, an adaptation of Emlyn Williams's 1930s play *Night Must Fall*. *Tom Jones* was a massive box-office hit, *Night Must Fall* considerably less so, suggesting that historical romance remained popular with the British public but the psychological thriller did not. Reisz also managed to reconnect with the radical impulse still present in British theatre when he filmed David Mercer's *Morgan: A Suitable Case for Treatment* (originally a TV play) in 1966. But *Morgan* was a comedy (albeit a very serious one) and was not played naturalistically. When Anderson finally got to make another feature, *If....*, in 1968, it was also not naturalistic; it was set in a boys' boarding school and enabled Anderson to give full rein to his hatred of the bourgeoisie without offering the audience the dubious benefit of his ambivalent feelings towards the working class.

What died in 1963, then, was something very specific, a particular type of class content allied to a particular, fairly traditional, realist form – a variant, in fact, of something the realist novel had been doing since Zola and Hardy but for which the cinema in the 1960s did not appear to have room. There were, I think, three major reasons why, with *This Sporting Life* in particular, the ex-Free Cinema film-makers found themselves in a dead end.

The first is that the films fell very uneasily into a gap between mass-audience and art cinema. Mass-audience cinema depends on attracting audiences which are not only large but, of necessity, varied, and it con-structs spectator positions which are comfortable for all sections of the likely audience. The American cinema, with the most varied audience to cater for, is particularly good at this. You do not have to be upper-class to enjoy an American high-society comedy such as *Philadelphia Story* or poor and dispossessed to enjoy *The Grapes of Wrath*. Indeed in each case it is better not to be, since the position designed for the spectator is one of curious detachment from the social circumstances and of engaged sympathy for what is 'human' or 'universal' in the events portrayed. Films which call for a precise class or other sectional identification on the part of the audience need either a public already identified in that way or one willing, for political reasons, to assume that identification while in the cinema if not throughout their everyday existence. Unfortunately for the ex-Free Cinema film-makers, such an audience did not exist in Britain in sufficient numbers, and to the extent that it did exist, was not easy to reach through the highly monopolized distribution and exhibition system which offered little space for films that needed a more than minority audience but not necessarily a huge one.

Secondly, both the mass and the art cinema audiences were shifting their allegiances, with criticism sometimes leading the way but sometimes following in their wake. The influential quarterly *Sight and Sound* continued to support Anderson and his friends and indeed featured Richard Harris in *This Sporting Life* on its front cover, along with an enthusiastic review. But this was more a gesture of personal solidarity than a statement of commitment to the aesthetic the film embodied, which had decisively fallen out of favour. In *Sight and Sound*'s case it was an enthusiasm for the new art cinema coming out of Europe – Truffaut and Resnais, Antonioni and Fellini – that prompted a turning away from the working-class realist school. But other critics did not merely turn away but attacked the realists head on. The first issue of the film magazine *Movie* in June 1962 launched an all-out attack on Richardson and his ex-Free Cinema colleagues, and just about the entire British cinema into the bargain. Heavily indebted to the *auteurist* tendency on *Cahiers du cinéma*, *Movie* promoted the values of *mise en scène* found in the work of directors such as Robert Aldrich, Otto Preminger, and (of course) Hitchcock and Hawks, by whose standards the ex-Free Cinema directors were found irredeemably deficient. Among directors working in the British cinema, *Movie* only really liked Joseph Losey and it was also quite keen on the Nouvelle Vague, though less so than *Sight and Sound*. Faced with this turnaround in critical attitudes, Britain's own New Wave found itself bereft of a crucial level of support.

Less visible, but ultimately far more important was the cultural change beginning to affect British society as the 1960s got underway. Popular culture in Britain was reconfiguring itself in ways which were (and have remained) opaque to most outside observers but certainly included a high level of self-assertion on the part of young people in particular. Before

1960, people in Britain were for the most part content to act out the roles assigned to them by society – or to be more precise, by the ideological apparatus which determined what these roles were and how they were represented. Individuals who publicly questioned the role assigned to them were few in number and generally categorized (in an ineffably British way) as eccentrics. Around 1960, this began to change. People realized that, even if there were limits to how much change they could effect in the basic conditions of their existence, they could at least rebel against how they were represented and be self-determining in some part of their life. By such simple acts as choosing what clothes to wear or what music to listen to, they could forge new group or individual identities for themselves. Always within some overall system of course, since the worlds of taste and fashion tend to constitute representational systems or sub-systems of their own, as Roland Barthes was already pointing out in the late 1950s,[8] but nevertheless with a much greater autonomy than had previously been thought possible. A further level of self-determination was reached when more and more young people realized you can not only choose what music to listen but, with a modicum of talent and effort, make it yourself.

British cinema was slow to pick up on the changes going on below the surface of popular cultural life. One thing that film-makers did twig was that London, rather than the North, was once again the focus of hopes and dreams for many people. In John Schlesinger's *Billy Liar* (1963), the hero Billy (Tom Courtenay) dreams of going to London to become a scriptwriter. He doesn't make it, but Liz, his girlfriend (Julie Christie), does. In the memorable phrase of Alexander Walker, with Julie Christie in 1963 'the British cinema took the train south'.[9] The immediate result of this historic train ride was Schlesinger's next and best film with Christie, *Darling* (1965). A more general and less happy outcome was to be a host of 'swinging London' films later in the decade, about which on the whole the less said the better.

For all its limitations, the movement issuing from Free Cinema was of major importance for the new cinemas worldwide. Alongside the Nouvelle Vague it was the first concerted attempt anywhere since the days of Italian neo-realism to create a new and different cinema, rather than just the occasional different or superior film. It also provided one of the few occasions when British cinema became a major focus of critical at-tention, to be admired and even imitated in different parts of the world.

Among those who took the proverbial train south (actually, in this case, a bus) was Nancy (Rita Tushingham), heroine of a comedy called, in full, *The Knack ... and How to Get It*, who arrives in London at Victoria Coach Station and is taken in tow by a couple of amiable young men. They take her back to their flat where a third man, Tolen (Ray Brooks), a rock musician who thinks himself sexually irresistible, decides to add her to his list of conquests. In the end it turns out that Tolen is resistible. Faced with this gawky provincial kid, he loses the 'knack' that had metropolitan dolly-birds queuing up at his bedroom door and is publicly humiliated at the Albert Hall in front of his former fan club. There is no moral to the film and, if there is a message, it seems to be that sexual success is a result of self-confidence: lose that for a moment, and you lose your power and (symbolically) potency. This cheerful amorality, virtually untouched by modern gender politics, came to typify the cinema of the 'swinging sixties', most of which was decidedly mediocre. What distinguishes *The Knack* is that its humour is partly situational (Tolen would make a good central character for a sitcom) but even more a matter of verbal and visual gags, mostly derived from classic American film comedy, from Buster Keaton, through the Marx Brothers, to 1930 and 40s screwball. It was directed by Richard Lester, a former American TV director, who had come to Britain where he first made a classic short, *The Running, Jumping and Standing Still Film* (1960), with the radio comedians the Goons, then a couple of second-rate features, before being invited to direct the first and best Beatles movie, *A Hard Day's Night*, the film which brought the new British rock scene to the screen and symbolically (by train) from Liverpool to London. *The Knack* was hastily put together in between the making of *A Hard Day's Night* and the second Beatles movie, *Help!*. It was produced by Woodfall Films, Tony Richardson's company.

What the British cinema was doing here was what it all too often does: catching up on a trend – in this case the growing popularity of rock music and a generalized atmosphere of sexual liberation – and seeing what mileage could be got out of it. It was not really at the forefront of anything.

The British cinema did however connect with world, or at any rate European trends through the alliance of director Joseph Losey and playwright Harold Pinter. This alliance took effect with *The Servant* in 1963, the year of the effective demise of working-class realism. Just ahead of *The Servant*, however, two very good films came out, one of them Pinter without Losey and the other Losey without Pinter.

Pinter without Losey was an adaptation, directed by Clive Donner, of Pinter's *The Caretaker*. Filmed cheaply in a derelict house in East London, with Alan Bates and Robert Shaw as the two brothers and Donald Pleasance as the tramp,[10] Donner's film is clearly 'filmed theatre', with all the pejorative connotations the phrase carries with it. But it is less theatrical (in the pejorative sense) than many adaptations of distinctive and successful plays. Donner replaces theatrical space with location filming, and thereby makes the effect necessarily more naturalistic. But by keeping almost all the action inside the house, and tightly framed, he retains, without needing to exaggerate, the strange threatening atmosphere engendered by Pinter's text.

Losey without Pinter was *Eva* (1962), a Franco-Italian co-production which was to transform his status in British cinema from that of an under-appreciated director of genre films to that of an almost unique exemplar of European art cinema in his adopted country.[11] And ironically for such a strange venture, it was a work of pulp fiction that provided the pretext.

What happened was that the veteran French producer Robert Hakim had acquired the rights to a James Hadley Chase novel and signed Stanley Baker and Jeanne Moreau to star in it. According to Michel Ciment,[12] it was Baker, who had recently played the lead in Losey's *Blind Date* (1959) and *The Criminal* (1960), who suggested Losey as director. Evan Jones, writer of another recent Losey film, *The Damned* (1961), was then brought in to develop the screenplay.

Although much interfered with by the producers during the writing and mangled by them on release, *Eva* remains Losey's most personal film and the one to which he was most attached. Baker plays a fraudulent Welsh writer brought low by his obsession with a high-class courtesan called Eve, played by Nouvelle Vague icon Moreau. The fluctuations of their relationship recall that of Belle (Melina Mercouri) and Deverill (Keith Michell) in *The Gypsy and the Gentleman* (1957), while the presence of a sinister third party (Giorgio Albertazzi) not only recalls *The Gypsy and the Gentleman* but also prefigures the figure of Barrett (Dirk Bogarde) in *The Servant*. *Eva* starts with a voiceover commenting on a statue of Adam and Eve, clearly implying that Moreau's character is representative of more than just herself. She is Woman, or Sexuality, or maybe just Temptation – but at any rate forced to bear a weight which Moreau herself found excessive.[13]

Tyvian, the Baker character in *Eva*, thinks himself hard but, as Eve soon discovers, is masochistic at the core. When we come to the first

Losey + Pinter film, *The Servant*, adapted by Pinter from a story by Robin Maugham, the central character, Tony (James Fox), is simply soft. The power he thinks he has derives from his wealth and upper-class background and manner and Barrett has no difficulty seeing through him. The power game that ensues has the sound of pure Pinter, but it is also pure Losey, particularly when Barrett's purported sister Vera (actually his mistress) is brought into the frame. Generally in Pinter the destructive intruder is male and the power struggle is between individuals or in a small group. Losey's world not only has a place for the *femme fatale* but shows a overt fascination with the British class system which in Pinter subtends what is happening but is rarely foregrounded. Both artists, moreover, are adept at holding things back, so there is always more going on than is either in the words or in the staging. Pinter brought a lot to Losey, but an equally large amount was already there. Losey's move into the new art cinema enabled him to foreground themes which in his genre films of the 1950s were already present but less overtly displayed because subordinated to the demands of action and plot.

To do this, however, he didn't necessarily need Pinter. His collaborations with Pinter were in fact only three: *The Servant, Accident* (1967), and *The Go-Between* (1971). Of these *Accident* is the most Pinterish. Far less fluid than either *Eva* or *The Servant*, it is a film in which characters pause (and pose) to deliver lines of piercingly resonant dialogue through which their shifting positions in the power plays are revealed. But for *King and Country* (1964) and *Modesty Blaise* (1966), he again turned to Evan Jones, successfully in the former case, less so in the latter. Not every film Losey made in the 1960s, with or without Pinter, was a masterpiece. But his career gave British cinema a distinction which it had lacked since the demise of the working-class realism movement.

There were other things going on in the British cinema. With *Poor Cow* in 1967, Ken Loach attempted to revive some of the political impetus of working-class realism. Antonioni visited swinging London and made *Blow Up* (1966). There was one great horror film, Michael Reeves's *Witchfinder General* (1968). But except in *Blow Up* and in the Richard Lester Beatles films there is little sense in British or British-made films of the middle and late 1960s that a cultural revolution was going on in Britain. And except in Peter Brook's remarkable *Tell Me Lies*, released at the beginning of 1968, there is little or nothing about Vietnam. As for revolutionary politics erupting into violence, there is Anderson's *If...*. But that is a revolution that takes place only in fantasy, in the confines of a boarding school. For a country where cinema was central to cultural and political change, one must turn to France.

Notes

1. Richardson also managed to find time to make a not very successful adaptation of William Faulkner's *Sanctuary* in the USA in 1960.

2. Alan Cooke, 'Free cinema', *Sequence* 13, New Year 1951, pp. 11–13.

3. Lindsay Anderson, 'Only connect: some aspects of the work of Humphrey Jennings', first published in *Sight and Sound*, April–June 1954. Reprinted with a new postscript in Mary Lou Jennings (ed), *Humphrey Jennings: Film-maker – Painter – Poet* (London: British Film Institute, 1982), pp. 53–9. The characterisation of Grierson comes from Anderson's 1982 postscript.

4. Lindsay Anderson, 'Get out and push!', in Tom Maschler (ed.), *Declaration* (London: McGibbon and Kee, 1957), pp. 153–78.

5. For *Room at the Top* and in particular its partially successful struggles with the British Board of Film Censors, see the essay by Tony Aldgate in Brian McFarlane (ed.), *The Cinema of Britain and Ireland* (London: Wallflower, 2005), pp. 105–12.

6. Salford, most Mancunians will tell you, is just a bit of Manchester down by the canal, but, as Salfordians never cease from wearily pointing out, it is in fact an independent city with its own university and a Catholic cathedral. As well as providing a setting and location for *A Taste of Honey*, it is also the (fictional) site of the long-running soap *Coronation Street*. The budget figure is as quoted in an interview with Richardson in *Sight and Sound*, summer 1961, p. 110.

7. In David Storey's original novel the character is called Arthur. This was changed to Frank in the film to avoid confusion with Arthur Seaton in *Saturday Night and Sunday Morning*. Had they known that another defiantly working-class Arthur was on the horizon, in the form of miners' leader Arthur Scargill, the film's makers would have even more reason to make the change.

8. For example in *Mythologies* (1957) and even more in *Le Système de la mode* (published 1967, but largely written around 1960).

9. Alexander Walker, *Hollywood England: The British Film Industry in the Sixties* (London: Michael Joseph, 1974), p. 167.

10. Bates and Pleasance were in the original stage production in 1960. Shaw joined the cast for its Broadway run in 1961. An interesting example of the tangled web of British cinema at the time is given by the fact that Donner's previous film *Some People* (1962) was a rock musical starring Ray Brooks (Tolen in *The Knack*).

11. Losey's admirers were mainly in France, on *Cahiers du cinéma* and even more on *Présence du cinéma*, which was the house magazine of the 'MacMahonnistes', so called because they used to hang out at the Cinéma MacMahon near the Champs Elysées. In Britain he was championed in the early 1960s by *Oxford Opinion* and its more important successor *Movie* – just as he was about to change tack.

12. In Michel Ciment, *Conversations with Losey* (London and New York: Methuen, 1985), p. 207.

13. See Edith de Rham, *Joseph Losey* (London: André Deutsch, 1991), p.126–7, cited by Colin Gardner in his book *Joseph Losey* (Manchester: Manchester University Press, 2004), p. 95. When and where Moreau said this is not stated, but she says similar things in the TV interview with Moreau by France Roche on 30 January 1972, relevant bits of which are included with the French DVD of the film. In Ciment, *Conversations with Losey*, p. 213, the director points out that he inserted further Adam and Eve references throughout the film, including a shot of Masaccio's painting of the expulsion from paradise.

11

France: From Nouvelle Vague to May '68

The French New Wave – the Nouvelle Vague – is the best known, best documented, and most discussed of all the new cinemas of the 1960s. Even so, a lot of confusion surrounds it. This chapter attempts to redress some of that confusion by looking at the background to the Nouvelle Vague as much as at the films which resulted from it. Although the Nouvelle Vague as such lasted for three or four years at most, the film-makers who emerged from it set the tone for the new cinema in France for the rest of the decade, up to the convulsions of May '68.

The idea of 'new waves' in cinema is now such a commonplace that it is easy to forget that the original French term, 'Nouvelle Vague', came into being with no application to cinema at all. It was coined in 1957 by the journalist Françoise Giroud in the French news weekly *L'Express*. In October of that year the paper launched an inquiry into French youth, by inviting readers aged between eighteen and thirty to answer a set of twenty-four questions about their habits, thoughts, and tastes. The topics chosen covered the Algerian War, attitudes to past events such as collaboration and resistance, the role of women, and favourite reading. The responses from readers were correlated with a more scientific survey undertaken by a market research organization and were then analysed – or rather resynthesized – by Giroud and eventually published in book form as *La Nouvelle Vague: portraits de la jeunesse* – 'The New Wave: portraits of the younger generation' – midway through 1958.[1] In her analysis Giroud detected a new spirit abroad in French cultural life. She found a generation impatient with the attitudes of its elders and eager to throw off many aspects of the legacy of the past. Giroud's book in fact makes no mention of cinema at all, which was curious because *L'Express* normally covered films quite well and had picked up on the novelty of Louis Malle's *Lift to the Scaffold* when it came out in 1957. But other writers soon began to ask the questions, beginning with Pierre Billard in the cine-club magazine *Cinéma 58*. If there is a new spirit abroad in French life, he wondered, when will it show itself in our cinema?[2]

Billard did not have long to wait. Even as he wrote, Claude Chabrol was already at work shooting *Le Beau Serge*, which was premiered at Locarno in the summer of 1958 and released in Paris the following January. Jacques Rivette was struggling with the logistics of making *Paris nous appartient*, which he began shooting in July 1958 but, sadly, took him over two years to complete. By the end of 1958 Chabrol had already completed his second feature, *Les Cousins*, and in May 1959 Truffaut's *Les Quatre cents coups*, Resnais's *Hiroshima mon amour*, and Marcel Camus' *Orfeu Negro* premiered at Cannes to worldwide acclaim. The film New Wave had definitely arrived, and thanks to a shrewd publicity campaign by the Centre National de la Cinématographie (CNC), the phrase 'Nouvelle Vague' attached itself to the cinema and stuck there – while its origins in sociological enquiry were forgotten.

Most film historians today tend to pay lip service to Giroud and her fortuitous phrasemaking and quickly pass on to discussing films made after the book was written and which she might have foreseen but could hardly have described. Also, within the films of 1958 to 1963 that had the New Wave label attached to them, they tend to concentrate on those by the *Cahiers du cinéma* group of Chabrol, Truffaut, Rivette, Godard, and their friends, at the expense of other new films which came out at the time. This is a mistake. What Giroud saw as a wide-ranging political and cultural movement, with its roots at the time of Dien Bien Phu, the Suez crisis, and the Soviet invasion of Hungary, thus gets reduced to a purely aesthetic and cinematic phenomenon whose origins are found in a critical doctrine rather than in the wider world. Giroud's survey may have had little to say directly about the cinema, or even about the viewing public, but what it says about the generation of French people who were soon to provide the audience for New Wave films is highly relevant to understanding how the French cinema came to renovate itself so radically in the years just before and just after 1960.

The generation on which Giroud focused was young people aged, at the time of the survey, between eighteen and thirty, that is to say born between 1928 and 1940. This was a generation too young to have been traumatized by the Fall of France, to have either collaborated with the Germans or taken part in the Resistance, or to be nostalgic about the 1930s. If they were interested in any war it was the war in Algeria, in which some of them had already served and for which others anxiously awaited call-up. Not surprisingly, their attitudes were found to be different from those of their elders, significantly but not outrageously so. The responses show them as emancipated and free-thinking, not overly in thrall to family values, and impatient with dogma even when loyal members of the Communist Party or Catholic Church. On the other hand they are not as hostile to the politicians who had saddled the country with the war in Algeria as Giroud had expected (or hoped) for them to be, and there is, as yet, no hint of the attitudes which will characterize the more rebellious generation that was to emerge ten years later, in 1968.

There is no definitive way of knowing whether young adults in France in 1958 were 'really' as portrayed in the survey, but there is no doubt that there was a widespread perception that change was taking place, even if it was not always easy to pin down. Alongside Giroud's survey, evidence was there in the form of the prodigious success of Françoise Sagan's novel *Bonjour tristesse*, published in 1954 when the author was nineteen years old, and the equal success of Roger Vadim's film *And God Created Woman* starring Brigitte Bardot two years later.

It is also fair to say that, if there was a wave of change rippling through French society in the mid-1950s, no one in the French cinema apart from Vadim seemed to be aware of it. French films, with few exceptions, continued to be nostalgic and ritualistic in their attitude to national life. The typical heroine of a French film, remarked Jacques Doniol-Valcroze in *Cahiers du cinéma* in 1954, is a 'petite bourgeoise bien tranquille'.[3] No French film-maker of the 1950s could have created a female character as original and alive as the heroine of Sagan's *Bonjour tristesse,* and when the novel came to be filmed in 1956 it was not as a French film but an American one, directed by Otto Preminger and starring Jean Seberg.

Among the people who welcomed both *Bonjour Tristesse* (film version) and *And God Created Woman* were François Truffaut, writing in *Arts*, and Jean-Luc Godard, who reviewed Vadim's next film *Sait-on jamais?* for *Cahiers du cinéma* and, famously, chose Seberg to play the heroine of his first feature *A bout de souffle* in 1959.[4] Vadim (b. 1928), Godard (b. 1930), Truffaut (b. 1932), Bardot (b. 1934), Sagan (b. 1935), and Seberg (b. 1938) were all members of the generation whose collective portrait is painted by Giroud.

What did Truffaut and Godard like about *And God Created Woman*? They liked Bardot, obviously, for being natural; they liked the film's youthfulness, they liked its choice of, as Truffaut put it, 'realism and life'. Meanwhile Godard, writing about *Sait-on jamais?*, pinpointed something equally essential to the emerging New Wave aesthetic: the fact that in Vadim the scene preceded the shot, rather than vice versa; something was going on between the characters, and how to express this something took precedence over what a shot should look like. Whether this was really a defining characteristic of Vadim's film is moot. What is perhaps more important is that Godard, in formulating his own aesthetic credo, saw enough of what he was looking for in *Sait-on jamais?* to use it to set down a marker for the future.

Although the young film-makers soon got tired of having the label 'Nouvelle Vague' attached to themselves and their work, there is no doubt that a wave existed and, furthermore, they were riding the crest of it. *Les Cousins, Les Quatre cents coups*, and *A bout de souffle* each attracted audiences of a quarter of a million people, predominantly young, on their first run, as well as being rapidly snatched up for export.[5] Other early Nouvelle Vague films did less well, but the impetus of the movement and its 'New Wave' branding was enormous and it launched the careers of many film-makers who went on to successful careers later, as well as many who did not.

The branding of the new cinema as Nouvelle Vague came about because it was not only the *Cahiers* critics who were sick of the old 'quality' cinema of the 1950s. The CNC itself had concluded that its system for supporting French cinema was simply encouraging the formulaic repetition of genres which might satisfy the more conservative elements of the public but were incapable of attracting new audiences into the cinemas. In the mid-1950s it had started channelling funds in the direction of short films in the hope of encouraging new talent. Then, when de Gaulle returned to power in 1958 and appointed André Malraux as Minister of Culture, the new minister was prevailed upon to change the subsidy system so that it no longer simply recycled money to producers on the basis of past performance but included a new element of 'selective aid' to film projects which showed both artistic promise and a reasonable chance of doing well enough to repay the loan on offer to them.

The new proposals became law early in 1959. They did not create the Nouvelle Vague which was already in the process of coming into being and some of the most famous Nouvelle Vague film-makers including

Godard and Rohmer never took advantage of them. But they greatly eased the birth pangs of the new movement by opening up the field to new producers and directors. Results were mixed. Production of debut feature films soared to unprecedented and unsustainable levels and many loans (or 'advances', as they were called) were made to films which never even made it into the cinemas. But the general effect was to create a climate in which innovation flourished over a wide spectrum of French production.

It was not only young or debutant film-makers who benefited from the new climate. Nor was innovation confined to the *Cahiers* group. Films came from quite unexpected quarters, Georges Franju being a case in point.

Franju's place in French cinema is a curious one. Born in 1913, as a young man he had helped Henri Langlois to found the Cinémathèque Française in 1936 and must therefore count as one of the godfathers of the Nouvelle Vague to the extent that without the Cinémathèque French film culture would never have taken the form it did. In the 1950s he achieved fame as a maker of short films which were left-wing in politics and often strongly surrealist in tone and were admired by *Positif* more than by *Cahiers du cinéma*. In 1959 he took everyone including his ad- mirers by surprise with two features, both in or close to the horror genre, *La Tête contre les murs* and *Eyes without a Face*, which owed their exquisitely realized claustrophobic atmosphere to the lighting and cam- erawork of the German-born veteran Eugen Schüfftan, famous for having been the cinematographer on Fritz Lang's *Metropolis* in 1927 and for his subsequent work for Max Ophuls and Marcel Carné in the 1930s. Stylis- tically, nothing could be further from the freewheeling style and fresh open-air feel of early Truffaut or Godard – or indeed any of the *Cahiers* directors except possibly Chabrol.

Although Franju was a good friend of Resnais, who was a good friend of Chris Marker, who in turn was a good friend of Agnès Varda, they never really formed a group, let alone a school, nor were there really any distinct groupings in Nouvelle Vague cinema, apart from the *Cahiers du cinéma* school. It has often been claimed that Resnais, Marker, and Varda formed a distinct 'Left Bank' group, living as they did on the left side of the Seine, being left-wing in politics, good friends of each other, and very fond of cats, as opposed to the *Cahiers* group who lived on the other side of the river, had suspect right-wing tendencies, and no recorded attitude to cats, for or against. Resnais and Marker had also collaborated on the documentary *Les Statues meurent aussi* in 1953 and Resnais had helped Varda with the editing of her experimental feature *La Pointe Courte* in 1955.

These personal links, however, are not enough to make them into a group, and certainly not a group opposed to *Cahiers*. This does not mean that there weren't tensions between *Cahiers* and the others. But Marker had been a regular contributor to *Cahiers* in the early days and the magazine had enthusiastically reviewed *La Pointe Courte* when it was released in 1956. And when Resnais's *Hiroshima mon anour* was shown at Cannes it provided the lead feature for the magazine's 97th issue under the title 'Hiroshima notre amour'.[6]

Resnais, in fact, was not like anyone else in the French (or any other) cinema. Furthermore, his type of cinema needed resources, which were provided for him by the doyen of French art cinema producers, Anatole Dauman. Thanks to Dauman, Resnais had few budgetary problems with his 1960s features, which were fully crewed and edited at leisure, unlike the majority of Nouvelle Vague films, which were shot and edited to very tight schedules (except where the money ran out completely, in which case schedules became very long but hardly leisurely). Resnais also had a unique relationship with his writers. Looking at the names of the writers he worked with, or who worked for him, all of them leading practitioners of the experimental 'Nouveau Roman' – Marguerite Duras for *Hiroshima mon amour*, Alain Robbe-Grillet for *Last Year at Marienbad*, Jean Cayrol for *Muriel*, Jorge Semprun for *La Guerre est finie* – one can easily be led to believe that these must be writers' films, for which the director provided only an admittedly spectacular *mise en images*. The themes elaborated in Resnais's early features – time and memory, the unreliability of memory and of narration – are all, it could be and has been argued, already present in the writers he has chosen, and the relative weakness of some of Resnais's later films when he didn't have writers of this type to rely on hints at a lack of true authorial originality on his part.

This argument is both false and foolish. It is true that Resnais chose writers with already distinctive styles and traces of those styles remain in the films, not only in the words uttered but also in their cinematic rendering. But this rendering is also quite distinct and Resnais goes way beyond his sources in the way the themes are developed. That memory is unreliable and the presentation of it by a narrational voice even more so is a Nouveau Roman commonplace, especially in Robbe-Grillet; that the absence of memory, or the unreliability of a narration which attempts to cover for this, might also be traumatic, is also present in Cayrol. But the weaving together of these themes, and the centering of traumatized memory or non-memory on a body rather than just a voice, is something which requires not only a film but a uniquely intelligent and scrupulous film-maker to bring out. Nor was Resnais overawed by the reputations of his writers. As François Thomas shows in his careful study of Resnais's working methods, the novelists may have provided the words but it was the director who had the overarching idea for the film and got them to come up with material to fit the idea and who then, alongside Henri Colpi at the editing table, established the hypnotic rhythm for which Resnais's early films are most often remembered.[7]

Resnais was unusual also in his choice of actors and performance style. He tended to use theatrically trained actors, rehearse them thoroughly, and encourage the use of theatrical gesture and delivery, though never to the point when it looked false on screen. (Delphine Seyrig in *Last Year in Marienbad* and *Muriel* is a perfect example: poised, seeming to wear a mask, but always a mask that fits her naturally.) By contrast the *Cahiers* group were more inclined to improvise on set and hated working with actors trained in the French theatrical tradition, much preferring the more natural style that they found in their favourite American films.[8] The Nouvelle Vague as a whole found what they wanted in actors with no or little theatre background, including Jeanne Moreau, Brigitte Bardot (when they could afford her), Catherine Deneuve, and Jean-Claude Brialy. If actors coming from theatre, such as Jean-Paul Belmondo and Michel Piccoli, were used they were expected to be flexible and adapt to the prevailing naturalistic style.

A panorama of the new French cinema a year or two after the Nouvelle Vague explosion would show a rough division into three camps. There was a new art cinema, with Resnais as its most prominent exemplar but a small number of film-makers following in his train, notably Henri Colpi (*Une aussi longue absence*, from a script by Marguerite Duras, 1960) and the versatile Peter Brook (*Moderato cantabile*, 1961, also with a Duras script). Those three film-makers certainly, but arguably others such as Pierre Kast (*La Morte Saison des amours*, 1961), were interested in time and duration and the representation of experience, and in pursuit of this broke radically with the purposive, linear action-narrative traditional in cinema. Secondly, there was the characteristic 'New Wave' cinema, spear-headed by the *Cahiers* group but also including Demy and Jacques Rozier (*Adieu Philippine*, 1962): low-budget films, roughly put together, trading on freshness and spontaneity, and generally endowed with a fairly traditional plot structure to provide narrative drive and cohesion. Then there were a few non-belongers. For example, there was Jean-Pierre Melville, who had pursued his own pioneering path since the early 1950s and continued to do so, but in more propitious circumstances, in the 1960s. There was Franju. There was Jean Rouch, pioneer of cinéma vérité with *Chronique d'un été*. And there was Louis Malle, also a pioneer in the sense that his two films from the late 1950s, *Lift to the Scaffold* and *Les Amants*, can be seen as paving the way for the Nouvelle Vague proper, but who, when the Nouvelle Vague came along, went off in various un-interpretable and contradictory directions. His *Zazie dans le métro* (1960) tried, and on the whole failed, to find cinematic equivalents for the extravagant wordplay that characterized the novel by Raymond Queneau from which it was adapted, while *Vie privée* (1961) was a film both with and about Bardot, interesting but in no way innovative. Varda, too, belongs with the non-belongers. Her *Cléo de 5 à 7* (1962) has its Godardian moments, including a cameo sequence performed by Godard and Karina, but it also explores the passing of time and the 'temps morts' when no action happens in a manner closer to Resnais, Colpi, or Brook.

When the Nouvelle Vague hit the placid shores of French cinema in 1959, critics rarely attempted to distinguish rigorously between the different tendencies or groups composing it. They were content to note that a lot was happening, that it was original, that it broke with the native 'quality tradition' and also with the tradition of Zavattinian neo-realism. It took a little while for the differences to sort themselves out, and by then the Nouvelle Vague had ceased to be a wave. Arguably it was no longer much of a wave as early as 1961, when Jacques Siclier published a little book reviewing current trends and noting the diffuse character of the movement and its declining impact.[9] If nothing else, figures showed that none of the subsequent films of Godard, Truffaut, or Chabrol came anywhere near to repeating the box-office success of *A bout de souffle*, *Les Quatre cents coups* or *Les Cousins* – let alone films with extra sex content such as Malle's *Les Amants* or Vadim's *Les Liaisons dangereuses*. A couple of years later in 1963, Luc Moullet noted in *Cahiers du cinéma* that the market had become saturated and numerous films by new directors were not even being released.[10]

Even if the wave was no longer a wave, however, it had done its job. It had launched not one but several new cinemas on the world, and it was the world as a whole that was to profit from what had happened. And, conversely, it was the world market, rather than the domestic one, which was to provide crucial support for the Nouvelle Vague film-makers for the rest of the decade. Pre-sales to foreign markets, particularly the United States, could earn a Nouvelle Vague film more than it was ever likely to get from the box office in its home country. International investment poured in – from Carlo Ponti in Italy, from Warner Bros. and United Artists in the United States, and other sources. A handful of 'name' directors, notably Truffaut, Godard, Chabrol, Demy, and Resnais, could rely on their worldwide reputation for continuing finance, even if their latest film had flopped at home.

The most durable component of the Nouvelle Vague, widely conceived, was undoubtedly the *Cahiers* group. Starting with a shared aesthetic, formulated in the pages of the magazine in the 1950s under the tutelage of André Bazin, the *Cahiers* directors diverged increasingly as the decade wore on. The core of the original doctrine lay in Bazin's phenomenology: reality was the world as it presented itself to consciousness, and the film-maker as perceiving consciousness was responsible for mastering the flow of this perceived reality and shaping it to make its truth visible. Truffaut, the least philosophically inclined of the group, was also the most loyal to the humanist side of Bazin's message. Throughout the 1960s his films continued to explore human situations and the problems people faced precisely through their situatedness in the phenomenal world. Truffaut's characters are not programmed, they are responsive to thoughts and to external stimuli (maybe just the texture of a woman's stocking), but are always basically self-determining, and they speak in the first instance for themselves, even when they are autobiographical, like Antoine in *Les Quatre cents coups*, or provide a shared focus of identification for author and audience (not to say the values of civilization itself) as with Montag in *Fahrenheit 451* (1966).

Eric Rohmer, who had great difficulty in getting films financed throughout the 1960s, was also intellectually close to Bazin, but his interest, when he got to make films, was in how the cinema could represent not consciousness in general but moral consciousness, or conscience. Beginning with *La Collectionneuse* in 1966 and *My Night with Maud* in 1969, Rohmer's cinema is a matter of ultra-precise *mise en scène* aimed at capturing the struggle that characters have with their conscience and the small acts by which they betray others and themselves.

The other *Cahiers* film-makers all moved in contrasting directions, which tended to take them further and further from the shared matrix of ideas formed around Bazin in the 1950s. They remained loyal to certain basic principles of what constituted good cinema, for example that scenes should be constructed according to what they had to say, not how they would look, or that audiences should not be teased, deceived, or bullied, but treated with respect. But outside the area covered by this handful of general principles, moral as much as aesthetic, inherited from the example set by Bazin in his criticism, there was ample scope for divergence and not surprisingly the film-makers diverged.

The main constraints on the directions available for the *Cahiers* or ex-*Cahiers* film-makers to take had to do with the audience they wished or needed to attract. Always a fan of genre films, Chabrol settled quite early on for a commercial audience. He didn't always find it, but after a while he successfully found himself a niche with crime thrillers which became increasingly stylish and accomplished as the decade went on. A faint aura of what can only be called evil hovers around all Chabrol's films, regardless of genre. It is metaphysical, as in Hitchcock, rather than psychological, and the smallest thing can set it off.

Apart from Bazin, the two most original thinkers on *Cahiers du cinéma* had been Godard and Rivette and they were also its most original film-makers. Godard kept on making films at breakneck speed throughout the 1960s, always managing to attract enough public and critical attention to be able to maintain momentum. Rivette, however, had a career in the 1960s consisting mostly of setbacks. Having managed with difficulty to finish *Paris nous appartient*, which received a limited release in 1961, he agreed with producer Georges de Beauregard on a project to adapt for the screen a scandalous 18th-century novel, Denis Diderot's *La Religieuse*. From the beginning this project ran into huge problems with the censorship. First it was vetoed, then it was allowed to be made, but once made it was given a single showing at Cannes on May 1966 before being banned not only from exhibition but from export. It was not until July 1967 that it was released in Paris.[11] It made no money for Beauregard, who had been forced to give up the rights, and left Rivette in a limbo from which he escaped by throwing himself into projects with no aspiration to be commercial. His next film *L'amour fou* was made in 1969; it is 255 minutes of pure fascination, mainly set in the rehearsal space for a staging of Racine's *Andromaque* (recalling the rehearsal of Shakespeare's *Pericles: Prince of Tyre* in *Paris nous appartient*), but when it goes outside it has the same magical feeling as is to be found in his next 'commercial' project, *Céline and Julie Go Boating*, which he did not make until 1974, nearly ten years after the travails of *La Religieuse*.

As the ex-*Cahiers* directors headed out in different directions, so did the magazine. During the 1960s French intellectual and political culture was changing. Existentialism was giving way to a revived, non-Stalinist Marxism. Marx's early *Economic and Philosophical Manuscripts* were pored over, as was Georg Lukács's *History and Class Consciousness*, written in 1922 but untranslated before 1960.[12] There were new theories of culture in general (Lévi-Strauss) and of modern capitalist culture in particular (Barthes, Debord). There was an attempted fusion of structuralism and Marxism in Louis Althusser's *Pour Marx* (1965) and of linguistics and filmology in Christian Metz's 'Le cinéma: langue ou langage' (1964). The war in Algeria was over but a new war had started in Vietnam (the second Indo-Chinese war, as far as the French were concerned, the first being the one that France had lost in the 1950s). *Cahiers* reacted at first in a piecemeal way to these changes. It found it harder and harder to reconcile its loyalty to favoured Hollywood 'auteurs' with a commitment to the new cinemas – not just the work of its Nouvelle Vague friends but new work emerging in Italy, the USA, and across the globe. Both auteurism and realism came under scrutiny. As early as 1960 it had devoted a special issue to Brecht. In 1963 it published a long interview with Roland Barthes, in which Brecht's theatre was again at issue, with all the challenges it provided to the phenomenological realism inherited from Bazin.[13] In 1965 it followed this up with an essay by Metz taking apart the 'impression of reality' generated by cinema.[14] New writers were also coming on to the magazine, including Jean-André Fieschi, Jean-Louis Comolli, and Jean Narboni. With these new writers on board the magazine was ready to take its leap into Marxism and semiotics in 1968.

As far as the cinema was concerned, 1968 began in February with the sacking of Henri Langlois from his post as director of the Cinémathèque Française. From an archival point of view, Langlois was an atrocious curator. Under his stewardship dangerous nitrate film was left to rot in unsuitable locations where it was at risk of catching fire with catastrophic results and many unique prints were damaged by repeated projection.[15] But the fact that he showed these unique prints, rather than stashing them away in vaults until an improbable good fairy came along with money to duplicate them, made him a hero to hundreds of French cinephiles. Truffaut and Godard led the demand for his reinstatement, with support from Jean Renoir and other distinguished figures. A demonstration on 14 February outside the Cinémathèque's premises at the Palais de Chaillot was roughly broken up by the police. Langlois was reinstated in April but the atmosphere of contestation had taken hold. When the first student protests began in Paris in May, the 'world of cinema' was at Cannes for the festival. The festival became a site of contestation. Film-makers who supported the protestors withdrew their films and the festival was suspended, with no prizes awarded.

The Cannes protestors returned to Paris, where the May Events were now in full swing. The 'Estates General of the Cinema', a motley crew but with a solid core of directors, technicians, and critics as well as eager but ignorant activists, came up with three different blueprints for the reorganization and renovation of French cinema. Film-makers took to the streets themselves, covering demonstrations and their repression, the vox pop of workers and students, etc., and issuing the footage under headings such as 'ciné-tracts'. Both Godard and Marker officially dissolved themselves into collectives – in Godard's case the 'groupe Dziga Vertov', in Marker's 'SLON', standing for 'Society [or Company] for Launching New Works'.[16] This heady period lasted for a few months, after which most of the film-makers involved returned to normal life, leaving only a handful of radicals, among them Godard and his associate Jean-Pierre Gorin, to pursue the '68 political agenda.

But May '68 was a cultural revolution as much as a political one. Slogans like 'Pouvoir à l'imagination' ('Power to the imagination') or 'Changez la vie' (i.e. life needs to change, not just social structures) shared space on the wall with demands for workers' control or a fairer distribution of income. It is not surprising therefore that the May Events were accompanied by a flurry of avant-garde artistic activity, expressed in the cinema mainly by a group called Zanzibar.

Zanzibar was the creation of the heiress Sylvina Boissonas, who channelled parts of her inheritance into production funds for a group of debutant film-makers including the actor Pierre Clémenti and make-up artist Jackie Reynal and not-quite-debutants such as the teenage prodigy Philippe Garrel whose *Marie pour mémoire*, made in 1967, was the big success of the Festival du Jeune Cinéma at the resort town of Hyères in April 1968. On the whole uninterested in the workers and peasants of Maoist sloganography, the Zanzibar film-makers shot a series of films during the May Events that capture much of the spirit of the time – at least as it appeared to the young bourgeois who joined in the events.[17]

Apart from that, the legacy of May 1968 in the cinema is slight. But in the period of reflection that followed a new seriousness came to the fore in the treatment of history. Except for the occasional costume picture, most of the films of the Nouvelle Vague and associated film-makers were set in the present. Only Resnais showed any interest in recent history and the traumas of occupation and collaboration or of the Algerian war. But with Marcel Ophuls's *The Sorrow and the Pity* (1969), Malle's *Lacombe Lucien* (1974), and Resnais's *Stavisky* (1974) some uncomfortable truths began to surface which no part of French society, radical or conservative, had up to then wanted to confront. Exactly how this phenomenon connects with the ups and downs of May 1968 is not easy to say. But is certain that after it, if not necessarily because of it, French cinema joins the belated exploration of painful themes also present in Italian and German cinema and which up to then only the Eastern Europeans had confronted with any honesty.

Notes

1. Françoise Giroud, *La Nouvelle Vague: portraits de la jeunesse* (Paris: L'Air du Temps, 1958).

2. Pierre Billard, *Cinéma 58*, February 1958. (To the perplexity of librarians, the journal changed its name, or rather number, with each new year, calling itself *Cinéma 57* in 1957, *Cinéma 58* in 1958, *Cinéma 59* in 1959, etc.)

3. Jacques Doniol-Valcroze, 'Une petite bourgeoise bien tranquille', *Cahiers du cinéma* 31, January 1954. This article was a companion piece to Truffaut's notorious 'A certain tendency' in the same issue. The flavour of Doniol's phrase is virtually impossible to render into English. Perhaps 'Little Ms Average'.

4. François Truffaut, '*Et Dieu . . . créa la femme* (Roger Vadim)', *Arts*, 5 December 1956, and '*Bonjour tristesse* (Otto Preminger)', *Arts*, 12 March 1958 (both in English translation in François Truffaut, *The Films in My Life* [New York: Da Capo Press, 1994], pp. 311–12 and 137–40, respectively); Jean-Luc Godard, '*Sait-on jamois?*', *Cahiers du cinéma* 73, July 1957 (English translation in *Godard on Godard*, pp. 55–7).

5. Michel Marie, *The French New Wave* (Oxford: Blackwell, 2003), p. 66.

6. 'Hiroshima notre amour', discussion among Jean Domarchi, Jacques Doniol-Valcroze, Jean-Luc Godard, Pierre Kast, Jacques Rivette, and Eric Rohmer, *Cahiers du cinéma* 97, July 1959. English translation (substantial but incomplete) in Hillier, *Cahiers du cinéma I*, pp. 59–69.

7. François Thomas, *L'Atelier d'Alain Resnais*. Colpi edited some of Resnais's early shorts and went on edit to *Hiroshima mon amour* and *Last Year at Marienbad*. But Resnais was a highly skilled editor in his own right. The editing of *Muriel* is credited to Kenout Peltier and that of the *La Guerre est finie* to Eric Pluet. It is likely, though, that Resnais had a major hand in editing both those films. From *Je t'aime, je t'aime* (1968) onwards, his favoured editor was Albert Jurgenson.

8. Jean Douchet, *Nouvelle Vague* (Paris: Hazan, 1998), p. 122. Speaking on behalf of his *Cahiers* friends, he describes the French actors against whom the Nouvelle Vague reacted: 'They adopt a pose, they "express", and have no ambition other than to be in view. They are a nuisance to the real film-maker and damage the spectator's involvement with the film.' Douchet also claims that even the films of Robert Bresson suffered from a similar lack of naturalness – though for different reasons.

9. Jacques Siclier, *Nouvelle Vague?* (Paris: Editions du Cerf, 1961), p. 142.

10. Luc Moullet, 'Trois points d'économie', *Cahiers du cinéma* 138, December 1962. Quoted in Marie, *The French New Wave*, p. 68.

11. See Nicole Vulser, 'La censure de *La Religieuse*', *Le Monde,* 26 August 2006. This article can be found on line by following the link in the entry on the film in the French edition of Wikipedia. The full title of the film, insisted on by the censors, is *Suzanne Simonin: La religieuse de Denis Diderot.*

12. Georg Lukács's *Geschichte und Klassenbewusstsein* (*History and Class Consciousness*) was published in German in 1923 but then disappeared from view throughout the Stalin period. Other writings by Lukács, mainly on aesthetics, began to appear in French and Italian translations in the 1950s, but *History and Class Consciousness* had to wait until 1960 before being republished in German and translated into French. It did not appear in English until 1967.

13. Brecht issue, no. 114, December 1960; Barthes interview in no. 147, September 1963. Translations of an article by Bernard Dort from the Brecht issue and the Barthes interview are in Jim Hillier (ed.), *Cahiers du Cinéma II* (London: Routledge, and Cambridge, MA: Harvard UP, 1986), pp. 236–47 and 276–85, respectively.

14. 'A propos de l'impression de réalité au cinéma', *Cahiers du cinema* 166–67, May– June 1965. Reprinted in *Essais sur la signification au cinéma* (Paris: Klincksieck, 1968), which also contains the essay 'Cinéma: langue ou langage' referred to above.

15. Langlois died of a heart attack in 1977. Three years later, in 1980, one of the Cinémathèque's warehouses did eventually catch fire, with the consequent loss of 7,000 prints, mainly nitrate.

16. SLON had been founded a couple of years earlier, but it came into its own in the anti-individualist and anti-bourgeois climate of 1968. The 'Groupe Dziga Vertov' was in fact a bit fictitious – rather like Vertov's own 'Council of Three', which consisted of himself, his wife, and his brother, with himself very much at the head.

17. For Zanzibar see Sally Shafto, *Zanzibar* (Paris: Editions Paris Expérimental, 2007).

12

Italy

Italy in the 1960s had the most thriving cinema in Europe, both old cinema and new cinema, and, crucially, films and film-makers who straddled the divide. What it did not have, because it did not really need, was a New Wave. Instead the new cinema (or cinemas) emerged, more or less organically, from the old. It (or they) emerged in disparate bits and remained disparate throughout the decade.

In the early 1960s Italian films were capturing an ever increasing percentage of a box office which numerically was not yet falling and in money terms, due to an increase in seat prices, was actually on the rise. In 1960, more than 130 Italian films (including co-productions in which Italian producers had a majority stake) were released on to the market, and accounted for over 50 per cent of box-office for the year, pushing the Hollywood share down to 35 per cent – the lowest since 1946. Production levels continued to increase throughout the decade, though by 1969 the market was beginning to shrink and many of the films made failed to live up to expectations, either financially or artistically, as too many fly-by-night companies entered the market in the illusory hope of easy profits. Around 1960, however, the mood among reputable producers was realistically optimistic. Favoured directors were receiving larger production budgets to work with and both large and small producers were prepared to back new talent, if not quite to the same extent as in France in the heady days of the early Nouvelle Vague.

As mentioned in Chapter 1, as the 1960s dawned the major Italian producers, including Dino De Laurentiis, Carlo Ponti, Angelo Rizzoli, Goffredo Lombardo, and newcomer Franco Cristaldi, were investing heavily in what came to be called the international art film. These were films with name directors, international casts, and a general if indefinable air of 'quality' about them. A slightly more realistic attitude to sex than would be allowed in an American film at the time was also a bonus. It is therefore not surprising if the first stirrings of a new cinema in Italy were obscured by the powerful presence of good but conventional Italian films entering the international market at the time.

If Cannes 1959 was the year of the Nouvelle Vague, Cannes 1960 was a harbinger of a new cinema in Italy. But it did not serve to launch a new film-making generation as had been the case in France. Instead it started by putting into the spotlight two established film-makers whose reputations in the 1950s had suffered from the long hangover of neo-realism. These were Federico Fellini, with *La dolce vita*, and Michelangelo Antonioni, with *L'avventura*.

Fellini was already quite well known internationally. *La strada* (1954) had won a Best Foreign Language Film Award at the Oscars in 1956 and art house audiences were still cooing over his most recent film, *Le notti di Cabiria* (1956 – known in Britain and the US simply as *Cabiria*), which featured his wife Giulietta Masina in the central role as a tart with an enormous heart of gold and not much brain. (In *La strada* she had played the sweet-natured simpleton brutalized by Anthony Quinn.) *La dolce vita*, which won the Palme d'Or at Cannes, defiantly shook off the detritus of the neo-realist legacy, especially its populism, while remaining broadly realist in its attempt to paint a collective portrait of Roman high life. It was in fact to be Fellini's last realist film for some time, though only in retrospect is it possible to see the way it connects to the assertively non-realist style inaugurated by his next film, *8½*, three years later in 1963. Its emotional colouring was familiar from previous Fellini films, but the dominant emotion in it is regret rather than the overwhelming nostalgia that was to become the hallmark of his later work. It was also a far more innovative film than was recognized at the time, but this again only became visible retrospectively.

By contrast, Antonioni was unknown outside Italy to all but a select handful of admirers. His previous film *Il grido* (1957) had a limited art-house release and a modest *succès d'estime*, culminating in a Prix de la Critique at the Locarno Festival in 1957. The film before that, *Le amiche* (1955), also had little exposure. Its resolutely low-key study of the unstable erotic relationships of a group of young or youngish bourgeois in many ways prefigures *L'avventura* and had it been better known the audience for the latter film might have been better prepared. As it was, *L'avventura* caused a furore at its premiere at Cannes in May 1960, and the dust took a long time to settle.

The scandal caused by *L'avventura* at that premiere can be seen as the watershed separating the world of the new cinemas from that of the old. On the one side was the sizeable handful of people who reacted with a mixture of anger and boredom at a film which took two and a half hours to tell a very slight story resolving itself, if at all, only in a rather unsatisfactory way. *La dolce vita*, it should be said, was even longer and its story was also low on narrative drive, but it had lots of sexy incident along the way and its resolution was comfortingly moral. *L'avventura*, however, challenged its audience all the way through, requiring a different form of attention and an acceptance of moral ambiguity that much of the festival audience found disturbing.

This vehement hostility had its own reaction. Critics and fellow film-makers rallied to Antonioni's defence. Audiences followed suit, especially in Paris. As a result Antonioni was easily able to get production finance for his next two films, *La notte* in 1961 and *The Eclipse* the following year.

Commercially the success of *L'avventura* was as nothing compared with that of *La dolce vita*, which topped the box office in Italy during the 1960/61 season, just ahead of *Ben-Hur*, with Visconti's *Rocco and His Brothers* following in third place. Both *Dolce vita* and *Rocco* also did very well in export markets, thus confirming the big Italian film producers in their strategy of concentrating their investment on the big-budget international art film. Fellini, Visconti, De Sica, Pietro Germi, and a number of other 'name' directors all profited from this strategy throughout the early 1960s, either for on-off productions or for more generic production such as the 'commedia all'italiana' or 'comedy Italian-style' which was beginning to coalesce as a distinct genre around that time.

The success of *L'avventura* was commercially far more modest, but in its way every bit as significant, since it proved that there was an audience not only for conventional 'quality' but for something actively different, as was the case in France. Antonioni founded no school and attempts to follow closely in his footsteps such as Giuseppe Patroni Griffi's *Il mare* (1962) only succeeded in aping his mannerisms while capturing nothing of the substance. But around the fringes films were beginning to appear with distinct aesthetic properties, owing little either to mainstream genre practices or to the quality art film.

The first of these in time was a tiny film called *Time Stood Still*, made in 1959 by a young man called Ermanno Olmi who was the in-house documentary film-maker for the Edison Volta electricity company. Produced by Edison Volta itself more for prestige than in expectation of profit, *Time Stood Still* was a simple story about the relationship of two men, one old and one young, stuck at the head of a mountain valley waiting for a repair to be carried out on the dam the old man is guarding. At a time when the rest of Italian cinema was struggling to shake off the remains of neo-realism, *Time Stood Still* was remarkable for its reassertion of the purest of the pure Zavattinian credo: ordinary life being watched happening at its own pace, which, of course, is normally far slower than the pace of life in the movies.

Olmi then went on to make two more small-scale but slightly better funded films with a similar laid-back rhythm and innocently conservative political stance, *Il posto* (*The Job*, 1961) and *I fidanzati* (*The Fiancés*, 1963) – the latter financed by De Laurentiis. Both films are remarkable in equal measure for their precise observation of ordinary situations and for their passivity in the face of what they report. Although they claim to draw inspiration from Zavattini, it is hard to imagine the old maestro constructing ordinary people so extraordinarily acquiescent or ordinary situations enveloped in such extraordinary inertia.

This observational vein was the one in which Olmi was most at home, but he had also grander ambitions to challenge the hegemony of the left in Italian cinema. In 1965 he made a film about the life of Pope John XXIII, *E venne un uomo*, starring Rod Steiger, which seemed purpose designed to rebut the eccentric portrayal of Christianity by Pasolini in his 1964 film *The Gospel According to Matthew*. Some years later, the film for which he is most famous, *The Tree of the Wooden Clogs* (1978), was an explicit response to the leftist interpretation of Italian history in Bernardo Bertolucci's epic *1900* which had been released two years earlier and had become instantly canonical.

Olmi was certainly right in noticing the way the Italian film scene in the early 1960s, even more than at the height of neo-realism just after the war, seemed to be dominated by the left. The left's cultural hegemony, originally constructed by and around the Italian Communist Party under its brilliant leader Palmiro Togliatti in the 1940s, had been fiercely contested by a resurgent right in the 1950s but was now reasserting itself in a new form, altogether more eclectic and diverse and less dependent on carefully crafted organizations for political sponsorship and patronage.

One part of the old left strategy had been the perpetuation of the neo-realist aesthetic well past the time when it had any grip on contemporary reality. The result of this had been that the aesthetic innovators of the 1950s – principally, in their different ways, Antonioni, Fellini, and Rossellini – had been excluded from the orthodox left-wing 'church'. To all intents and purposes, there had been no new left-wing cinema in the 1950s, and the left itself was as much to blame as were its enemies.

The leftward swing in the cinema of the early 1960s was a mixture of old and new and its first symptom was a revived interest in the 'Southern Question', that is to say the much debated issue of the deep seated inequality between the industrial north of the country and the mainly agrarian south. For the old, Visconti returned in 1960 to the social concerns of his neo-realist period, forging the grandiose melodrama *Rocco and His Brothers* out of the problem of south to north migration. In between old and new, Francesco Rosi, who had been Visconti's assistant on *La terra trema* in 1948, investigated the *mafioso* character of Sicily in *Salvatore Giuliano* (1962) and the endemic corruption of his native city of Naples in *Hands over the City* (1963). And among the new, Vittorio De Seta set his debut feature *Banditi a Orgosolo* (1961) in what was probably the most backward part of Italy, the mountainous interior of the Mediterranean island of Sardinia.

The most radical innovator in Italian cinema, however, was Pier Paolo Pasolini. His first two films as director – *Accattone* (1961) and *Mamma Roma* (1962) – were set in Rome, but a Rome which was a microcosm of every possible contrast between new and old, rich and poor, developed and primitive, north and south. When *Accattone* first came out, its originality was not appreciated. It seemed like a hangover from neo-realism, whereas in fact it was barely realist at all in a conventional sense and was far more uncompromising in its social message than any film from the neo-realist period.

Like Antonioni, Pasolini neither belonged to a school nor founded one. But he had two protégés, one major and one minor. The minor one was Sergio Citti, elder brother of the actor Franco Citti who plays the eponymous hero of *Accattone*. Sergio, described by Pasolini as 'my living dictionary of Roman dialect', was encouraged by his mentor to develop his talents beyond the mere supply of authentic dialogue to actual scriptwriting, but none of his scripts became a successful film and his attempts at direction were even less impressive. His first effort, however, did lead somewhere. In 1962, working from an idea supplied by Pasolini,

Citti began to flesh out a script which was then handed over to a young friend of Pasolini's, the twenty-one-year-old Bernardo Bertolucci, who had been an assistant on *Accattone,* to direct. The result was *La commare secca,* known in English as *The Grim Reaper,* very much in the mould of the sort of film for which Pasolini had been writing scripts a few years earlier.

Bertolucci's next film, *Before the Revolution* (1964) was much more personal, and owed little to his mentor. It was personal not in the sense of having a distinctive signature belonging to its maker but in the sense of being clearly autobiographical, in a way that is common in literature but very rare in cinema before the 1960s. Of course there are autobiographical elements of many kinds in earlier films but for various reasons the genre is not prevalent, the most obvious of these reasons being that most films have a writer and a director who are different people. In the 1960s, however, the personal film suddenly became far more realizable than it had been previously. The principal reason for this was the fact that cinema (or sections of it) was increasingly regarded as part of high culture so that criteria regularly applied to poetry or the novel seemed applicable to the cinema too. This in turn led to the promotion of the director as author and the increasing practice of directors making films from their own scripts or without much of a formal script at all. If a young novelist, if only because as yet unable to construct characters in any other way, decided to write largely out of personal experience, why should a young film-maker not do likewise? The so called 'auteur' theory, whose original purpose had mainly been to claim authorial status for Hollywood directors struggling to express their personality in a regime dominated by writers and producers, was adapted after the success of the French Nouvelle Vague as a rationale for pure artistic individualism. Hard-headed producers, who in earlier decades would not have allowed a writer with no film production experience to direct, or a director to film what he chose without the benefit of a sage industry scriptwriter at his shoulder to ensure the dialogue was up to scratch, now signed up virtual unknowns to do their own thing in the hope that one of them would become the next Truffaut or Chabrol.

Meanwhile a precedent for film as lightly disguised autobiography had been provided by Fellini, whose *8½* in 1963 was about the creative dilemmas of a film-maker who can only make a film by drawing on the resources of private memories – the memories in question being in part fictional and in part clearly to be referred to the memories of Fellini himself.

Thus it came about that Bertolucci, at the ripe age of twenty-three, was able to get finance from Fellini's producers, Cineriz, to make a film whose hero is a young man who stands in for the film-maker and resembles him in a number of biographical respects, most notably a provincial, bourgeois background in Parma. Fictional elements intervene: the hero's affair with his aunt is borrowed from Stendhal's *Charterhouse of Parma* rather than (one supposes) real life. What matters is that the problems of life-choice facing the hero, which are the classic problems of the romantic hero in literature – to conform or not to conform, to accept or not to accept a class-bound destiny, how to value the life of the intellect as against that of the senses, that of others as against one's own, that of one's family against society at large – could all be traced back to the artist himself, for whom the hero becomes a spokesman.

Before the Revolution was a gamble which did not pay off. The audience, it turned out, was not that keen to identify with the specific problems of its hero presented as if they were problems of humanity as a whole. It was four years before Bertolucci could make another feature and when he did it was less subjective but even more idiosyncratic than *Before the Revolution* had been. *Partner*, as this film was titled, was a farrago of Godardian tropes, hitting out wildly and sometimes wittily at various targets, from consumerism to the academy. Shot in the spring of 1968, it had a skittish almost carnavalesque quality, well suited to the time of its production. By the time it was released in the autumn, however, it was out of touch with the harsher political climate that followed the restabilization of France after the May Events and the invasion of Czechoslovakia.

Bertolucci's move from the fringe to the mainstream dates from the very end of the decade when, back to back, he made *The Spider's Stratagem*, produced by the state broadcaster RAI, and *The Conformist*, from the novel of that title by Alberto Moravia, an Italo-Franco-German co-production for worldwide cinema release. Both these films look back over the Fascist period, raising ghosts which the Italian cinema (and much of the rest of Italian culture likewise) had preferred throughout the 1950s and 60s not to resurrect. The problem of coming to terms with a Fascist past was not as severe in Italy as in Germany, but it was still a troubling one. *The Spider's Stratagem* deals subtly with one aspect of the problem – the idealization of the Resistance. *The Conformist* is less subtle and at times reductive. Vittorio Storaro's photography and Ferdinando Scarfiotti's set designs make it a memorable visual experience. Intellectually, it suffers from the fashion (which it in part initiated) for seeking the origins of Fascism in sexual psychopathology.

By the time *The Spider's Stratagem* and *The Conformist* were made, the Italian cinema had substantially reconfigured itself. The great producers like Ponti and De Laurentiis no longer dominated the scene as they had done ten years earlier. De Laurentiis ran into financial difficulty and eventually left Italy for the USA. Ponti continued to exert an influence but his interests were increasingly international so that alongside important Italian films such as Marco Ferreri's *The Ape Woman* (1964) and Elio Petri's *The 10th Victim* (1965), he was also producer or co-producer of Godard's *Contempt* and *Les Carabiniers* (1963), David Lean's *Doctor Zhivago* (1965), Miloš Forman's *The Fireman's Ball* (1967), and Antonioni's three English-language films for MGM, *Blow Up* (1966), *Zabriskie Point* (1970), and *The Passenger* (1975). The places of the great swashbuckling moguls were taken on the one hand by more modest men such as Franco Cristaldi, producer of Rosi's early films and (among others) of Marco Bellocchio's *China Is Near* (1967), and on the other hand by adventurers like Alberto Grimaldi, who made his money in the spaghetti western and thereafter backed a number of 'art cinema' directors including Pasolini (*The Decameron*, 1971) and Bertolucci (*Last Tango in Paris*, 1972), but only on condition that their films contained plenty of sex.

Meanwhile, as elsewhere in Europe, the mass audience was beginning to fall apart. This posed problems for producers, but it also contributed to the variety of films jostling for position in the new fragmented market. High-budget films had to be made for the widest possible international distribution, with an inevitable loss of national specificity. But smaller films could be made which addressed self-selected audiences, mixing genre tropes with a variety of political or quasi-political statements. Crime films in particular would hint at the existence of hidden worlds of *mafia* and corruption and even the western was often a vehicle for anti-imperialist messages.

In general in Italy in the mid-1960s imagination was beginning to outrun reality. Economic growth (the 'miracolo economico') had not been matched by substantial changes in social relations. Italian society remained deeply conservative. The Christian Democrats stood solid and immobile at the heart of government, though from 1963 onwards they had to share power with the Socialists in a so-called *centro-sinistra* or centre-left coalition. The Catholic Church retained enormous influence. Divorce was not permitted. Female contraception was almost unheard of. Censorship was not only powerful but arbitrary and arcane.

The most common reaction to this state of affairs was a resigned and ironic acceptance, which found expression in the plethora of comedies Italian-style which continued to be produced in large numbers. These comedies satirized the quirks of Italian life, particularly its backward sexual morality, but on the whole with a gentleness which created space neither for extravagant hope nor overwhelming despair. Outside the industrial mainstream, however, a deeper negativity was fermenting and burst forth in films by Paolo and Vittorio Taviani, Marco Ferreri, and Marco Bellocchio.

In 1962, in a film co-written and directed by the Taviani brothers and Valentino Orsini entitled *Un uomo da bruciare* (*A Man for Burning*), the first 'angry young man' appears in the Italian cinema. Salvatore (played by Gian Maria Volontè) is a working-class militant who decides, off his own bat, to take on the power structure in Sicily, employers, *mafia*, the lot. No way, however, is he a positive hero of socialist folklore and there is nothing redemptive in his defeat and death. The team's next film, *I fuorilegge del matrimonio* (1963 – the title translates literally as 'The outlaws of marriage'), mounted a furious onslaught on Italy's archaic marriage laws and, unlike Germi (*Divorce Italian Style*, 1961) or De Sica (*Marriage Italian Style*, 1964), found nothing funny about them.

A similar rawness also animates *I sovversivi* ('The subversives'), made in 1967 by the Tavianis but this time on their own without Orsini. Mixing footage of the funeral of the Communist leader Palmiro Togliatti in 1964 with interlacing stories about characters in various states of discontent with their existence. *I sovversivi* is a muddled film, unsure of its targets and uninventive in the way it is put together. But it has a prophetic element. Whatever catharsis the characters are seeking they will find a year later, when Italy is hit with the repercussions of the Paris May Events.

May 1968 is also foreshadowed in Bellocchio's *China Is Near*, at least to the extent that some of the characters embrace the utopian spirit of western Maoism in their futile revolt against the reactionary absurdities of the bourgeois institutions which envelop them. Bellocchio's critique of provincial bourgeoisdom is unashamedly subjective. It is not displaced on to problems which, whatever their importance in the global scheme of things, are always those of someone else. This gives his films a focus and intensity which, however well intentioned, the Tavianis lack.

For both the Tavianis and Bellocchio (and the same could be said of Bertolucci too), Italy in the 1960s appears as a country recalcitrant to progress, beyond reform yet not ripe for revolution. By contrast, the world as represented in the films of Marco Ferreri has a negativity unredeemable by any imaginable political solution. Ferreri is best known internationally for the sex-and-gluttony extravaganza *La Grande Bouffe*, made in France in 1973. Italian by birth, he actually began his career as a film director in Spain, teaming up with the Spanish writer Rafael Azcona to make the bizarre comedy *El cochecito* (*The Wheelchair*) in 1961. Ferreri returned to Italy in 1962 but the partnership continued for the best part of twenty years. The Ferreri/Azcona universe is one in which abnormal actions, choices, or events are viewed and presented with ironic detachment, as if they were not abnormal at all. As Lino Micciché puts it, there are no villains in these films but this is because all the characters are, in their own way, as monstrous as each other.[1] This mask of detachment cannot disguise a deep structural imbalance. Though men may behave in monstrous ways it is woman who is, herself and in her very being, the monster, whether physically, as in *The Ape Woman* from 1964, or in the vagaries of her sexual appetite as in Ferreri's previous film *The Queen Bee* (1963).

Ferreri is not unique in exhibiting this fear of the feminine. Fellini too creates monstrous women, desirable and fearful at the same time, though his portrayals are both more affectionate and more self-aware than Ferreri's. The presence of an underlying strand of castration anxiety in Italian culture was to be exploited and turned on its head in the films of Lina Wertmüller and Liliana Cavani in the 1970s.

The disparate strands making up the new cinema in Italy in the 1960s are perhaps more connected than they might seem at first sight. For the sexual question, as it emerges in Ferreri and Fellini but also more widely in comedy Italian-style, is inseparable from the southern question, which is in turn inseparable from the question of corruption, which is also the question of the immobility of political and social institutions.

The sexual question connects to the southern question to the extent that retarded patriarchal sexual mores, as satirized in 1960s cinema, were more entrenched in the south of Italy than further north. The emancipated heroines in Antonioni films belong to the Roman, Torinese, or Milanese bourgeoisie, and would be unthinkable in a small-town environment in Sicily or Calabria. Conversely, the *delitto d'onore* or crime of honour was (or was seen as) a southern custom and Simone's murder of Nadia in Visconti's *Rocco and His Brothers* is clearly marked as a sign of his inadaptation to life in the north. Corruption, too, though widespread throughout the country, was intensified in the south by the power of the Sicilian *Mafia* and its counterparts in Naples and other southern cities. Neapolitan or Sicilian-based criminality or corruption, sometimes spreading its tentacles to the heart of the government in Rome, is a regular theme of Rosi's films from *La sfida* (1957) onwards. Petri, too, was to shift his attention to Sicily in the black comedy *A ciascuno il suo* ('To each his own') in 1967 and again in *Todo modo* in 1976, both adaptations of novels by the master analyst of Sicilian peculiarities, Leonardo Sciascia. By contrast, films examining the (generally rather superficial) effects of modernization and gap between aspiration and reality can be set anywhere, but most often either in Rome or to the north of it.

While the contents of many Italian films of the 1960s can be related to broadly shared notions of the state of the nation in the period, there is complete diversity when it comes to style. Where Antonioni is sparse, Fellini is exuberant; where Olmi is reticent, Visconti is operatic; where Pasolini is rough-edged and moves progressively away from naturalism towards the hieratic, Mario Monicelli and other industry stalwarts remain loyal to slick and on the whole naturalistic stagings. The general lack of homogeneity is particularly visible in the many episode films of the period which often seemed purpose-designed to showcase the difference in style among the directors selected to film each episode. There was, however one constant. With few exceptions, producers did not give author-directors free rein. They insisted on high professional standards of screenwriting and cinematography, which was generally to the good, since the Italian cinema excelled in both areas. But they also insisted on what they regarded as a proper soundtrack, which meant lifeless studio sound effects and dubbed voices chosen for clarity rather than authenticity. Directors protested, but to no avail. Whatever else the new cinema achieved in Italy, it did not produce a Nouvelle Vague.

Notes

1. Lino Micciché, *Cinema italiano: gli anni '60 e oltre* (Venice: Marsilio, 2002), p. 164.

13

From Polish School to Czech New Wave and Beyond

The life of the Czech New Wave (as it came to be called) was brief and brilliant. It came into being quite rapidly in 1963 or 1964 and was throttled to death within months of the Soviet invasion of Czechoslovakia in September 1968.

The emergence of this New Wave took most people outside Czechoslovakia by surprise. If any country east of the Iron Curtain was going to produce a new cinema, the most likely candidates, it was thought, would be either Poland or Yugoslavia – Yugoslavia because it was the least Stalinized of the Eastern bloc countries, and Poland because it had the strongest and most independent-minded cinema already in existence. In the event, Yugoslavia produced a radical new cinema, but it was small and soon fell victim to one of the waves of repression which punctuated political and cultural activity in all countries with Communist regimes. And, for a complex of reasons, Poland somehow missed the boat. It entered the 1960s with a very dominant old guard, and the new cinema, when it did emerge, was late and fragmentary.

Before turning to the remarkable case of Czechoslovakia, it is therefore worth looking also at the general context in Eastern Europe and the on the whole less remarkable cases of some of the other countries in the Soviet orbit.

The bloc of countries in Eastern Europe comprising East Germany, Poland, Czechoslovakia, Hungary, Romania, Bulgaria, Yugoslavia, and Albania all had Communist regimes of a broadly similar type, which (except in Yugoslavia and Albania) had been forced on them by the Soviet Union after the end of the Second World War. They had also all been under Nazi occupation during the War, from which they were liberated partly by their own efforts and partly by the Red Army. The regimes in power were totalitarian in the sense of attempting to control all aspects of life, including cultural life, and an orthodox doctrine going by the name of Socialist Realism was imposed on the cinema, following the Soviet model, when the new regimes came to power, lasting until 1956 if not later.

That much said, all these countries were profoundly different. They were different before the Communist takeover and they remained different afterwards. Czechoslovakia (or at least the Czech part of it) was an advanced industrialized country, Albania was rural and feudal. Poland could boast a strong non- or even anti-Communist resistance movement during the war, whereas in Yugoslavia the main resistance was Communist and liberated the country without Soviet help (but quite a bit of help from the western Allies). German-speaking and Jewish intellectuals played an important role in cultural and political life in Czechoslovakia and Hungary before the War and their influence survived into the postwar period. The Holocaust was also differently experienced in different countries. Bulgaria's Jews were protected by the Government. Elsewhere, local anti-Semites bore varying degrees of responsibility for handing Jews over to the Nazis. And when the Communists came to power, the degree and form of opposition to their rule was very different in countries with a solid Social-Democratic tradition such as Czechoslovakia and in countries with a history of powerful and often virulent nationalism, such as Poland. In spite of all the levelling imposed by the new regimes, these differences were to surface in the films made throughout the so-called bloc, particularly after 1956, when cinemas in Poland and Hungary in particular felt free to examine their own past and present it in a critical way.

It also needs to be said that, although Socialist Realism was imposed as official doctrine throughout the Soviet bloc, its reign was brief and its effects were far less harmful in the satellite countries than in the Soviet Union itself. In Czechoslovakia, for instance, the Communist takeover did not happen until 1948 – five years before the death of Stalin and eight years before the first tentative steps were taken to demolish parts of the Stalinist system, including the iron grip exerted by the Party on the arts. In East Germany, which was under direct Soviet rule from 1945 to 1949, the Russians did not bother too much with artistic directives and it was only when German Communists themselves took over the cultural apparatus that Socialist Realist norms were seriously imposed.[1] Even during the height of the Stalinist period, moreover, it was difficult for the authorities to staff the bureaucracy solidly with *apparatchiki* and there were always (especially in Poland and Yugoslavia) pockets within the apparatus sympathetic to the need of artists to deviate from the strict norms of official doctrine.

As mentioned in Chapter 3, 1956 was a dramatic year throughout Europe, and especially in the East. Yugoslavia confirmed its detachment from the Soviet bloc, and Hungary threatened to follow suit in declaring its neutrality. Internally, both Hungary and Poland took steps to liberalize society and the economy. Liberalization was stopped in its tracks in Hungary by the Soviet invasion in November 1956, but in Poland it was able to continue after a tense stand-off between Khrushchev and the reforming Polish leader Władyslaw Gomulka. Although well aware of the dangers of defying its powerful neighbour, the Polish government continued with a cautious reform programme in most spheres of life. When it came to the cinema, the bureaucratic transmission belts were long and slow and there were enough reform-minded intellectuals inside the administration to make the continued imposition of a stultifying and unpopular aesthetic doctrine virtually impossible. Besides, the authorities wanted both to have their cake and eat it. They wanted Polish films to be admired abroad, both for their artistic merit and for the picture they gave of People's Poland, not to mention the hard currency they might earn. But they also had to cope with the problem that the films admired in the west were not always the ones of which they approved for internal consumption.

The trials and tribulations – and occasional satisfactions – of being a film-maker in Poland at the time are well illustrated by the career of Andrzej Wajda.

Wajda was the central figure, alongside Wojciech Has, Jerzy Kawalerowicz, Andrzej Munk, and others, of what came to be called the 'Polish School' that flourished in the late 1950s. Spanning the watershed year of 1956, Wajda made three films about the Polish resistance towards the end of the Second World War. The first of these, *A Generation* (1955), is politically orthodox; it ascribes the leading role in the resistance to the Communists and it shows the hero, in true Socialist Realist fashion, developing political consciousness as the story progresses. The second, *Kanal* (1957), about the 1944 Warsaw uprising, is still orthodox, though formally more unusual in that most of the action takes place in the sewers beneath the beleaguered city. But it is the third, *Ashes and Diamonds*, made in 1958 and generally released the following year, that made Wajda's international reputation. Set in the very last days of the war, and adapted from the already controversial novel of the same title by Jerzy Andrzejewski, it overthrows Socialist Realist convention by making a romantic hero of the nominal villain. Maciek, played by Zbygniew Cybulski in leather jacket and dark glasses and looking like Marlon Brando in *The Wild One* mysteriously transported into a European war zone, is a member of the nationalist and anti-Communist resistance who has been assigned the job of assassinating the nominal hero, Szczuka, an intelligent Communist. In the end (it could hardly be otherwise) the assassination attempt is bungled. Szczuka dies, but so does Maciek.

This romanticization of the Cybulski character created tremors in the apparatus. The film was shown to senior Party figures who reluctantly approved it and it was premiered in October 1958. It was decided not to enter it for Cannes the following spring but it was sent to Venice in September, though not in competition. At Venice it received an award from the international critics' circle, FIPRESCI, rather to the embarrassment of the authorities who had wanted a small amount of prestige and possibly an export sale but above all no controversy.[2]

Cannes 1959, the festival to which *Ashes and Diamonds* did not go, was of course the occasion of the revelation to an astonished world of the French Nouvelle Vague. Poland was among the countries caught up in the general excitement this provoked and Wajda was one of the first filmmakers to respond. In 1960 he settled down with Andrzejewski to plan a 'new wave' film of his own. Since the film was to be about young people, he drafted in a young writer called Jerzy Skolimowski initially to help with the dialogues but eventually to rewrite much of the script. The leads were played by Tadeusz Lomnicki (from *A Generation*) and Krystyna Stypulkowska, but a recently graduated film student named Roman Polanski, whose short film *Two Men and a Wardrobe* had been shown in London as part of Free Cinema in 1958, was invited to play the role of one of the hero's friends. (Cybulski and Skolimowski also had parts in the film.) Entitled *Innocent Sorcerers*, the film tells a new-wavish story about a couple who can't quite decide to get it together; they sit around in the man's apartment, they tease, they play strip poker, but for some reason avoid going the whole way. He goes out for a moment, returns to find her gone, searches for and discovers her, and then – improbably – they decide that their apprehensions about each other were misplaced and they hook up together again.

Innocent though this story is (and as the title insists), the film was profoundly shocking to official sensibilities. But it earned plenty of hard currency through export sales and led to Wajda being invited to make an episode for the compilation film *Love at Twenty* (other episodes were by Truffaut, Shintaro Ishihara, Marcel Ophuls, and Renzo Rossellini). From now on Wajda could count himself an international director as well as a Polish one, a fact which would stand him in good stead in the future.

The year of *Love at Twenty*, 1962, was also the year of what is sometimes called the 'small stabilization' in Poland, when a halt was called to some of the reforms that had been taking place since 1956.[3] Just before the clamp-down Roman Polanski had been able to make a brilliant first feature film, *Knife in the Water* (co-scripted by Skolimowski), which was found even more suspect and decadent than *Innocent Sorcerers*. Seeing no future for himself in Poland, Polanski emigrated. Meanwhile, in September 1961, Munk died in a car crash in the middle of making *Passenger*, a film about the relationship between two women, one a guard and the other a prisoner, in the Auschwitz concentration camp. Assembled by Munk's friend Witold Lesiewicz in a form as close as possible to Munk's intentions, but still bearing signs of its unfinished state. *Passenger* is a powerful and disturbing film, all the more so for being fragmentary and inconclusive. With Munk's death and Polanski's decision to emigrate, the 'small stabilization' did not have all that much to stabilize. The years between 1963 and 1967, so fertile elsewhere in East Central Europe, in Poland were mainly barren.

A new cinema did in fact spring up in Poland and again the film school at Łódź was of seminal importance. Skolimowski spent the years of the stabilization there, making student exercises which he strung together on graduation to form the autobiographical feature-length *Rysopis* (1964). The hero of *Rysopis* is a drifter; that of Skolimowski's next film, *Walkover* (1965), is a loser, a boxer who has lost the will to win. The story of *Walkover* is told in thirty-five shots and, like *Rysopis*, it is autobiographical (as well as a writer, painter, and jazz musician, Skolimowski had been a semi-professional boxer), but in both films the autobiography serves a wider, anti-establishment purpose. It would be over-interpretation to say that the films are political allegories – that Poland is only worth drifting through and certainly not worth fighting for – but they do forcibly stake out a claim for an existence outside of official social structures and approved patterns of thought. It was not surprising that after one more film made in Poland, the even more radically non-conformist *Barrier* (1966), Skolimowski left for the west. Skolimowski was that rare thing in the cinema anywhere, a genuine avant-garde artist who was able to push open the frontiers of what the medium can do. He came at the right time, but in the wrong place. By the time he made this first film in the west, *Le Départ* (1967), it was still the right time, but only just.

Skolimowski was a one-man bridge between the Polish School that fell apart in the early 1960s and the 'cinema of moral concern' inaugurated by Krzysztof Zanussi, another Łódź graduate, whose first film, *The Structure of Crystals*, was released in 1969. Meanwhile the rest of East Central Europe worked to a different timetable and the mid and late 1960s were a period of innovation, especially in Czechoslovakia but also on a small scale in Hungary and Yugoslavia.

One major irony in the Czech situation was that the clamp-down which hit Poland in 1962 happened there much earlier – to be precise in February 1959, when a conference called by the authorities in the Slovakian spa town of Banská Bystrica was the occasion for the government to announce a reimposition of more or less the same norms as had prevailed in the Stalin period. They could not be quite the same but they were sufficiently restrictive to create panic in reform-minded film circles. Then in 1963, just as Poland was 'stabilizing', Czechoslovakia began cautiously to liberalize, the change in climate symbolized by the belated official recognition that Franz Kafka was both Czech and a great writer.

Not all forms of potentially radical film-making were hit by the 1959 clamp-down, only those in which the official mind discerned a threat to national morale or the construction of the socialist order. Films set in the 19th century or earlier were generally safe, as were comedies that indulged the traditional Czech taste for irony with suitable discretion. The film-makers hardest hit were those who actually believed in building socialism and wished to tackle controversial subjects, but in an unorthodox way. Writing from Canadian exile in 1971, the dissident writer Josef Škvorecký described this group of film-makers, who included Jan Kadár, Voytěch Jasný, and Jaromil Jireš, as an 'Ur-Wave' preceding the real New Wave of the mid-1960. 'All the creators of the Ur-Wave,' Škvorecký wryly observes, 'were members of the Communist Party; this is why they took the questions of public conscience more to heart than non-members who, having no claim on the merits of the revolution, did not feel responsible for its less meritorious aspects'.[4] By contrast the New Wave in waiting was to consist almost entirely of younger people who were not Party members: Miloš Forman, Evald Schorm, Věra Chytilová, Ivan Passer, Jan Němec, Jiři Menzel, to name but the most famous. These were people who had no particular interest in building a socialist culture. As far as they were concerned this so-called socialism was something that was there; they had grown up with it, it existed, and on the whole they didn't like it. If they were socialists, Škvorecký remarks, 'they were socialists without complexes'.[5]

Another thing that immediately distinguished this New Wave was that its members were already the children of other new waves. They were not in a position to see all that many of the new films coming out western Europe and North America, but as students at the national film school, FAMU, or as visitors to the festival at Karlovy Vary, they had been able to see a fair number – some French, some British, but above all new documentaries from various sources in direct cinema mode, films in which the camera watched and waited and eventually something happened.

When this new generation began to make films it did so at first in a small way, and one which was not likely to draw undue attention from the authorities. The New Wave proper is sometimes held to begin with a small-scale featurette by Forman entitled *Konkurs* and variously translated as 'The Audition', 'The Competition', and 'Talent Competition'. *Konkurs* started life in 1963, when Forman had just graduated from film school, as a medium-length quasi-documentary about singers taking part in an audition. In that form it attracted very little attention, either favourable or unfavourable. Forman then added to it two loosely connected narrative strands, one of a couple of bands in rehearsal and one of boys taking part in a motor-cycle rally while girls look on. A flimsy plot device has two of the boys involved in both the rehearsal and the rally, but it is hardly necessary, such is the fascination of the barely narrativized footage of the two conductors haranguing the musicians, the boys trying to extract extra performance from their underpowered bikes, and the girls anxious not to blow their moment of glory in front of the microphone.

By the time the new version of *Konkurs* came out, Forman was already controversial. In his first proper feature film, *Peter and Pavla* (1964), teenage Peter is employed as a security guard in a grocery store, a dead-end job that he is not much good at. On duty, he fails to catch an elderly shoplifter; off duty he flirts with Pavla and is shouted at by his father who treats him as a lazy good-for-nothing. There is nothing unusual, under any political system, about young people doing jobs they don't like and not getting on brilliantly with their parents. But working-class youth in socialist Czechoslovakia were not supposed to be lazy good-for-nothings or row with their elders and betters. Unwittingly, Forman found himself at the centre of a storm, in which he was cast as Peter and the authorities played the role of Peter's father. There was nothing in the film that could be censored, but the official critics found it deeply offensive.

Low-level controversy of this type continued to dog not only Forman but other New Wave film-makers for the next four years. Rarely were films made which were a deliberate provocation to the authorities, but they gave offence none the less and even without seeking it the film-makers were resigned to this as a likely outcome. Interpreting the politics (or the political implications) of the New Wave is not easy but one way of putting it would be to say that the film-makers were trying to be apolitical in a situation when being apolitical was not an option. They knew this, but went on trying.

At least two films, however, made in the heady period between 1963 and the Soviet invasion in 1968, decidedly did court controversy. One was Forman's *The Firemen's Ball* and the other was Věra Chytilová's *Daisies*. Chytilová had earlier scored a modest success with *Something Else*, a film about two women, a gymnast and a housewife, one who had sacrificed her personal life in pursuit of a career and one who had settled for a life of domestic tedium. Chytilová was both a feminist and a formalist, and one of the striking things about *Something Else* was the sheer beauty of the images, particularly those of Eva Bosáková as the gymnast, endlessly performing routines on the bars and responding equally routinely to the questions of journalists.

Made in 1963 and a prize-winner at Mannheim that autumn, *Something Else* has a better claim than *Konkurs* to be the inauguration of the Czech New Wave. Its success on the festival circuit earned Chytilová the privilege of being allowed to make her next film, *Daisies*, in Eastmancolor. This was a privilege that the studio came to regret, for *Daisies* is a completely anarchic film, one of the most anarchic films ever made. Two girls, referred to as Marie I and Marie II, go on a spree. They hang out for a while in their bikinis and then, having determined that 'the world ruins everything' and that the only antidote is to ruin the world in its turn, they engage in various mischievous acts. They tease a couple of middle-aged men with the promise of sex and leave them stranded at the railway station before carrying on with their mayhem, eventually turning up in a building where an enormous banquet is spread out for the benefit of some distinguished personages. They then proceed to demolish the banquet and what they can't eat they throw around the room. In a fit of conscience, they attempt to clear up the mess, but the damage has been done. The level of damage, it should be said, is nowhere near enough to threaten the stability of a whole society, but the energy with which the two innocents throw themselves into it created shock waves which were not easy to contain.

Forman's manner was generally as restrained as Chytilová's was extravagant. But in *The Firemen's Ball* he used his deadpan style to devastating effect. Co-written with Ivan Passer and Jaroslav Papoušek, it is ostensibly a semi-affectionate satire on provincial small-mindedness and petty officialdom, but it was interpreted as if its target was the political system as a whole. A retired fireman is dying and his former workmates decide to use the occasion of the annual ball to give him a present. The ball is a disaster in every conceivable way and when a fire breaks out which the assembled firemen cannot extinguish, guests seize the opportunity to steal the tombola prizes. Whether this was really an allegory of the kleptocratic Communist Party bosses can be debated. But it was taken to be one, and the film was banned 'in perpetuity' when the old guard returned to power after the dousing of the Prague Spring of 1968.

The New Wave was not instantly crushed with the return of the old guard following the Soviet invasion. A few film-makers fled the country. These included Forman, for whom a successful Hollywood career beckoned, and Passer, who was less successful. Among those who stayed, Papoušek struggled to complete a project already in production and went on to make the singularly bitter comedy *Ecce Homo Homolka*, in which an ordinary Czech family distinguishes itself by failing to go to the help of a woman who is being assaulted. For most, however, it was a matter of grinding one's teeth and waiting to see if things would get better, which they did, but only eventually.

The legacy of the Czech New Wave consists mainly in films about contemporary life which were obstinately unglamorous. With rare exceptions, they tended to have provincial settings. Rather as the British New Wave had found the heart of England in its northern cities, the Czech film-makers found the heart of their country not in the metropolis but in the countryside and provincial towns (Forman's *Loves of a Blonde* does have scenes in Prague, but only in a drab suburb). In the work of Forman and Passer (for example *Intimate Lighting*) in particular, small events, happening to insignificant people, and recounted in the most understated way possible, are preferred to drama and heroics. In a country whose most memorable literary figurations are Jaroslav Hašek's Good Soldier Švejk and Franz Kafka's Joseph K., this is perhaps not surprising.

The New Wave also applied its understatement and irony to the Second World War. The problems of facing up to the less heroic aspects of the wartime past were broadly the same as in other countries which had been under Nazi occupation. But they were less acute than, for example, in Poland, where matters were complicated by the division of the resistance into Communist and anti-Communist factions and where certain questions about the role of the Soviet Union, such as the Katyn massacre and the Red Army's failure to come to the aid of the Warsaw uprising, were still taboo. Czech New Wave film-makers such as Jan Němec with *Diamonds in the Night* (1964) and Jiří Menzel with *Closely Observed Trains* (1966), revisited the occupation period without feeling the need for excessive piety or mock heroics. In the former, two Jewish boys trying to escape the Germans are captured by a group of old men who seem quite prepared to kill them or hand them over but then mysteriously appear to let them go. And in the latter the hero is more concerned with his attempts to lose his virginity (and his premature ejaculation when he is in the process of doing so) than with the role assigned to him in the resistance.[6]

No other Eastern European cinema had the confidence (though some might say it was cowardice) to ironize in this way about what was by any reckoning a national trauma. All countries, however, had to do their reckoning. In Bulgaria the landmark film was Vulo Radev's *The Peach Thief* (1964). In Hungary a similar honour would appear to belong to András Kovács's *Cold Days* (1966), which deals with a massacre carried out by Hungarian troops in Serbia in 1942.[7] It is worth pointing out that when it came to facing up to unsavoury aspects of the national past, the cinemas of Eastern Europe had a much more honourable record than those in the west. In French and Italian films before 1970 the Resistance is almost always glorified in a completely uncritical way. West Germany had yet to begin on its 'coming to terms with the past' referred to in Chapter 9. Comment on the British and American war films of almost any period would be superfluous.

In Hungary, the great critical chronicler of national epic was Miklós Jancsó. The most striking feature of his films from *The Round Up* (1965) onwards is the use of the long take and constantly moving crane-mounted camera, which swoops and zooms as it scans flat and dusty landscapes out of which horsemen mysteriously emerge (or even more mysteriously, naked peasant women endeavour unsuccessfully to take shelter). Admired in the west mainly for their pyrotechnics and apparently exotic content, Jancsó's films of the 1960s are treatments of very particular moments in Hungarian history, usually the aftermath of civil war or attempted revolution. Thus *The Round Up* is set after the failure of the 1848 revolution, when revolutionary struggle had left banditry in its wake. *The Red and the White* (1967), a Hungarian-Soviet co-production, deals with an episode in the civil war in Russia that followed the Bolshevik Revolution and the end of the First World War. Hungary, too, had its own short-lived revolution at that time, the so-called Republic of the Councils or Béla Kun Soviet, and this provides the background to *The Silence and the Cry* (1968). Finally, with *The Confrontation* in 1969, Jancsó approached a more topical theme: the film is set at the end of the Second World War, when radical and conservative students have a face-out over the future of Hungary after the defeat of Nazism. As in 1848 and 1919, the hopes of the revolutionaries are dashed – as they were to be again in 1956.

No study of the new cinemas of Eastern Europe in the 1960s would be complete without at least a mention of Yugoslavia and the 'novi film' (sometimes referred to as 'crni film' – 'black film') movement, whose leading figures were Aleksandar Petrović, Živojin Pavlović, and Dušan Makavejev. From the mid-1950s onwards, Yugoslavia had followed its own distinctive path to socialism. In foreign policy it was non-aligned and the intellectuals were kept on a far longer leash than was the rule in the Soviet bloc proper. The 'novi film' started about the same time as the Czech New Wave, which influenced it considerably, but it survived longer, being finally called to order by the authorities only around 1972.

The 'novi film' was part of Yugoslavia's general intellectual ferment in the period. Stalinist orthodoxy had been almost totally discarded in favour of 'western' Marxism – the ideas of George Lukács, Antonio Gramsci, and Yugoslavia's own dissident intellectuals around the Journal *Praxis* – with a heavy dose of Sartrean existentialism thrown in for good measure. This mix of ideas undoubtedly shaped the cinema of Pavlović and Makavejev, but Petrović (best known for *I Even Met Happy*

Gypsies, 1967) probably less so.[8] In Makavejev's case there was an added element: the utopianism of the Marxist Freudians Herbert Marcuse and Wilhelm Reich, with their almost messianic belief that no social revolution was possible without a sexual one or vice versa. In four feature films made during the heyday of 'novi film' between 1965 and 1971, Makavejev explored various aspects of the links between sexual repression and social order. Of these film *W. R. Mysteries of the Organism* (1971 – the 'W.R.' of the title is Wilhelm Reich and 'organism' is a euphemism for orgasm) is the most notorious, but *Switchboard Operator* (1967) must surely be regarded as the better film, if only because it combines its liberationist message with a sharp (if depressing) analysis of the state of Yugoslav society in the period. Isabela, the switchboard operator of the title, is an emancipated girl from the Hungarian minority in the north of the country who falls in love with Ahmed, a Muslim from the South (presumably either Bosnia or Kosovo). When Isabela gets pregnant – probably by another man – Ahmed attempts to kill himself. Isabela drowns in attempting to rescue him and Ahmed is arrested for her murder. The narrative is interrupted, in typical Makavejev fashion, by a lecture from a sexologist demonstrative of the ignorance and human ineptitude of the purveyors of official science in Yugoslavia – and by implication elsewhere.

The demise of 'novi film' brought to an end a glorious period in the history of cinema in Eastern Europe, in which most countries in the region took part. Makavejev joined Forman and Jancsó in seeking at least temporary refuge in the west. But it was not the end of everything. Slovakia, which had played a very minor role in the nominally Czechslovak New Wave, escaped the worst of the repression and produced interesting films in the 1970s. Polish cinema revived. Some at least of the émigrés returned to their homelands. But the sense of the cinema as a vanguard in the struggle to enable the peoples of Eastern Europe to 'live in truth' in Václav Havel's phrase, disappeared and did not return.

Notes

1. See Hans Michael Bock, 'East Germany: The DEFA story', in Geoffrey Nowell-Smith (ed.), *The Oxford History of World Cinema* (Oxford and New York: Oxford University Press, 1996), pp. 627–32.

2. According to Paul Coates, Jerzy Lewiński, the official who took the film to Venice, had a hard time on his return explaining to his superiors why a film not entered in

competition nevertheless got awarded a prize. See Paul Coates, *The Red and the White: The Cinema of People's Poland* (London: Wallflower Press, 2005), pp. 39–40.

3. According to Marek Haltof in his book *Polish National Cinema* (New York and Oxford: Berghahn, 2002), p. 103, a resolution of the pompously named Central Committee Secretariat of the Polish United Workers Party in June 1960 already signalled the impending end for the Polish school of film-makers. But it was not for another couple of years that the climate became such that the shutters really came down, in the cinema as elsewhere in Polish cultural life.

4. Josef Škvorecký, *All the Bright Young Men and Women* (Toronto: Peter Martin Associates, 1971), p. 45.

5. Ibid.

6. Also in a similar vein is Jan Kadár and Elmar Klos's *A Shop on the High Street* (1965), set in a small town in Slovakia, in which an old Jewish shopkeeper is deprived of her property but sheltered by the man who takes over the shop; to save her from the Nazis he locks her in a cupboard, where she is later found dead.

7. See John Cunningham, *Hungarian Cinema from Coffee House to Multiplex* (London: Wallflower, 2004), p. 105.

8. The original title of the film is *Skupljači perja* which means 'The feather buyer'. Petrović's earlier film *Three* (1965) is discussed by Vlastimar Sudar in a chapter in *The Cinema of the Balkans* (Dina Iordanova [ed.] [London: Wallflower, 2006]) which also contains a chapter on Pavlović's *When I Am Dead and Pale* (1968). For Makavejev, Robin Wood's essay on *Man Is Not a Bird* (1965) in Cameron et al., *Second Wave* (London: Studio Vista, 1970) remains a classic.

14

Latin America

Before 1960 there was no such thing as Latin American cinema. It was not that there were no films or even film industries, but they were dispersed and disconnected. The three most populous and urbanized countries in the region, Mexico, Brazil, and Argentina, had national cinemas of some substance, supported by a large internal market and thriving on the basis of strong native cultural traditions. Mexico in particular – in spite or perhaps because of the looming presence of the United States just across the border – had a powerful presence in world cinema from the 1930s onwards, first through the work of Fernando de Fuentes and then through that of the combination of director Emilio Fernandez and cinematographer Gabriel Figueroa. And of course, there was the Spanish exile Luis Buñuel, who made Mexico his home in the 1940s and remained attached to it until his death. Brazilian cinema had less international resonance, but Argentina had both a popular cinema and at least one distinguished 'art cinema' director in the form of Leopoldo Torre Nilsson, whose dissection of Argentine bourgeois life – notably in *La casa del ángel* (1957) – was much admired (though not widely distributed) in Europe as well as at home.

But these were cinemas in Latin America, not Latin American cinema. The countries in question were geographically far apart. Even within Spanish-speaking Latin America there was little circulation of films between one country and another, while Portuguese-speaking Brazil had no natural export outlet for its production. Simon Bolívar's 19th-century vision of a united continent had no grip on early and mid-20th-century reality, at least as far as the cinema was concerned.

Around 1960, all this changed. There were two major developments, which eventually merged. During the left-wing presidency of Arturo Frondizi (1958–62) in Argentina, there was a small wave of new art cinema ('bourgeois', according to its detractors). Alongside the established Torre Nilsson, other film-makers emerged – or, if established, changed course. These included David Kohon with *Tres veces Ana* ('Anna, three times over', 1961) and Miguel Antín with *La cifra impar* ('Odd number', 1962), while Fernando Ayala, best known for the crime film *El jefe* ('The boss', 1958), went through a rapid 'New Wave' phase before settling on sex comedies in the late 1960s. Largely forgotten by historians enraptured of the radical cinema that was to erupt on the scene the scene a few years later, this new art cinema demonstrated that there was room on the market for something different from either American imports or the by now rather tired indigenous genre cinema.

Meanwhile, in a contrasting development, another new cinema was taking shape, more influenced by Italian neo-realism than by the example of the European new waves. Fernando Birri, a poet and film-maker who had left Argentina in the early 1950s to study at the Centro Sperimentale di Cinematografia in Rome, returned home to found a film school of his own in the city of Santa Fe. In 1958, loosely inspired by neo-realist example, he and his students made a documentary about the slum-dwellers of Santa Fe entitled *Tire die* ('Throw us a dime'), which was shown at a festival in neighbouring Uruguay at the same time as a film by the Brazilian Nelson Pereira dos Santos, *Rio zona norte* ('Rio, north zone'), made in 1957. Both films were influenced by neo-realism but, as dos Santos put it, more as an example of how to produce films on the fly than as an aesthetic or an ideology.[1]

Then, in 1959, came the Cuban revolution. Within months of its establishment, the revolutionary government set up ICAIC, the Instituto Cubano de Arte e Indusria Cinematográficos. Among its founders were Julio García Espinosa and Tomás Gutiérrez Alea, both of whom, like Birri, had studied at the Centro Sperimentale. Cesare Zavattini was invited from Italy to assist in the formation of the new institute and the globetrotting Joris Ivens to advise on documentary. In 1960 ICAIC produced its first feature films, Espinosa's *Cuba baila* ('Cuba dances') and Alea's *Historias de la revolución*, neither of them aggressively political and both clearly affected by Zavattini's example.

But it was not Cuban films, which at first were little seen outside their home country, that provided the inspiration for a new Latin

American cinema so much as the example of the revolution itself. The self-affirmation of Cuba as the 'primero territorio libre de América' – the first free territory of America – revived all the dreams of commonality of the Spanish and Portuguese-speaking territories of the Americas, united in their common state of underdevelopment and a shared hostility to a new oppressor north of the Rio Grande. Events in a small island off the shores of this oppressive power were to generate a new continental consciousness. From now on films about poverty, whether in Argentina or Brazil, in the *barrios* and *favelas* or in the countryside, would henceforward be films not only about particular states of impoverishment but about the enforced poverty and underdevelopment of a whole continent.

The first radical expression of this new mood came in a film called *Barravento* (sometimes known in English as *The Turning Wind*), made in 1961 by a young man called Glauber Rocha and released in Brazil the following year. Shown at the Karlovy Vary festival in 1962 and again at Sestri Levante, but otherwise hardly seen outside Brazil before 1970, *Barravento* tells the story of an educated black man who returns from the city to his native seaside village and sets about trying to combat the power exercised by a local magician over his fellow villagers. The film is in a mode that probably deserves the much abused label magical realist, since it is basically realist but the magician does in fact have magical powers (which he loses if he engages in sexual intercourse). As well as being both magical and realist, *Barravento* is on the one hand very Brazilian but on the other hand harks back to Italian neo-realist models (De Sica and Zavattini's *Miracle in Milan* springs to mind).

At the same time Rocha was in the process of discovering *Cahiers du cinéma* and the Nouvelle Vague and in a book published in 1965 and entitled *Revisão critica do cinema brasileiro* or 'Critical revision of the Brazilian cinema' gives an account of Brazilian cinema to date which sets great store by the notion of the *auteur* as propounded by Truffaut in the 1950s.[2] For Rocha at this point in his career there is no reason to excoriate the author as bourgeois in the manner of Birri or later writers such as Fernando Solanas and Octavio Getino. On the contrary, a cinema of individual expression, such one finds in *Barravento* and Rocha's subsequent films, is the only possible counterweight to a commercial cinema in thrall to folkloric clichés about 'the people' and which treated the audience as irredeemably petty bourgeois in mentality. Among previous Brazilian film-makers, Rocha expresses particular scorn for Lima Barreto, maker of the acclaimed and extremely popular *O cangaceiro* ('The outlaw', 1953), while reserving his praise for the veterans Alberto Cavalcanti and Humberto Mauro. In pursuit of the aim of sweeping the native quality tradition off the Brazilian cinematic map, he quotes from an article by Truffaut in 1958: 'There are not even good or bad films: there are just film authors and their politique, necessarily beyond reproach.'[3]

But Rocha was not just in love with ideas of cinema as self-expression. He also thought that the cinema should speak to the condition of Brazil and the underdeveloped and colonized world in general. Also in 1965 he published his famous manifesto 'The aesthetics of hunger', in which he argued that the politics of the underdeveloped world was of necessity a politics of hunger and that, again of necessity, there had to be an aesthetic of hunger to match it.[4] This aesthetic, Rocha claimed, was beginning to manifest itself in what was now coming to be referred to as the Brazilian Cinema Novo. Films from this new cinema began to appear on the European festival circuit. Pereira dos Santos's *Vidas secas* (*Barren Lives*, 1964), about poverty in the Brazil's rural north-east, and Carlos Diegues's *Ganga Zumba* (1963), about a rebellion of African slaves against their Portuguese masters in the 17th century, caused a sensation when they were shown at the Festival del Cinema Libero at Porretta Terme in 1964, with *Ganga Zumba* narrowly beating *Vidas secas* to the top prize.

Rocha himself contributed to the distinctiveness of the new movement with *Black God, White Devil* (1964). Like Diegues, he was keen to highlight the country's often suppressed African heritage but he was less interested in the history of slavery than in the traces it had left in Brazilian culture. In *Black God, White Devil* (whose full title translates as 'God and the devil in the land of the sun'), a displaced peasant couple, Rosa and Manuel, attach themselves first to Sebastião, the charismatic black leader of a strange millennial cult, and then, when Sebastião and most of his followers are massacred by the agents of the landowning class, transfer their loyalty to a *cangaceiro* or bandit called Corisco. But Corisco's less religious and more social revolt suffers the same fate as Sebastião's, and his followers too are mown down by the notorious bandit-hunter popularly known as Antonio das Mortes – Antonio bringer of death. Neither the cultists with their drumming and chanting and magic charms, nor the bandits with their improvised weaponry are a match for the ruthlessness of Antonio and his paymasters. Stylistically, the film attempts to match the exaltation of Sebastião and his followers and Rocha makes little attempt to explain the actions of Manuel and Rosa in terms of rational psychology. The world of *Black God, White Devil* is a world in a state of collective delirium, a world in trance.

'Land in Trance' – *Terra em tramse* – is in fact the title of Rocha's next film, released in 1967. The setting is modern, and the central character is an intellectual not a peasant, but the structure is remarkably similar to that of *Black God, White Devil*. Paulo, the hero, is a poet who hesitates between two possible political masters, the ineffectual liberal populist Vieira and the right-wing authoritarian Diáz. Disillusioned by Vieira, he betrays him and facilitates Diáz's resistible rise to power. The story is set in an imaginary province of Brazil and all the usual disclaimers can be assumed to apply about how none of the characters is based on any real-life original, but the political message of the film, made when Brazil had recently undergone a military coup, albeit of a relatively civilized kind, could hardly be clearer. Or rather, the political dilemma is clear enough, but the solution isn't. If Paulo is representative of the liberal intelligentsia of his country – and Rocha seems to suggest that he is – and if the people are too abject and oppressed to revolt on their own, what hope is there for their survival, let alone for revolution? Fortunately, *Terra em tramse*, like all of Rocha's films, is not designed to be read in a purely realistic key. The accentuated emotionality, the generalized atmosphere of corruption and seduction (whether political or sexual), the overall ex-altation of hope and despair transport the spectator to a world which, yes, is Brazil in the mid-20th century but is also that of a thought-experiment where, as in *Black God, White Devil*, delirium is the order of the day and the pieties of conventional political discourse do not hold.

Black God, White Devil and *Terra em tramse* can both be counted exercises in political pessimism that nevertheless hold inside them a tiny message of hope. By contrast, *Antonio das Mortes* (properly entitled *O dragão da maldade contra o santo guerreiro* – 'the dragon of evil against the holy warrior') is a positively feel-good film – with, however, a bitter twist towards the end. Released in 1969, by which time a second and more brutal military coup was about to bring an end to the whole Cinema Novo experiment, *Antonio das Mortes* returns to the world of millennial cults and social banditry featured in *Black God, White Devil*. But this time Antonio, already in the earlier film a reluctant executioner, changes side to join the rebels and turn his lethal shotgun on his evil paymasters. His ally is a local schoolteacher of pacific temperament, who joins in the final shootout in spite of being told by Antonio that the intellectuals should stick to the word and leave the shooting to the gunmen. A final coda has Antonio and the teacher walking along a dusty highway next to a gigantic column of stationary trucks. Having slain the dragon of feudal oppression, they enter the world of capitalist modernity more displaced than ever.

In 1970 Rocha moved to Europe where he made two more films, *Cabezas cortadas* ('Off with their heads') and *Der Leone habe sept cabezas* ('The lion has seven heads'), while remaining loosely in touch with his home country. He then spent four years in exile, returning to Brazil in 1975. By this time Cinema Novo had ceased to exist. It only every really consisted of a handful of film-makers – basically, Rocha, Diegues, Pereira dos Santos, Ruy Guerra, and Joaquim Pedro de Andrade – none of whom was at all prolific. Few of their films, apart from *Antonio das Mortes*, were international box-office successes. But as a movement it was immensely important. Rocha's writings were widely read and contributed to a sense of common purpose across Latin America, even where his films, for commercial or censorship reasons, failed to penetrate. Along with manifestos and polemical articles by other film-makers, they helped to define Latin American cinema as a more extensive and coherent entity than the films of the period would themselves suggest.

Cinema Novo, moreover, was far from typical of Latin American cinema as a whole, and Rocha's ideas were by no means the same as those of fellow film-maker-intellectuals elsewhere on the continent – or even in Brazil itself. Certain generically Third-Worldist political propositions were common currency throughout the area, notably an insistence on the fact that underdevelopment was not an accident but a product of imperialism. Aesthetically, too, there was an increasingly widespread recognition of the need to escape from pre-existing European models, whether Italian neo-realism or the Nouvelle Vague. But many differences remained. Rocha was unique in breaking not just with neo-realism but with realism of any kind. Dos Santos's *Vidas secas*, with its attempted fusion of subjective narration and elements of documentary, is both original and eclectic and in so far as it has sources, neo-realism would not be the main one; but it operates entirely within a realist frame of reference, which the film-maker sees no need to challenge.

Meanwhile in Argentina, a military coup in 1962 led to the break-up Birri's Santa Fe school. Birri himself left the country shortly afterwards, but not before the group had completed a feature, *Los inundados*

('Flooded out'), which by all accounts (I have not seen the film) would appear to be a bridge between neo-realism and Gutiérrez Alea's *Death of a Bureaucrat*, made in Cuba a few years later. From Brazilian and later European exile, Birri continued to agitate for a radical new cinema in Latin America, but with military governments in power in both Argentina and Brazil, his ability to influence the situation was limited.

Military dictatorship, however, did not prevent Fernando Solanas and Octavio Getino from making the massive three-part documentary *The Hour of the Furnaces* in mainly clandestine conditions between 1966 and 1968. *The Hour of the Furnaces* is an impassioned and often strident denunciation of western imperialism which is both generically Third-Worldist in calling for revolution throughout the underdeveloped world and quite nationalistic in relation to Argentina itself. Particularly in the second and third parts of the film, Solanas and Getino make no secret of their Peronist leanings, combining the general progressive message of the film with a nostalgia for the days of the authoritarian leader, overthrown in 1955, who had acquired political credit at home (and in certain circles abroad) by nationalizing large amounts of British- and American-owned businesses during his time in power. Culturally too the film had a nationalist message, singling out imported western rock music as a threat to a national tradition embodied in the tango.

Solans and Getino followed up the film with a manifesto. 'Towards a Third Cinema', first published in Cuba in 1969, which was probably more influential than the film itself.[5] For Solanas and Getino, 'first' cinema is Hollywood and its epigones in other countries ('Hollywood–Mosfilm' as Godard called it), overtly and obviously commercial and reactionary, but 'second cinema', which is art or *auteur* cinema or cinema of individual expression as practised in Europe and sometimes imitated in Latin America, is not much better, at least from a political point of view. Against these two models the authors propose the notion of a Third Cinema, more appropriate to the social and political situation of the Third World, a cinema directly in the service of the people with neither commercial interest nor bourgeois vanity to satisfy. This notion of Third Cinema came to be adapted in Europe and the USA as a catch-all phrase for all sorts and kinds of cinema which were neither commercial nor self-proclaimedly artistic and neither 'national cinemas' nor simple extensions of global capitalism[6]; but in its original application the term was mainly reserved for a cinema of political militancy, and not only that but one where the militants were working in the hostile conditions imposed by dictatorship.

Given the prevailing political conditions, it is not surprising if the new Latin American cinema in the mid and late 1960s often seemed to exist more in aspiration in reality. But the aspiration was not ineffective. Film-makers who had previously worked in isolation began to meet together at festivals such as that at Viña del Mar in Chile in 1967, or at the Pesaro Mostra del Nuovo Cinema in Italy.[7] Revolutionary Cuba, as well as producing its own cinema, acted as a clearing house for ideas. It was in Cuba that Birri's 'Cinema and underdevelopment' and Solanas and Getino's 'Towards a third cinema' were first published, along with a Spanish translation of Rocha's *Revisão crítica do cine brasileiro*, and it was a Cuban film-maker, Julio García Espinosa, who wrote the most politically lucid of all the manifestos of the period, 'For an imperfect cinema'.[8]

Cuba was unique in Latin America, and indeed in the world, in that its new cinema was also the dominant cinema. It had no commercial competition, nor was it stifled by officialdom. American films were no longer being imported, their place being taken by cheaply acquired and often unappealing product from the socialist bloc. And on the whole, at least during the 1960s, what the film-makers at ICAIC wanted to make, got made. Along with privilege came responsibility. With automatic access to the mass market, the ICAIC film-makers felt they had to make films that pleased the masses, while keeping a wary eye out for possible negative responses from higher up the political chain. They were also very aware of the multiple advantages that could accrue if the films did well abroad, ranging from trips to Europe for film-makers, to earnings in hard currency pumped back into the economy, to national prestige and spreading the message of the Revolution.

Faced with these choices, the ICAIC film-makers decided to concentrate on making films for popular audiences at home, a number of which went on to enjoy success abroad as part of the wave of enthusiasm for revolutionary Latin America felt by young intellectuals in Europe and elsewhere. Throughout the 1960s Cuban film-makers experimented with a number of hybrid styles, adapting both European and American models to what seemed to them to be the needs of the Cuban audience. Hollywood films were pastiched, sometimes in a Godardian manner. The basic staples of any cinema, comedy and melodrama, were pressed into service. The melodramatic strand culminated in Humberto Solás's historical epic *Lucia* (1968), two and a half hours long and heavily indebted to Visconti's *Senso*. Not surprisingly, given its ambitions, *Lucia* was ICAIC's most expensive film to date and an experiment that was not repeated.

Comedies were better value for money. Alea adapted a Russian play, Ilf and Petrov's *The Twelve Chairs* (later borrowed in Hollywood by Mel Brooks), in 1962 to satirize surviving pre-revolutionary attitudes and continued in similar vein with *Death of a Bureaucrat* in 1966. Especially in the latter, the whole tradition of American comedy is pillaged for ideas and gags, from Chaplin to Jerry Lewis. Not to be outdone, Espinosa made the picaresque *Adventures of Juan Quin Quin* (1967), which not only borrowed tropes from film comedy but parodied other film genres from westerns to romance. *Juan Quin Quin* was not an entirely successful film. It tried to do too much – to indulge stereotypes, to play with them, and to subject them to political criticism – and it was not easy for audiences to engage with the film at all levels simultaneously. It was nevertheless a good example of the Cubans' determination to learn from past experience and make a revolutionary cinema that escaped the monotony of socialist realism and other traditional models.

The most intellectually ambitious of all Cuban films of the 1960s was Alea's 1968 *Memories of Underdevelopment*. It is a film which uses the process of making a film as a way of looking at the formation of revolutionary consciousness – or, more accurately, since we are not in the neverneverland of socialist realism, at the failure of its formation. Sergio is a would-be writer who fancies himself as both within the Revolution and above it. He is shown as a spectator of a process whereby a novel is being turned into a film. Meanwhile in his mind he goes back over recent events and experiences, the Cuban missile crisis, his wife leaving him to go to the United States, the various other women he made it with or not. Sergio is increasingly torn between a hopeful feeling that he has a place in the new revolutionary society and a masochistic sense of himself as too irredeemably bourgeois ever to fit in. Gradually it emerges that the film being shot is in fact Sergio's own life story – in other words precisely the film that the audience is now watching, rather as Fellini's *8½* is the film that Guido, the director, cannot make.

Sergio is a complex and appealing character. He is also a self-indulgent parasite. Alea wanted audiences to be aware of the seductiveness of characters like Sergio but to see them for what, in the eyes of the Revolution, they nevertheless were. He probably also knew that many people in the audience, especially in the west, had more than a little of Sergio in their own make-up. In the event the reception of the film in Europe (it was for a long time prevented from being shown in the USA) was both enthusiastic and misguided. Critics and audiences identified with Sergio's ambivalence towards the Revolution more than with the criticism of the character that the film-makers intended (and was taken for granted by audiences at home).

No such confusion is possible in relation to the documentaries of Santiago Alvarez. Brilliant, punchy, and for the most part montages of already existing materials, they make no secret of their status as propaganda – for the Revolution and against the United States. As the Vietnam War escalated, Cuba found itself more and more in the forefront of anti-imperialist struggle and solidarity with the Vietnamese. *Hanoi, martes 13* (1967), one of the few films for which Alvarez shot his own original footage, is a particularly vivid testimony to this feeling, the negative of which, a visceral anti-Americanism, appears in his savage montage *LBJ* (1968). In between he made *Hasta la victoria siempre* ('Always until victory'), a tribute to Che Guevara put together in haste after the news came through of the revolutionary hero's death in Bolivia on 9 October 1967.

1967 and 1968 were in all respects the highpoint of the new Cuban cinema. They were the years of the best films and of the country's highest standing in world opinion. By 1970 it was becoming clear that the economy was in trouble. A siege mentality began to develop. In 1971, the poet Heberto Padilla was placed under house arrest for a month without charge. Intellectuals across the world interpreted this as a sign that Cuba was no longer true to the principles that had made it different from other socialist countries. Although, as Michael Chanan points out, strictly speaking the Padilla 'affair' was marginal to ICAIC, it was a symptom of a change that was taking place in the relationship between the regime and its generally loyal but occasionally critical artists.[9] There were interesting films yet to come for a number of years, notably Sara Gómez's *De cierta manera* ('One way or another', 1977), but the Cuban cinema never recaptured the élan that it had possessed in the early years of the revolution.

It did, however, succeed in spreading the spirit of the revolution elsewhere in Latin America. Although revolutionary filmmaking was sporadic, more an isolated guerrilla than a concerted war of position, it could happen anywhere. In landlocked Bolivia, Jorge Sanjinés and a small group of collaborators made two films in the 1960s, *Ukamau* (1966) and *Blood of the Condor* (1969), set among the majority Aymara and Quechua population, and continued into the 1970s and even the 1980s, using the most modest of means. The electoral victory of the socialist forces in Chile led by Salvador Allende in 1970 held out a brief promise of a new cinema, but this was dashed by the US-backed coup three years later. Chile's most innovative film-makers, Miguel Littin and Raúl Ruiz, went into exile, repeating the pattern set in Argentina and Brazil in the previous decade. What remains, however, is a very substantial legacy.

Notes

1. Quoted in Randal Johnson and Robert Stam (eds.), *Brazilian Cinema* (New York: Columbia University Press, 1995), p. 122.

2. Glauber Rocha, *Revisão crítica do cinema brasileiro* (São Paulo: Cosac & Naify, 2003). I have not been able to trace the original Portuguese edition of this work, which was translated into Spanish and published in Havana in 1965 as *Revisión crítica del cine brasilero*.

3. 'Il n'y a pas davantage ni bons ni mauvais films. Il y a seulement des auteurs de films et leur politique, par la force même des choses, irréprochable'. François Truffaut in *La Revue des lettres modernes*, summer 1958. Quoted by Rocha in *Revisión crítica*, p. 11.

4. In *Revista civilização brasileira* 3, July 1965. English translation in Michael Chanan (ed.), *Twenty-five Years of the New Latin American Cinema* (London: British Film Institute/Channel 4, 1983), pp. 13–14.

5. Fernando Solanas and Octavio Getino, 'Hacia un tercer cine', *Tricontinental* 13, October 1969. In English as 'Towards a Third Cinema' in *Afterimage* 3 (London), summer 1971, pp. 16– 35, and in Chanan, *Twenty-five Years*, pp. 17–27.

6. See in particular Jim Pines and Paul Willemen (eds.), *Questions of Third Cinema* (London: British Film Institute, 1989).

7. John King, *Magical Reels* (London: Verso, 1990), p. 71. According to King, the 1967 Viña del Mar festival was followed by one in Mérida (Venezuela) in 1968 and a return to Viña del Mar in 1969.

8. First published in *Cine Cubano* 66–67, 1970. In English in *Afterimage* 3 (London), summer 1971, pp. 56–67, and in Chanan, *Twenty-five Years*, pp. 28–33.

9. Michael Chanan, *The Cuban Image* (London: British Film Institute, 1985), p. 257.

Part IV

Three Auteurs

15

Young Godard

Jean-Luc Godard is the most important and revolutionary film-maker of the last fifty years. Though still making films in the 21st century, the revolution he carried out in how films could be made and how the cinema could be thought about belongs mainly in the 1960s. Born in Paris in 1930 to a well-to-do Franco-Swiss family, he spent the war in the safety of neutral Switzerland and then chugged to and fro between Switzerland and Paris in the early postwar years in halfhearted attempts to complete his Baccalauréat and start university studies at the Sorbonne. Once settled in Paris he soon became a denizen, along with Truffaut, Rohmer, and others, of the Cinéclub du Quartier Latin, where he helped to found the seminal film magazine *La Gazette du cinéma*. He left university after two years without a degree, having acquired a superficial knowledge of sociology and a profound distaste for it. Disowned by his family, with whom he was never to be properly reconciled, he gave himself over to the *vie de bohème*, to reading books (many of them stolen), and to ever more assiduous immersion in the cinema.

When Bazin and Doniol-Valcroze founded *Cahiers du cinéma* in 1951 he became an occasional contributor, writing at first under the pseudonym Hans Lucas (a Germanization of Jean-Luc). At *Cahiers* he was the joker in the pack. He wrote two trademark pieces for early issues of the magazine – a review of *Strangers on a Train* (issue 7, March 1952) which placed him precociously among the group who were to become the Hitchcocko-Hawksians, and an article entitled 'Defence and illustration of classical construction' (issue 15, September 1952) which showed him equally precociously taking his distance from Bazin and the mainstream

Cahiers aesthetic. He then disappeared for three years, travelled, made a documentary about the construction of a dam in the Swiss Alps, and only returned to Paris and film criticism late in 1956. His insults were now more tempered (he no longer declared that popular heart throb Gérard Philipe was not only a bad actor but positively ugly) but his enthusiasms became even more delirious. He announced that Rossellini's *India* was 'the creation of the world' (issue 96, June 1959), that 'the cinema is Nicholas Ray' (issue 79, January 1958) and conversely that Ray is 'the whole cinema and nothing but the cinema' (issue 68, February 1957). He communicated his enthusiasm for Ingmar Bergman in an article called 'Bergmanorama' (issue 85, July 1958, concluding 'I adore *Summer Interlude*'), and in a telegram from Berlin (issue 86, August 1958) which breathlessly declared, 'HEIDEGGER + GIRAUDOUX = BERGMAN'. (He seems to have been fairly well acquainted with Giraudoux, but it is uncertain whether he had actually read very deeply in Heidegger.) Meanwhile he was slowly developing a theory of cinema, which was taking him further and further from Bazin and the mainstream. The article 'Montage my fine care' (issue 65, December 1956) is a direct riposte to Bazin's principled opposition to the very idea of montage cinema. Godard was prepared to follow Bazin in the belief that the film-maker must first and foremost seek to capture reality as it reveals itself, but he challenged the aprioristic idea that reality is just there and that the uninterrupted long take automatically reveals it, arguing instead that the film-maker's intervention in the form of strategically placed cuts can be even more important in order for the crucial truth to be elicited.

As the 1950s progressed, his criticism – like that of his great friend François Truffaut – was increasingly that of the film-maker in the making, animated by a sense of how he would shoot a scene if he got the chance rather than just the effect it had on him as a spectator. Already in his 'Defence and illustration of classical construction' he had begun to assert that the nature of the scene to be staged should dictate the form taken by the shots that make it up but now his eye was more and more telling him how this should actually be done. Between 1956 and 1958 he directed and edited a number of short films, acquiring valuable experience of what this meant in practice. But this experience was not enough to stop him making a mess of his first attempt at a full-length feature, *A bout de souffle*, made in 1959. Brilliantly shot by Raoul Coutard in natural locations, the resultant footage proved difficult to post-synchronize and practically impossible to edit according to the rules of classical construction whose praises Godard had sung seven years earlier. In order to bring it down to manageable proportions, Godard and his editor Cécile Décugis threw away the rule book and strung together the interesting bits of footage, consigning shots and parts of shots that were necessary only for continuity to the editing bin. Although largely unintended, the result was revolutionary, a collage rather than a montage of actions, conversations, and scraps of monologue. Godard became an overnight sensation, as did his star, Jean-Paul Belmondo. *A bout de souffle*'s success at the box office (259,000 admissions in Paris alone) meant that its producer, Georges de Beauregard, was able to bring in co-production finance from the Italian magnate Carlo Ponti for Godard's next few features, none of which, however netted them any money.

The first lesson of *A bout de souffle* for Godard was the need to monitor continuity throughout the shoot and for his next films he employed a top-class continuity editor (and close friend and collaborator of Truffaut), Suzanne Schiffman, to keep that aspect of the production in order. But it also forced him into a definitive break with the legacy of Bazin and the whole Bazinian school. From his newly acquired point of view as a film-maker, he realized that, basically, film was stuff. Cinema was not the world itself magically appearing on a screen in the form of an image, nor was it a clever simulation giving the illusion of reality; it was bits of stuff, celluloid and magnetic tape, on which real things had left their stamp but which now needed to be patched together as the film-maker desired. This was not in itself an earthshattering discovery, because at some level every film-maker knows it and so too, if they come to think about it, do most spectators. Godard's genius lay in the conclusions he drew from it. What he retains from Bazin is the preference for stuff which is imprinted with the real world, rather than concocted in a studio or with special effects.

Godard's second feature, *Le Petit Soldat*, was banned in France because of its implication that right-wing terrorists were engaged in a dirty war to help the French defeat the Algerian insurgency. Even now it is rarely screened and is mainly famous – or notorious – for the statement put into the mouth of its hero, Bruno, 'Cinema is truth, twenty-four times a second.' Whether this is what Godard himself believed at the time is hard to say. What is certain is that by the time he made his third feature, *Une femme est une femme* – in his own view his first real film[1] – he had moved on. From the very beginning of *Une femme est une femme* he sets out to show the audience that film is stuff and that what lies behind the magical illusions of cinema is a set of choices by the film-maker about how to put stuff together.

During the opening credit sequence there is the sound of an orchestra warming up and a female voice shouts (in English), 'Lights – camera – action.' We then see Anna Karina enter a café to the strains of a song by Charles Aznavour whose source is revealed to be a jukebox. She drinks her coffee, realizes she is late and leaves the café, winking at the camera as she goes. Cut to the street. Karina is walking along, traffic is going by, but there is no sound except the faint tip-tap of her (dubbed) footsteps. Cut to another angle and this time there is loud street noise. Cut again, and again silence, then in the middle of the shot the music returns. In the next shot Karina says 'Ça va?' over the music, but there is no live background noise.

This spectacular opening employs a number of devices which Godard will return to later, most famously in the 'one-minute silence' in *Bande à part* three years later. Here in *Une femme est une femme* they are not foregrounded in the same way and, coming as they do at the beginning of the film when the spectator is still looking for clues as to what the story is going to be, they can easily pass unnoticed.

What they show is Godard thinking aloud about cinema, what its components are, and how they fit together. Here's some natural sound, here's some that's studio, here's some music that seems to be background, but let's give it an onscreen source and make it diegetic; and, for the hell of it, why not dispense with a soundtrack entirely? In *Une femme est une femme* the pyrotechnics seem merely playful, but within a few years they will have acquired a purpose, as Godard makes 'baring the device' a central part of his aesthetic.

Godard continued to think aloud with *Vivre sa vie* (1962), but this time his focus was content as well as form. Again there are moments where the sound is simply switched off, or the camera performs a seemingly meaningless movement, but every formal gesture is carefully calibrated to mark changes in the discursive level – from objective to subjective, from narrative to reflection, from immediacy to quotation. The subject matter of the film is prostitution, which is treated alternately with pathos and with scientific detachment and also as a metaphor for capitalism. But Godard is still some distance away from the radical anti-capitalist and quasi-Marxist position taken up in *Two or Three Things I Know about Her* (1967), which also treats prostitution as a form of capitalist exchange. In *Vivre sa vie* his thinking is humanist and existentialist. The heroine, Nana, makes an existential choice to become a prostitute, imagining that this act of self-alienation is not decisive and that, like the heroine of Ophuls's *Lola Montès*, she will 'give her body, but keep her soul.'

The question of the soul is introduced early on in *Vivre sa vie* when Nana's husband quotes from a schoolchild's essay: 'The hen is an animal made up of an outside and an inside. If you remove the outside, the inside is left. If you remove the inside, what is left is the soul.' (Hen in French is *poule*, which is also slang for prostitute.) A similar question about what it means to be a person is raised in *Contempt* when Camille (Brigitte Bardot), lying naked on a bed, asks Paul (Michel Piccoli) which of her body parts he loves best, and when he says he loves all of them, she declares: 'So you love me totally.' And in *Alphaville* (1965) the same theme recurs, only cast more in terms of consciousness. Here Lemmy Caution, played by Eddie Constantine, is interrogated by Alpha 60, the giant computer which runs the city of Alphaville. After first responding with quotes from Pascal ('The eternal silence of these infinite spaces terrifies me') and Bergson ('I believe in the immediate data of consciousness'),[2] Lemmy eventually succeeds in forcing Alpha 60 into an existential crisis because it cannot say who or what it is. As Alpha 60 and its systems unravel, Lemmy is able to rouse Natacha (Karina) from her status as automaton seductress and to pronounce with conviction the hitherto meaningless words 'I love you'.

Godard's next film after *Alphaville*, made later the same year, was *Pierrot le fou* – the story, in his words, of 'the last romantic couple'. This was also to be his last romantic film and the last for some time in which the search for truth behind appearances is conducted in humanist and existentialist terms. In the films which follow, beginning with *Masculin Féminin* in 1966, the issue is no longer consciousness and the soul but the status of fiction and of the image in relation to social reality. From now on Godard, whose politics had previously been somewhat ambiguous, is clearly identified with the left, with Marxism, and with opposition to the war in Vietnam.

What happens to Godard about 1966 is best described as an epistemological shift. It is not as if the elements with which he is now working are entirely new. An interest in political revolution can be traced back to *Les Carabiniers* – in particular the scene with the woman partisan who quotes from Mayakovsky before being shot. The appeal to the theatre of Bertolt Brecht in *Two or Three Things* has a forerunner in *Contempt*, where Fritz Lang quotes Brecht to Piccoli and Jack Palance. Nor does he repudiate his old enthusiasm for the Hollywood B-picture, to which he continues to pay homage in *Made in USA* (1966). But the elements are newly configured. Brecht's example becomes central rather than peripheral. Hollywood remains seductive, but the seduction is now seen as dangerous. Most importantly, the early intuition that cinema was stuff ceases to be an excuse for play and now has a political purpose.

At the beginning of *Masculin Féminin* a title declares, 'This film could be called / the children of Marx and Coca Cola / Make of it what you will'. But the intellectual impulse behind Godard's work in this period is only partly Marxist. His target, here and in *Two or Three Things*, is on the one hand the structures of power and of commodity production as analysed by Marx but on the other hand the world of capitalist appearance, the 'society of spectacle' denounced by Guy Debord and the International Situationists.[3] But unlike the Situationists, Godard does not respond puritanically to the seductions of advertising-led consumerism. From a pure aesthetic standpoint, *Two or Three Things* is one of the most beautiful of all Godard's films. The soundtrack is a delight. In a typical Godardian way, the din of a construction site alternates with complete silence. There is no musical score, just the repetition at key moments of phrases from Beethoven's string quartet Opus 135. The images too are striking, most famously the extreme close-ups of the swirling bubbles dissolving and reforming on a cup of espresso.

For a more angry take on capitalism one must turn to *Week-end*, and for a picture of the world of the little ultra-left groups which were preparing to take on the power of the State, to *La Chinoise*. By mid-1967, when these films were made, Godard's turbulent marriage with Karina, which had lasted since the time of *Le Petit Soldat*, had come to an end. Meanwhile a new and greater disorder was about to descend, in the form of the 'events' of May 1968.

Up to 1968, Godard had made films for the cinema, that is for a public of people who paid money to be entertained, moved, educated, or whatever they thought worth paying their money for. Sometimes, as with *A bout de souflle* or *Contempt*, a large number of people thronged to see his films; at other times, as with *Une femme est une femme* or *Les Carabiniers*, very few showed any interest. But, success or flop, the relationship between film-maker and audience was basically the same. Godard felt he was ahead of the audience and hoped they would follow him. If they didn't wish to follow, that was up to them, and financially the producer would carry the can. In *Two or Three Things* and to some extent *La Chinoise* there is a hint of the film-maker wishing to draw the audience towards him and to be cajoled to accept a point of view that is not necessarily theirs, but the relationship remains one of cordial exchange. With 1968 and its aftermath, this all changes. Godard turns his back on the bourgeois audience, that is not just on the bourgeois people who frequent the first-run cinemas in Paris and elsewhere, but on any audience which accepts the bourgeois principle of commodity exchange. Excited by the atmosphere of sectarian debate, he embarks on a strategy of aggression towards the audience, haranguing them for their reactionary attitudes. He stops making films for the cinema and for audiences caught up in the circuits of capital. Instead he made films on 16 mm for militant audiences and turned to (mainly state run) television networks in the hope of getting support for projects aimed at a wider audience. When they saw what they had let themselves in for, however, the television networks generally refused to broadcast the films, which were shown, if at all, mainly on 16 mm to leftish cinephiles and film students.

The legacy of this turbulent period consists, basically, of two films. One is *Le Gai Savoir* (1969), an intellectually ferocious but also ravishingly beautiful essay on the relationship of sounds, images, ideology, and politics; and the other is *Wind from the East* (1970), nominally directed by a collective, the 'Groupe Dziga Vertov', but in practice by Godard with support from Jean-Pierre Gorin. *Wind from the East* for a long time enjoyed a high reputation as an example of counter-cinema and of 'making films politically'.[4] Thirty years on, its exemplary properties as political cinema are less apparent, and it differs from rest of Godard's work at the time in being slightly less arrogant and narcissistic and in being occasionally quite humorous (not always intentionally). *Le Gai Savoir*, meanwhile, continues to amaze.

In June 1971, Godard was badly injured in a motorcycle accident. This became an occasion for him to slow down and take stock. The immediate result was *Tout va bien* (1972), co-written and directed with Gorin, a film which sums up the politics of immediately post-1968 industrial militancy in an exemplary Brechtian manner. Starring Jane Fonda and Yves Montand, it was his first actual cinema film since 1968. But it was also the end of an era, both for Godard and for the rest of the world. Formally inventive, it is politically stale, marching boldly down a cul-de-sac of generic ultra-leftism. After *Tout va bien* Godard withdrew from the cinema for another eight years, to return refreshed with *Sauve qui peut (la vie)* (known variously in English as *Slow Motion* and *Everyone for Himself*) in 1980. Since then he has made some extraordinary films, but none as remarkable as those contained within the trajectory that led him from *A bout de souffle* in 1960 to *Tout va bien* in 1972.

Notes

1. Interview, *Cahiers du cinéma* 138, December 1962. *Godard on Godard*, p. 182.

2. 'Les données immédiates de la conscience' (1889) is the title of a work by Henri Bergson, known in English as 'Time and free will'.

3. Guy Debord, *La Société du spectacle* (Paris: Buchet-Chastel, 1967).

4. See Peter Wollen, 'Countercinema: *Vent d'Est*', *Afterimage* 4 (London), autumn 1972. Reprinted in Peter Wollen, *Readings and Writings: Semiotic Counter-Strategies* (London: Verso, 1982), pp. 79–91.

16

Antonioni

In the late 1950s the name of Michelangelo Antonioni was known only to a select handful of people. After the release of his film *Le amiche* ('The Girlfriends') in 1955, the writer Italo Calvino congratulated him on turning a lurid and moralistic novel (Cesare Pavese's *Tra donne sole* – actually rather good) into a sober and intelligent film. A critics' jury at the Locarno Film Festival in 1958 awarded a prize to his next film *Il grido* ('The cry', 1957). And Alain Resnais was so impressed by the laid-back modernist scores for both those films that he chose their composer, Giovanni Fusco, to write the music for *Hiroshima mon amour*. But as far as wider audiences were concerned, in Italy or abroad, Antonioni was nobody in particular. His films were judged too cold and too refined either for the mass audience or for a mainstream critical consensus still in thrall to the warm-hearted populism of neo-realism.

In the 1960s this all changed. *L'avventura*, shot in the autumn of 1959 and premiered at Cannes in May 1960, was a huge critical and even box-office success, especially in France. It was followed by three similar films, *La notte* (1961), *The Eclipse* (1962), and *Red Desert* (1964), all starring Monica Vitti, the actress whose strange mixture of melancholy and infectious laughter had been revealed to audiences in *L'avventura*. But it was touch-and-go. *L'avventura* nearly never made it to the screen and when it arrived it was nearly stifled at birth. Halfway through shooting the producers went bankrupt. Cast and crew were marooned on a volcanic island, living on credit from reluctant lodging-house keepers, while the director conducted negotiations on an antediluvian telephone to secure new financing. Shooting was held up for several weeks. Scenes

supposed to take place in the summer were not shot until well into
November, giving an accidental mystery to the eerie light that suffuses
the island sequences, as the idle-rich protagonists splash in the no-longer
warm waters off the Sicilian coast. Then, at the Cannes premiere, it was
roundly booed by sections of the audience disappointed that the unknown Vitti turned out to be the star of the film, rather than the better
known Lea Massari who plays a major role at the beginning before disappearing halfway through the film, never to return.

In the event, it was the Cannes audience rather than Antonioni who
were out of touch with the *Zeitgeist*. *L'avventura* and then *La Notte* and
The Eclipse proved to be the iconic films of the early 1960s, alongside
Jules et Jim and *A bout de souffle*. But although they clearly caught the
spirit of the time, they were hard to explain even for their admirers. They
were films in which very little happened, or appeared to happen, and it
wasn't even clear what, if anything, they were supposed to be about. A
favoured explanation was that, precisely in their inability to be about
anything concrete and tangible, they were in fact about alienation, and
their listless and purposeless protagonists were emblems of the alienated
state of modern society. This explanation is not that wide of the mark,
but it is too generic and metaphysical to account either for the films'
immediate success or for their enduring appeal.

Although many people at the time complained that these were films
in which nothing happened, on closer inspection this proves not to be
the case. In *L'avventura*, in the space of four or five days, Claudia (Vitti)
experiences the loss of her best friend, enters into an affair with her
friend's lover, is betrayed by him (as she has perhaps betrayed her friend)
but seems prepared to accept a reconciliation. In *La notte*, in less than
twenty-four hours, Giovanni (Marcello Mastroianni) and Lidia (Jeanne
Moreau) also experience the loss of a close friend, which triggers a crisis
in their relationship; both are tempted by adultery (he with a rich heiress
played by Vitti, she with a playboy nonentity), but decide against it,
and they end up dubiously together. In *The Eclipse*, Vittoria (Vitti) ter-
minates a longstanding relationship, enters into a frenzied affair with
Piero (Alain Delon), but decides (or appears to decide) not to continue
it. By the standards of ordinary life (if not necessarily the cinema), this is
not exactly nothing.

In Antonioni's presentation of them, however, these potentially quite
dramatic events are not dramatic at all. The disappearance of Anna
in *L'avventura* might be an accident, it might be suicide, or it might be

kidnap or even murder (like the murder of Janet Leigh that violently disposes of the heroine in Hitchcock's *Psycho* which appeared the same year), but we are not shown what happens, nor is the mystery ever explained; nothing is ever more than a possibility, a shadow hanging over the plot. In *La notte* we do not learn that the dying friend, Tommaso, has actually died, until Lidia lets drop in conversation that a phone call she received earlier was to tell her about his death. Nor does any drama attach to the crisis in the marriage or the tempted adulteries. The couple do not row: they are just palpably unhappy. When Lidia goes off in the car with her playboy, we see the car stop outside a hotel, and then move on, but we do not hear their conversation, nor can we even see their faces, which are obscured by the rain beating on the car windows as they talk. As for Giovanni's flirtation with Valentina (Vitti), it is just allowed to peter out after Lidia has eavesdropped on it. And in *The Eclipse* we assume that Vittoria and Piero have each decided to bring their affair to an end, but only because neither of them comes to the rendezvous they have set up.

It is not the case, therefore, that nothing has happened, but that the status of what has happened (and something undoubtedly has happened) remains uncertain. Narrative expectations are set up, and then defeated. (It is this, rather than mere boredom, that provoked the hostile reaction of the Cannes audience.) On the one hand this can be seen as elementary realism, a reproduction of the messiness and uncertainty of everyday life as against the conventional predictability of melodrama, and there is no doubt that part of the appeal of Antonioni's films lies in this unexpected lifelikeness. But the lifelikeness is also an effect of art, the result of a deliberate play with narrative conventions. What holds the rambling plot of *L'avventura* together is not what happens but the expectation of something happening – the return of Anna or an explanation of her disappearance – which, if it *were* to happen would give the narrative sense, but since it *doesn't* happen leaves the story poised uncomfortably over a void. And in *The Eclipse* it is again the expectation of a resolution – that Piero and Vittoria's affair will continue and formally be sealed as a 'happy end' – that holds the audience's attention during the extraordinary last sequence, in which time passes and the lovers never show. On the one side, something lifelike, two characters uncertain whether the affair they have drifted into is one they would like to continue. On the other, something that has nothing to do with Piero and Vittoria as characters at all: a meditation on transience provoked by teasing the audience into expecting the story to do what stories usually do – and then not delivering.

In underplaying narrative in this way in order to foreground some-thing else, Antonioni nevertheless definitely plays with it. From his first feature film, *Cronaca di un amore*, in 1950, to *Identification of a Woman* in 1982, passing through *L'avventura* and *Blow Up* (1966), he makes consistent and tantalizing references to the mystery or detective format, in which a narrative is set in motion by a suspected crime, which the rest of the story then sorts out. The difference, of course, is that in Antonioni films the mystery is not sorted out but is left in the air, a pos-sibly important, possibly unimportant shadow hanging over the charac-ters and leaving the audience in deliberately mild suspense. By means of this play with expectations, Antonioni can maintain interest in a story which in almost all respects rejects the normal criteria of how stories should push forward and how they should end. Antonioni's characters tend to live only in the present, carrying with them very little baggage from the past and with few if any ambitions for the future. They don't hold historic grudges and they don't make projects. This makes them on the face of it poor narrative material, since the stuff of narrative is moti-vation, and Antonioni's characters on the whole have very little of it.

The characters are not entirely devoid of motivation but its direction tends to be uncertain. The women tend to be more lucid and reflective than the men, but their intelligence only tells them that life is full of problems, not how those problems can be solved. And although some of the male characters are languid or inert (for example Giovanni in *La notte* and Ugo, the husband in *Red Desert*), others are compulsively active. Piero is a dealer, frenziedly buying and selling shares on behalf of clients. But the deals mean nothing to him and there is more than a hint that his sex life is like his work: he picks up women and drops them as easily as he trades in any other commodity. Thomas in *Blow Up* is equally com-pulsive; life for him is a flurry of photo sessions, of bending objects – especially models – to his will. But none of these characters, whether active or passive, blind or observant, knows where they are going, unless something happens, provoked by the narrative, to give them pause. They have few social, family, or workplace ties and live relatively unconstrained by conventional moral codes. This does not mean that they have no morality, but rather that they have to make their own moral choices as they go along, which they sometimes do and sometimes don't. It is the seeming rootlessness of these characters, accentuated by a *mise en scène* which isolates them within the frame, which has given rise to the label 'alienated' being attached to them. There is also something distinctly modern about it, in the sense that they inhabit situations which sociologists, then as now, characterize as typical of modern societies.

The modernity of Antonioni's characters may have reflected a sociological commonplace, but for the cinema it was something new. For all sorts of reasons, the mainstream cinema was deeply resistant to modernity in this form. A kind of existential listlessness occasionally surfaces in American films of the 1940s and 50s (in *They Live by Night* and other Nicholas Ray films, for example), but only as a property of lone individuals. It is not generalized across an entire social world, nor is it disabling to individuals. The American hero, especially, remains an action hero and his actions are endowed with meaning. But in the entropic world of Antonioni's films there is little scope for meaningful action offered to the hero or heroine to engage in – unless, like Mark in *Zabriskie Point* (1970) or David Locke in *The Passenger* (1975), they invent new roles for themselves to perform.

Antonioni's characters, like those in films generally, are not freestanding entities. They are brought into being by story and *mise en scène*, and both story and *mise en scène* are elusive in the extreme. Mysteries are evoked but never solved and the narrative never reaches the moment of truth that a solution would provide. What happened to Anna in *L'avventura*? We never find out. Nor do we find out if there really was a murder in *Blow Up* or exactly who the people were who murder first Robertson and then Locke in *The Passenger*. Even in films which do not have a mystery written into the plot, facts are withheld from the audience or the characters or both – not so that they can be revealed in due time but because they have no real pertinent existence. The world of the films is the fleeting world the audience sees and there is no more solid world underlying it and capable of acting as a guarantor of its truth. In the epigraph to Sam Rohdie's book on Antonioni, the director is quoted as saying, 'the world, the reality in which we live is invisible … hence we have to be satisfied with what we see.'[1]

What we see in Antonioni films is a pared-down narration, consisting of a series of views of spaces where characters enter, perform their actions, and depart. In conventional film narration, spaces are defined by the characters who occupy them and by the actions performed in them, and the succession of spaces (the editing of shots) is determined by the continuity of the action. In Antonioni's films space precedes the action and asserts its reality independently of the action performed within it. Although there are conventional matched-action cuts in the films, there are also many shots which begin or end with no character in frame at all (most notably in *The Eclipse*). The character makes an appearance in the shot, redefines the space as the space of an action, then disappears, restoring to the space its original independent reality. What anchors the narration is not a story but a composition.

This foundational quality of the filmic space means that the action of the film often takes the form of an interaction between the characters and the space they move in and out of. Characters are often presented as sensitive to landscape, sometimes more to it than they are to each other, or drawing solace from it as a refuge from social existence. This is as much true of the sane and balanced Vittoria in *The Eclipse* as of the palpably neurotic Giuliana in *Red Desert*. Landscape and elements – mud, fog, rain, deserts – are powerful determinants of the action, but so are smaller spaces, the emptiness or constriction of a room, the closeness of a blank wall. The physical prevails over the social, and landscape cuts characters down to size. In *Red Desert* Corrado (Richard Harris) tries to persuade a group of refinery workers to join him on a drilling expedition to Patagonia. The workers listen but are not convinced. The camera lingers on their faces, traces the lines of brightly painted pipework, focuses on huge jars used for storing acid. The sheer presence of the immediate environment is overpowering, and against it Corrado's vision seems insubstantial, a mere will-o'-the-wisp.

If place and space are important, so is time and duration, There are indeed times in Antonioni films when nothing much happens, or at any rate nothing of obvious narrative significance. But it is never actually nothing. Rather, the action slackens to allow the audience to take in the sensation of time passing and the things that continue to happen when plot action is suspended. At the end of *The Eclipse* a montage of shots shows people coming into frame who might be Piero and Vittorio but turn out not to be; then afternoon shifting into evening, water running out of a waterbutt, hoses being turned off and streetlights being switched on. At the end of *The Passenger* the action ends with a spectacular seven-minute shot in which the camera observes David Locke lying on his bed in a hotel room, passes out through the window, circles a courtyard where a learner driver is practising, watches the arrival of some gangsters and then Locke's wife and the police, and returns along a corridor to reveal his now dead body in the room where the shot started. But the film does not end there. There is one more shot, showing a sunset and the learner driver continuing to practise his turns. The world continues to exist, and life goes on within it.

On the occasion of an award given to Antonioni by the City of Bologna in 1980, Roland Barthes gave a address in which he defined the three cardinal virtues of Antonioni's cinema as vigilance, wisdom (*sagesse*), and fragility.[2] That is to say, it is a cinema which observes and awaits (desiringly, Barthes says); which is reflective; and which in its refusal to be judgmental is a challenge to the exercise of power. It is also, Barthes concludes, the kind of cinema which justifies the existence of the artist in a world in which art has been desanctified.

Notes

1. Sam Rohdie, *Antonioni* (London: British Film Institute, 1990), p. iv.

2. Roland Barthes, 'Cher Antonioni', *Cahiers du cinéma* 311, May 1980. English translation in Geoffrey Nowell-Smith, *L'avventura* (London: British Film Institute, 1997), pp. 63–68.

17

Pasolini

Pier Paolo Pasolini was already a well known literary figure in Italy long before he directed his first film, *Accattone*, in 1961. He was the author of two novels and four volumes of poetry and was much in demand as a scriptwriter for films set in the Roman underworld. Although his novels and scripts make brilliant use of *romanesco*, the dialect of the shantytowns and shabby estates on the outskirts of Rome, he was not in fact a native of the city. He was born in 1922 in Bologna and went on to do his university studies there, but most of his childhood and youth were spent in Friuli, a mainly rural region in the far northeast of Italy. (His first literary efforts had been an attempt to revive the dialect of the region as a vehicle for poetry.) In Friuli he joined the Communist Party in part as a gesture of rebellion against his authoritarian and Fascist-minded father, an officer in the Carabinieri, and in spite of the fact that his beloved bother Guido had been killed by rival Communist partisans in a feud with Guido's own Socialist faction. But in October 1949, a murky (though probably pretty innocent) homosexual episode involving some teenage boys resulted in him being arrested for indecency and promptly expelled from the local Party. This incident, coupled with the increasingly violent behaviour of his drunken father, led him to escape, with his mother, to the safety – and excitement – of Rome. There he rapidly found a name for himself in literary circles, becoming a close friend of the poet Attilio Bertolucci (father of film-maker Bernardo), of the novelist Alberto Moravia, and other leading lights of the period. He also paid frequent visits to impoverished shantytowns on the edge of the city, partly no doubt in pursuit of boys but more respectably in search of material for his novels.

His early novels, *Ragazzi di vita* (1955) and *Une vita violenta* (1959), are distinguished by their density of texture and the way they integrate the dialect of the shantytowns with standard literary Italian. His best poetry, meanwhile, contained in the volumes *Le ceneri di Gramsci* (1957) and *La religione del mio tempo* (1961), combines a public subject matter with a highly personal speaking voice. This was in sharp distinction to the prevailing hermeticism as found for example in the work of Italy's greatest 20th-century poet, Eugenio Montale, where the subject is private but the tone reserved and almost impersonal. By contrast Pasolini's voice was assertive, even shrill, and one emphatically demanding to be heard.

In the late 1950s Italy was desperately in need of dissenting voices, and Pasolini provided one. But he could hardly make a living out of poetry, or even novel writing, and he survived at first as a private tutor and then, when his literary skills began to be recognized, by writing dialogues and eventually entire scripts for films set in the Roman underworld. Most of these films were mediocre but among other tasks he provided dialogues for Fellini's *Le notti di Cabiria* (1956), which led to a long-standing friendship.

In 1961, Pasolini directed his first film, *Accattone*, a story about an idler and pimp known to his friends as 'Accattone' (scrounger), who eventually dies when trying to escape after a bungled robbery. He followed this up with *Mamma Roma* (1962). The title is again a nickname – this time that of a former prostitute, played by Anna Magnani, who is trying to go straight while providing for her son who is being looked after in a charitable boarding school. Again the story ends badly, with the death of the son.

Both films are remarkable for a refusal of the grammar of the well made film – a grammar which was a bit less strict in Italy than in Hollywood but which earlier Italian film-makers, including the neo-realists, had generally respected. Pasolini, however, saw no more reason to pedantically respect supposed film grammar than the grammar of language, which he had subverted to great effect in his novels and poems. Bertolucci, who worked as an assistant on *Accattone*, later claimed that when Pasolini lined up a shot it was as if he was inventing the cinema from scratch, with nothing to guide him other than an awareness that one or two forebears such as Carl Theodor Dreyer had been there before him. Pasolini's raw material was dual: people (especially their faces), and environments – dusty and sundrenched by day and luridly lit by night. These are then crudely put together in such a way as to accentuate their physicality. If there exists anything beyond this bare physical existence – human culture, perhaps, or the human soul – this is left to be inferred, for example in the form of Roman ruins breaking surface in a wasteground, or the incongruous presence of Bach or Vivaldi on the soundtrack.

What is most striking about the images is their isolation. Distance shots and close-ups abound but there is not much in between and certainly none of the smooth transitions normally achieved by the adroit use of two-shots and medium shots. Broadly speaking the editing respects continuity but it does not subordinate itself to its demands. Each shot stands on its own as an image, expressive in itself and with minimal relationship to the other shots next to it. When *Accattone* and *Mamma Roma* first came out, Pasolini and his editor Nino Baragli were widely condemned as amateurish and incompetent, which was rather like saying that Cézanne's brushstrokes showed that he couldn't paint. By 1960 nobody would say that of Cézanne, but film criticism lagged a good half century behind. The purpose of what he and Baragli were doing, however, became clearer with Pasolini's next feature, *The Gospel according to Matthew*, in 1964. Large sections of this film do not even bother to respect continuity, let alone pay obeisance to it. No sleight of hand is deployed to make the miracles reported by Matthew even remotely realistic. Each shot simply presents itself as reality in its own right but there is no attempt to maintain the realistic illusion that has been the foundation of cinema since the early 1920s if not before.

About the time that he finished the Gospel film Pasolini discovered the newly emerging theory of semiotics, which he engaged with in the hope of finding a theoretical rationale for his distinctive mode of making cinema. He had always been interested in linguistics and in a series of essays written between 1965 and 1968 (later collected together under the title *Heretical Empiricism*)[1] he set out among other things to theorize the differences between prose and poetry and between language and cinema (or between the languages of cinema and of writing and speech). These essays are always interesting and often brilliant, but what they do not come up with is a semiotic theory of cinema. Pasolini realized that in order to communicate films must signify and coined the word *im-segno* (i.e. *immagine-segno* or image-sign) to name the elements with which they do so. But he saw these *im-segni* or image-signs as chunks of reality to which the cinema provided a form of articulation. Cinema for him was 'the written language of reality' but it was a language with few everyday prosaic uses and a natural propensity for poetic expression. As a theoretical model to explain aspects of his own practice this was extremely illuminating, but it did not require the conceptual apparatus of semiotics to come up with it.

While Pasolini's semiotic explorations help to illuminate the form of his films, it is more helpful to look at his life and at his journalistic writings for a guide to their content. He was not an author for whom life and art, or theory and practice, could be kept apart. He regularly inscribed himself, his voice or body or both, in his films, and cast his mother as the Virgin Mary in the Gospel film – a gesture which might be held to imply an embarrassingly exalted role for himself in the global scheme of things. In an attempt to synthesize his manifold contradictions, critics sometimes described him as a Catholic Marxist. But this better describes the kind of sensibility which warmed to his work than it does his own actual ideas. He was brought up a Catholic and remained (particularly during the brief pontificate of John XXIII between 1958 and 1963) sympathetic to the Church's humane mission. He also retained a profound sense of the sacred – what he called the *sacrale* – but unattached to any particular institution. Politically he sided with the left and the Communist Party in particular, always regarding himself as a communist with a small c, even though he never attempted to rejoin the Party. But he supported the Communist Party as the representative of the poor and the dispossessed rather than as the political vanguard of the organized working class and he was deeply suspicious of any form of Marxism which announced the inevitable triumph of the proletariat. The classes he identified with were the peasantry and the subproletariat, in whom he saw vestiges of an alternative to the bourgeois capitalist order, whereas the working class proper he saw as increasingly prone to embourgeoisement as it grew more prosperous.

The irreducible core of Pasolini's critique of modern society was a profound sense that the world, and individuals in the world, had lost their innocence. If innocence survived it was to be looked for among the subproletariat, or in the Third World, and if, as Pasolini suspected, it was no longer to be found anywhere in the present then it could be imagined as something located in the past – in the Middle Ages, or in pre-history – which could be imaginatively recreated through film.

Pasolini's films start by being about thieves, pimps, and prostitutes. Then, after the gospel film and a wonderful exploration of the state of popular culture in Italy (*Hawks and Sparrows*, 1966), he embarks in the late 1960s on a series of films which explores themes of parricide and incest (*Oedipus Rex*, 1967), bi- or pan-sexuality (*Theorem*, 1968), parricide (again) and cannibalism (*Pigsty*, 1969), and infanticide (*Medea*, 1970). A trilogy of films derived from medieval tales and devoted (mainly) to natural and instinctive sexuality (*The Decameron*, 1971; *The Canterbury Tales*, 1972; and *The Arabian Nights*, 1974) is then followed by his last film, *Salò* (1975), an orgy of sex and death based on the Marquis de Sade's *120 Days of Sodom*. In spite of this often lurid subject matter, the main theme of all these films is innocence, what it is, and how it has been lost.

In Pasolini's films a model of innocence is provided by the characters played by Ninetto Davoli. Ninetto was a young man who Pasolini loved, leaving his lover and mentor heartbroken when he first had to go and do his military service and then, shortly afterwards, went off to get married.

There are then two models of semi-innocence in the form of characters played by Franco Citti and by the great comedian Totò. Whether as Accattone or as Oedipus, Citti strides boldly through the film, thieving, seducing, killing, his handsome features untroubled by consciousness of morality or guilt. Totò in *Hawks and Sparrows* is the same, only older and uglier. His lack of conscience is disturbing, but he is not bad. He has just muddled through to a ripe old age without learning anything, least of all the nature of his own place in a corrupt social order.

Totò as semi-innocent and Ninetto as total innocent are paired together as father and son in *Hawks and Sparrows* and again in a wonderful short 'The Earth Seen from the Moon' from the 1967 compilation film *Le streghe*. In the former they traverse a stretch of countryside outside Rome, acting as rent collectors for a bunch of oppressive landlords. On the way they meet a talking crow who tries to educate them in Marxist theory. Hungry and infuriated by the crow's incessant and moralizing prattle, they eventually kill and eat it, thus belatedly ingesting a little wisdom. In the latter, Totò marries a deaf-mute Silvana Mangano, who dies, comes back to life and dies again: 'Dead or alive, what's the difference?' the film asks in conclusion. In another, even more wonderful short, 'What Are the Clouds?' (from the 1968 *Capriccio all'italiana*), they are life-size marionettes in a popular puppet theatre, where they play the roles of Iago and Othello in total unawareness of what they are doing or what existence they might have outside of their roles. But the audience takes sides in favour of Cassio and Desdemona, rises in revolt and smashes the puppets, which are then thrown on the scrapheap outside the theatre. Only then, staring up into the sky, do the puppets realize, too late, that there could be another life.

Ninetto on his own features in yet another marvellous short, 'The Paper Flower Sequence' from *Amore e rabbia* (1970). We see him skipping gaily down the via Nazionale in Rome without a care in the world clutching a giant paper flower, chatting up girls and hitching rides from a delivery man and a man on a scooter. Interspersed are images of the public sphere – politicians speaking, bombs falling, the war in Vietnam. The audience sees these images, but Ninetto, of course, does not. An increasingly exasperated God speaks to Ninetto in voice off: 'Curly-head, listen to me. How can you be so blind with the world suffering all about you? Why don't you listen?' But Curly-head still doesn't listen. God invokes the parable of the Barren Fig Tree, struck down for not bearing fruit even though it was still only springtime. As he hops through the traffic, Curly-head is then struck down by a truck. Innocence is no protection.

In Pasolini's universe it is not really God who makes the life of the innocent an impossibility. It is the iniquities of the social and economic system with which the west has saddled itself. All his films represent a turning away from some or other aspect of modern society. They turn away from modernity into the past, from technology to nature, from the industrial west to the Third World, from the bourgeoisie to the peasantry and subproletariat, from the patriarchal to the maternal, from repression and heterosexism to the polymorphous sexuality of childhood – in short to a world before the Fall. This prelapsarian world, of course, does not exist, but it is evoked as the negation, piece by piece, of a world which all too emphatically does exist, and which Pasolini hated. There is no coherence to the universe the films portray except in the form of this negation. And the only recoverable part of the lost world would appear to lie in sexual revolution, which might – just – restore to the modern world some sense of the freedom it had forgone. Such, as least, would appear to be the lesson of *Theorem* (1968), in which the mysterious stranger played by Terence Stamp gets off with all four members of a bourgeois nuclear family (plus the maid), with ambiguous results.

How the world lost its innocence is explored in the films set in mythic prehistory (*Oedipus Rex*, *Medea*, and half of *Pigsty*) and in their present-day counterparts (*Theorem* and the modern sections of *Pigsty*). The so-called 'trilogy of life' which follows can be seen as an enactment of how the lost innocence might be recreated. But by the time Pasolini came to the end of the trilogy he had ceased to believe even in the liberatory potential of sex. The sexual 'revolution' of the 1960s was no such thing but just a new form of embourgeoisement which normatized adolescent heterosexuality, while the gay movement (or what little he saw of it, which was not much) was just a way of channelling homosexuality into another bourgeois ghetto.

It was in this frame of mind that he first 'abjured' the trilogy and then prepared to shoot what turned out to be his last film, *Salò* (1975). In this adaptation of Sade's *120 Days of Sodom* he transfers the action to Italy in 1944, when the Nazis had set up Mussolini as head of a puppet republic with its headquarters in a small town of that name on Lake Garda. The round-up and torture of the victims is overseen by senior Fascists and aided and abetted by troops loyal to the dictator and allied with the Nazis. To make the political parallel even more explicit, during the round-up the camera lingers on a road sign pointing to Marzabotto, site of a notorious Nazi massacre in the closing stages of the war. The aim of the Fascist 'gerarchi' is surrogate sexual satisfaction to be obtained from the humiliation and torture of their victims, and the realization (in the literal sense of its 'making-real' for the camera) of the Sadean orgy emphasizes the impotence of the libertines. The more orgiastic the scene, the more they seem driven by their own hatred of Eros and subservience to the death drive.

Salò is a horrific film, illuminated by flashes of beauty. It was also the last film Pasolini was to make and therefore can easily be taken (though this would be a mistake) to be his testament. On the morning of 2 November 1975 the film-maker's battered body was discovered on waste ground outside the seaside resort of Ostia near Rome (a site revisited in Nanni Moretti's 1993 film *Dear Diary*). A young male prostitute was tried and convicted of his murder in 1976, but the death continues even today to cause controversy. Pasolini had many enemies and there were widespread suspicions of a right-wing conspiracy. A more outlandish, but quite plausible theory, maintains that it was a 'death foretold', a quasi-suicide in which the young lad was the unwitting instrument of Pasolini's wish to die a ritual death so that from his sacrifice something could be reborn.[2] Whatever story one chooses to believe. Pasolini's death, like that of Fassbinder seven years later, was a tragic event from which nobody, not even his enemies, could draw any comfort.

Notes

1. *Empirismo eretico* (Milan: Garzanti, 1972). English translation by Ben Lawton and Louise K. Barnett as *Heretical Empiricism* (Bloomington: Indiana University Press, 1988).

2. Giuseppe Zigaina, *Pasolini tra enigma e profezia* (Venice: Marsilio, 1989).

Conclusion

There was no day the music died, no single point at the end of the 1960s at which there was no more new cinema or the new cinema there had been suddenly lost its magic. There were continuities. There were even advances. But gradually over the years between 1968 and 1972, most of the new cinemas either lost their novelty or disappeared or transmuted into something different and on the whole less vital. The early new waves, of course, had come and gone long ago, in the British case leaving very little legacy and in the French case leaving behind some established film-makers who, with the exceptions of Godard and Rivette, became increasingly conservative as time went on. Of the new cinemas flourishing in mid-decade, the Czech New Wave and Brazil's Cinema Novo were both struck down by political repression in 1968. Yugoslavia and, arguably, Cuba followed in a year or two. 1968 also changed the alignment of cinemas in western Europe, not always in the ways that might have been predicted. Whatever it was – and it was many things at once – the spirit of 1960s cinema did not long survive the turn of the decade.

There were, however, substantial bridges between the cinemas of the 1960s and what came after. There was Buñuel, whose films got if anything more radical and outrageous as the 1970s went on. There was Oshima, who outraged the censors with *Empire of the Senses* in 1976, but who before that had continued his formal experimentation of the 1960s in *The Ceremony* (1971) and *Dear Summer Sister* (1972). There was Fassbinder, who shot to fame around 1970 with a string of films which jolted a new German cinema into existence and addressed the malaise of West Germany with unprecedented directness. And there was the husband-and-wife team of Jean-Marie Straub and Danièle Huillet, whose purity and rigour made them a perfect foil for Fassbinder's rough-edged exuberance. Straub and Huillet's films never reached a wide audience, but they were very influential, not always for the reasons one might expect.

The Straubs were, after their fashion, almost pedantically realist. When shooting live sound, Jean-Marie used for example to insist on placing the microphone directly on top of the camera so that it only captured the sound heard from the precise spot the picture was taken from.[1] They were also rarely overtly political, choosing subjects like the life of Johann Sebastian Bach (*Chronicle of Anna Magdalena Bach*, 1968) or filmed versions of a play by Corneille (*Othon*, 1970) or a Schoenberg opera (*Moses and Aaron*, 1974) in preference to what would normally be regarded as political themes. Nevertheless, as their reputation migrated from cinephile circles to political ones they were taken up by the post-1968 left as models of anti-realist, political film-making. This reputation was not unjustified, since the films were not realist in the sense of creating any form of illusion of reality in the style of ordinary realistic fiction films. They were also always political in implication and sometimes (as in *Fortini/Cani*, 1976) these politics were brought to the surface. But the way these finely crafted, beautiful but always minoritarian films were promoted and even imitated can be taken as symbolic of a fragmentation that was taking place in the world of the new cinemas.

The new cinemas of the 1960s were always more or less commercial. This might matter less in the socialist countries or in those which had some sort of safety net for commercial failures and the degrees of more or less covered a wide spectrum. But as a general rule, films were made for a cinematic release which would be mainstream at least in their country of origin though probably more of an 'art house' type in export markets. Some films might fail, but it was rare for a film to be made without some expectation of a commercial career if not outright success. This not unreasonable expectation tended to channel films into an area of broad consensus: audiences wanted stories but they were broadminded in their attitude to what the stories contained and open-minded in their attitude to how they were told. The anti-capitalist politics of *Week-end*, the explorations of sexual fantasy in *Belle de Jour* and the non-resolving narrative of *Blow Up* all fell within the broad consensual area where producers and distributors were unafraid to tread.

1968 affected the system on its edges as a handful of film-makers, led by Godard, took to making films aimed at political rather than generically art house audiences. If these films were to circulate at all, they needed alternative circuits to circulate on. This gave a boost to 16 mm distribution, previously a reach-me-down outlet for already released mainstream and art house films but now a way in which smaller films could bypass the theatrical market entirely. More important, however, as it turned out, was television. In Italy, West Germany, and France, public broadcasting took on a role of patron for experimental work. Producers and commissioning editors were even prepared to take on films which were politically close to the edge, but then, if the film seemed to go beyond the edge, orders would come from above to have the film pulled from the schedules. But by then the film would have been made and could be released on the 16 mm circuit. At the same time more and more countries took to funding non-commercial films with production subsidies of one kind of another. This was welcomed by aspirant film-makers but it led in many cases to films being made which were not then commercially distributed. 'Alternative' cinemas grew, but outside the world of commercial release.

Meanwhile the new cinemas were being eroded from the other side. In a process that had already started in the 1960s, the international art film became increasingly attractive to major releasing companies as a business proposition and more and more film-makers were tempted into the high-budget international arena. MGM, Fox, Warner Bros., and United Artists stepped up their investment in films 'helmed' (as the trade journal *Variety* put it) by prestigious European, and especially Italian, directors. This development can be traced back to 1963 with Fox's investment in Visconti's *The Leopard*. But *The Leopard* was still an Italian film, set in Italy and adapted by an Italian director and scriptwriters from an Italian novel, and with a mainly Italian cast. The three films made by Antonioni for MGM (*Blow Up*, 1966; *Zabriskie Point*, 1970; and *The Passenger*, 1975), however, had practically nothing Italian about them except their director. They were shot in English and set respectively in London (with British actors), in California (with American actors), and in various locations in Europe and in the Sahara (with an international cast). MGM had final cut. Bertolucci's *Last Tango in Paris* (1972) was, if possible, even more international – set in Paris, with Marlon Brando, Maria Schneider, and a bewildered looking Jean-Pierre Léaud in the leading roles.

Stepping out of the limited world of national industries or European co-production into that of multinational (in effect, American) finance had obvious advantages. Not only were production budgets more generous, but the burden of how to get international distribution was lifted: provided the film had an English-language soundtrack in the first instance, it could be released by an American studio all over the world, dubbed or subtitled as the case might be. The distance from the local worlds of *Les Quatre cents coups*, *Fists in the Pocket*, *Konkurs*, or *Black God, White Devil* was enormous.

Rather than die, then, the new cinemas dispersed. But they had created a legacy, even more widespread than that of neo-realism a decade and more earlier. And unlike neo-realism, they stand today, forty years on, as representatives of modernity. More valuable still, the modernity they bespeak is that of liberation. And the message of modernity as liberation is not one locked up in a bottle; it may no longer be available in the cinemas, but it is there for the asking when you unwrap that DVD and place it in your player.

Notes

1. Although it is now customary to attribute the films to Jean-Marie Straub and Danièle Huillet equally, this was not the case in the 1960s, when they were usually credited to Jean-Marie on his own. The collaboration was always close and became more egalitarian as time went on. Danièle was largely responsible for the editing from quite an early date, but does not receive a (co-)direction credit until *Othon* (more properly, if indigestibly, known as *Les Yeux ne veulent pas en tout temps se fermer*) in 1970. Decisions relating to camera placement and the like would normally be taken by Jean-Marie, who was also spokesperson for the partnership. When I interviewed them for *Enthusiasm* (issue 1, December 1975), she said practically nothing, except to correct him from time to time.

Bibliography

Aitken, Ian. *Encyclopedia of the Documentary Film*. 3 vols. London: Routledge, 2006.

Aldgate, Anthony, and James C. Robertson. *Censorship in Theatre and Cinema*. Edinburgh: Edinburgh University Press, 2005.

Althusser, Louis. *Pour Marx*. Paris: Maspéro, 1965. In English as *For Marx*, translated by Ben Brewster, London: Allen Lane, 1969.

Anderson, Lindsay. 'Get out and push!', in Tom Maschler, ed., *Declaration*. London: McGibbon & Kee, 1957, pp. 153–78.

——. 'Only connect: some aspects of the work of Humphrey Jennings', in Mary Lou Jennings, ed., *Humphrey Jennings*. London: British Film Institute, 1982.

Antonioni, Michelangelo. *Fare un film è per me vivere*. Venice: Marsilio, 1994.

Astruc, Alexandre. 'Naissance d'une nouvelle avant-garde: la caméra stylo', *L'Ecran français* 144, 1948. In English in Graham, *The New Wave*, 1968, pp. 17–23.

Austin, Guy. *Claude Chabrol*. Manchester: Manchester University Press, 1999.

Baecque, Antoine de. *La Nouvelle Vague: portrait d'une jeunesse*. Paris: Flammarion, 1995.

Baecque, Antoine de, and Serge Toubiana. *Truffaut: A Biography*. New York: Alfred A. Knopf, 1999.

Barthes, Roland. *Mythologies*. Paris: Seuil, 1957. English translation by Annette Lavers, London: Cape, 1962.

——. *Le Système la de mode*. Paris: Seuil, 1967.

Barton, Ruth. *Irish National Cinema*. London: Routledge, 2004.

Bazin, André. *Qu'est-ce que le cinéma*, vol. 4. Paris: Editions du Cerf, 1962.

——. *What Is Cinema*, vol. 2. San Francisco: University of California Press, 1971.

Beevor, Anthony, and Artemis Cooper. *Paris after the Liberation: 1944–1949*. London: Penguin, 1995.

Belton, John. *Widescreen Cinema*. Cambridge, MA: Harvard University Press, 1992.

Bernardini, Aldo, ed. *Il cinema sonoro, 1930–1969*. Rome: ANICA, 1992.

Bock, Hans-Michael. 'East Germany: the DEFA story', in Nowell-Smith, ed., *The Oxford History of World Cinema*, pp. 627–32.

Bordwell, David. *Narration in the Fiction Film*. Madison, WI: University of Wisconsin Press, and London: Methuen, 1985.

Cameron, Ian, et al. *Second Wave*. London: Studio Vista, 1970.

Caute, David. *Communism and the French Intellectuals*. London: André Deutsch, 1964.

Chanan, Michael. *The Cuban Image*. London: British Film Institute, 1985.

——, ed. *Twenty-five Years of the New Latin American Cinema*. London: British Film Institute/Channel 4, 1983.

Ciment, Michel. *Conversations with Losey*. London and New York: Methuen, 1985.

Coates, Paul. *The Red and the White: The Cinema of People's Poland*. London: Wallflower Press, 2005.

Cowie, Peter. *Revolution! The Explosion of World Cinema in the 60s*. London: Faber & Faber, 2004.

Crisp, Colin. *The Classic French Cinema*. Bloomington: Indiana University Press, 1997.

Crofts, Stephen. 'Concepts of National Cinema', in Hill and Church Gibson, *The Oxford Guide to Film Studies*, pp. 385–94.

Cunningham, John. *Hungarian Cinema from Coffee House to Multiplex*. London: Wallflower, 2004.

Darke, Chris. *Alphaville*. London: I. B. Tauris, 2005.

Debord, Guy. *La Société du spectacle*. Paris: Buchet-Chastel, 1967.

Deleuze, Gilles. *Cinéma 1: l'image-mouvement*. Paris: Editions de Minuit, 1983. Translated as *Cinema 1: The Movement-Image*. London: Athlone Press, 1986.

——. *Cinéma 2: l'image-temps*. Paris: Éditions de Minuit, 1985. Translated as *Cinema 2: The Time-Image*. London: Athlone Press, 1989.

Douchet, Jean (with Cédric Anger). *Nouvelle Vague*. Paris: Cinémathèque Française/Hazan, 1998.

Eaton, Michael. *Anthropology – Reality – Cinema: The Films of Jean Rouch*. London: British Film Institute, 1979.

Elsaesser, Thomas. *The New German Cinema: A History*. Basingstoke: Macmillan, 1989.

Espinosa, Julio García. 'Por un cine imperfecto'. *Cine cubano* 42-3-4, 1967. English translation as 'For an imperfect cinema' in Chanan, *Twenty-five Years*, 1983.

Evans, Peter William, and Isobel Santoalalla, eds. *Luis Buñuel: New Readings*. London: British Film Institute, 2004.

Gardner, Colin. *Joseph Losey*. Manchester: Manchester University Press, 2004.

Giroud, Françoise. *La Nouvelle Vague: portraits de la jeunesse*. Paris: L'Air du Temps, 1958.

Godard, Jean-Luc. 'Bergmanorama'. *Cahiers du cinéma* 85, July 1958.

Godard on Godard. See Milne.

Gozlan, Gérard. 'In Praise of André Bazin', in Graham, *The New Wave*. Originally in *Positif* 47, 1962.

Graham, Peter, ed. *The New Wave*. London: Secker & Warburg, 1968.

Haltof, Marek. *Polish National Cinema*. New York and Oxford: Berghahn, 2002.

Hill, John, and Pamela Church Gibson. *The Oxford Guide to Film Studies*. Oxford: Oxford University Press, 1998.

Hillier, Jim, ed. *Cahiers du Cinéma: Vol. I, the 1950s – Neo-Realism, Hollywood, New Wave*. London: Routledge, and Cambridge, MA: Harvard University Press, 1985.

——. *Cahiers du Cinéma: Vol II, the 1960s*. London: Routledge, and Cambridge, MA: Harvard University Press, 1986.

Iordanova, Dina, ed. *The Cinema of the Balkans*. London: Wallflower, 2006.

Jennings, Mary Lou, ed. *Humphrey Jennings: Film-maker – Painter – Poet*. London: British Film Institute, 1982.

Johnson, Randal, and Robert Stam, eds. *Brazilian Cinema*. Expanded edition. New York: Columbia University Press, 1995.

King, John. *Magical Reels: A History of Cinema in Latin America*. London: Verso, 1990. Revised edition, 2000.

Lassally, Walter. *Itinerant Cameraman*. London: John Murray, 1987.

Leenhardt, Roger. 'A bas Ford! Vive Wyler'. *L'Ecran français*, 13 April 1948.

Lukács, George. *History and Class Consciousness*. Translated by Rodney Livingstone. London: Merlin Press, 1967.

MacCabe, Colin. *Godard: A Portrait of the Artist at 70*. London: Bloomsbury, 2003.

Maltby, Richard. 'Censorship and Self-regulation', in Nowell-Smith, ed., *The Oxford History of World Cinema*, pp. 235–48.

Mamber, Stephen. *Cinéma Vérité in America*. Cambridge, MA: MIT Press, 1974.

Marie, Michel. *Le Mépris: Jean-Luc Godard*. Paris: Nathan, 1990.

——. *The French New Wave: An Artistic School*. Translated by Richard Neupert. Oxford: Blackwell, 2003.

Maschler, Tom, ed. *Declaration*. London: McGibbon & Kie, 1957.

Mathews, Tom Dewe. *Censored*. London: Chatto & Windus, 1996.

McFarlane, Brian, ed. *The Cinema of Britain and Ireland*. London: Wallflower Press, 2005.

Mekas, Jonas. *Movie Journal. The Rise of the New American Cinema 1959–1971*. New York: Macmillan, 1972.

Metz, Christian. *Essais sur la signification au cinéma*. Paris: Klincksieck, 1968.

Micciché, Lino. *Il cinema italiano degli anni '60*. Venice: Marsilio, 1975.

Milne, Tom, ed. *Godard on Godard*. London: Secker & Warburg, 1972.

Müller, Jürgen, ed. *Movies of the 60s*. Cologne: Taschen, 2004.

Neupert, Richard. *A History of the French New Wave Cinema*. Madison, WI: University of Wisconsin Press, 2002.

Nowell-Smith, Geoffrey, ed. *The Oxford History of World Cinema*. Oxford: Oxford University Press, 1996.

——. *L'avventura*. BFI Film Classics. London: British Film Institute, 1997.

Nowell-Smith, Geoffrey, and Ricci, Steven, eds. *Hollywood and Europe: Economics, Politics, National Identity, 1945–1995*. London: British Film Institute, 1998.

O'Regan, Tom. *Australian National Cinema*. London: Routledge, 1996.

Orr, John, and Elzbieta Ostrowska, eds. *The Cinema of Andrzej Wajda: The Art of Irony and Defiance*. London: Wallflower Press, 2003.

Pasolini, Pier Paolo. *Empirismo eretico*. Milan: Garzanti, 1972. English translation by Ben Lawton and Louise K. Barnett, *Heretical Empiricism*. Bloomington: Indiana University Press, 1988.

Pines, Jim, and Paul Willemen, eds. *Questions of Third Cinema*. London: British Film Institute, 1989.

Pistagnesi, Patrizia, ed. *Poetiche delle Nouvelles Vagues: 2, Italia*. Venice: Marsilio, 1991.

Rham, Edith de. *Joseph Losey*. London: André Deutsch, 1991.

Richardson, Tony. *The Long Distance Runner: An Autobiography*. New York: William Morrow & Co., 1993.

Rivette, Jacques. 'Génie de Howard Hawks'. *Cahiers du cinéma* 23, May 1953.

——. 'L'âme au ventre'. *Cahiers du cinéma* 84, June 1958.

Robertson, James C. *The Hidden Cinema: British Film Censorship in Action, 1913–1975.* London: Routledge, 1989.

Rocha, Glauber. *Revisão critica do cine brasileiro.* São Paulo: Cosac & Naify, 2003 (originally published in 1965). Spanish edition *Revisión crítica del cine brasilero.* Havana: ICAIC, 1965.

——. 'The aesthetics of hunger' in Chanan, *Twenty-five Years*, pp. 13–14.

Rohdie, Sam. *Antonioni.* London: British Film Institute, 1990.

——. *The Passion of Pier Paolo Pasolini.* London: British Film Institute, 1995.

Rohmer, Eric. *The Taste for Beauty.* Translated by Carol Volk. Cambridge: Cambridge University Press, 1989.

Rouch, Jean. *Ciné Ethnography.* Edited and translated by Steven Feld. Minneapolis: University of Minnesota Press, 2003.

Rouch, Jean, and Edgar Morin. *Chronique d'un été.* Domaine Cinéma 1. Paris: Interspectacles, 1962.

Roud, Richard. *Cinema: A Critical Dictionary.* Two volumes. London: Secker & Warburg, 1980.

Rowbotham, Sheila. *Promise of a Dream: Remembering the Sixties.* London: Allen Lane, Penguin Press, 2000.

Solanas, Fernando, and Octavio Getino. 'Hacia un tercer cine'. *Tricontinental* 13 (Havana). English translation as 'Towards a Third Cinema' in *Afterimage* 3 (London), summer 1971, and in Chanan, *Twenty-five Years*, pp. 28–33.

Shafto, Sally. *Zanzibar: les films Zanzibar et les Dandys de Mai 1968.* Paris: Editions Paris Expérimental, 2007.

Siclier, Jacques. *Nouvelle Vague?* Paris: Editions du Cerf, 1961.

Škvorecký, Josef. *All the Bright Young Men and Women: A Personal History of the Czech Cinema.* Translated by Michael Schonberg. Toronto: Peter Martin Associates, 1971.

Sontag, Susan. *Against Interpretation and Other Essays.* New York: Farrar, Straus & Giroux, 1966, and London: Eyre & Spottiswoode, 1967.

Taylor, B. F. *The British New Wave: A Certain Tendency.* Manchester: Manchester University Press, 2006.

Thomas, François. *L'Atelier d'Alain Resnais.* Paris: Flammarion, 1989.

Truffaut, François. 'Une certaine tendance du cinéma français'. *Cahiers du cinéma* 31, January 1954.

Vian, Boris. *Et on tuera tous les affreux.* Paris: Pauvert, 1997. First published in Paris by Editions du Scorpion in 1948 under the name Vernon Sullivan.

Walker, Alexander. *Hollywood, England: The British Film Industry in the Sixties.* London: Michael Joseph, 1974.

Williams, Alan. *Republic of Images.* Cambridge, MA: Harvard University Press, 1992.

Wilson, Emma. *Alain Resnais.* Manchester: Manchester University Press, 2006.

Winston, Brian. *Claiming the Real: The Griersonian Documentary and its Legitimations.* London: British Film Institute, 1995.

Wollen, Peter. 'Countercinema: *Vent d'Est*'. *Afterimage* 4 (London), 1972.

——. *Readings and Writings: Semiotic Counter-Strategies.* London: Verso, 1982.

Wood, Michael. *Belle de Jour.* BFI Film Classics. London: British Film Institute, 2000.

Zigaina, Giuseppe. *Pasolini tra enigma e profezia.* Venice: Marsilio, 1989.

Index of Film Titles

General Index